# When **Big Blue** Went to War

A History of the IBM Corporation's Mission in
Southeast Asia during the Vietnam War (1965–1975)

*Dan E. Feltham*

In memory of R. L. (Bob) Tanner, the man
who put our mission all together.

**And dedicated to all the fighting men and
women we were there to help.**

**abbott press**®
A DIVISION OF WRITER'S DIGEST

# When Big Blue Went to War

*ISBN: 978-1-4582-0440-0 (e)*
*ISBN: 978-1-4582-0441-7 (sc)*

*Library of Congress Control Number: 2012910626*

*Abbott Press books may be ordered through booksellers or by contacting:*

*Abbott Press*
*1663 Liberty Drive*
*Bloomington, IN 47403*
*www.abbottpress.com*
*Phone: 1-866-697-5310*

*Printed in the United States of America*

*Abbott Press rev. date: 06/21/12*

# Contents

Preface............................................................................ vii

Chapter 1: Inward Bound.............................................1

Chapter 2: Welcome Home.............................................12

Chapter 3: Keep A Low Profile, But Experience Everything...........................36

Chapter 4: Processing The Information Of War .........54

Chapter 5: Special Customer Situations.....................78

Chapter 6: White Shirts And Ties .......................... 106

Chapter 7: Recreation ............................................. 124

Chapter 8: Angkor Wat, Cambodia ........................ 148

Chapter 9: Fears And Tears....................................... 162

Chapter 10: The Sail Of The "Demasiado"................ 179

Chapter 11: War Zone Memoirs By Ed Baker .......... 193

Chapter 12: My Vietnam Years, By Curtis Maxwell ............................. 210

Chapter 13: Life In The War Zone By Stu Schmidt............ 237

Chapter 14: The General's Boat Trip ...................... 254

Chapter 15: Vietnamization & De-Escalation............ 262

Chapter 16: Send The Computers (And The IBMers) Home............ 277

Chapter 17: The Last Phone Call – The Fall Of Saigon ...................... 293

Epilogue ....................................................................317

Acknowledgements.......................................................323

Bibliography .............................................................325

# Preface

THIS IS NOT A DIFFICULT story to tell, and I have enjoyed the telling. In fact, I have felt a compulsion, an obligation, to tell this story for far too many years. Thousands upon thousands of Americans and Vietnamese lost their lives in Vietnam but the experiences as told here are not the typical war time horrors of guns or bombings or bloody battles and loved ones won and lost. Hundreds of American contractors also lived and worked in Vietnam. I was one of those contractors, serving the U.S. military forces, and this is my story and the stories of other IBM civilians in Southeast Asia. I have never fired a gun and have never been asked to do so. Thank goodness! My job was a peaceful one. There were many people like me, working in the war zone, making good money, experiencing untold adventures, but also risking their lives with the effort, and learning about life, chaos, danger and death.

This story is also about the 'business side of war'. It has been said that the IBM Corporation did not want to profit from the Vietnam War, but I believe they did. The expenses to manufacture, ship, staff and manage the thousands of machines sent to Southeast Asia over an eight-year span were enormous. The expenses to maintain the 250 resident bachelor technicians, administrators and managers in multiple foreign countries for their overseas assignments were also enormous. So were the rental, purchase and service fee revenues flowing into IBM's coffers during what was called the System/360 Era.

In writing this story, I realize that I may be opening a can of worms by telling of our extraordinary life styles, and may be subject to some criticism by the very men that we held in awe and respect - the troops fighting in the jungle highlands and rice paddies - those who risked and gave their lives and limbs so that civilians like me could continue to celebrate Freedom - those who we were there to help. However, I truly hope that such is not the case.

I also especially respect those military men and women who volunteered for additional tours in 'Nam' because they believed in a cause and what they had been told the war was all about. By comparison, we contractors had easier life styles in the cities and on the bases and for the most part we enjoyed and profited from our Vietnam experiences - profited monetarily but also in 'life's lessons learned'. Nevertheless, I cannot change history and we all had a job to do. Those who may criticize would have acted no differently than we. In my defense, I should also state that the civilian way of life as portrayed in this book was not all that much different from many of the military officers and support troops who were assigned to rear echelon headquarters positions such as at MACV HQ or USARV HQ, most of whom served a single year. We can all say, "We were there", with either shame or pride, depending on one's point of view and convictions. I choose pride for what little I helped to accomplish.

There are many experts on the Vietnam War. I do not claim to be one. I have only written what I can remember and what other IBM professionals have told me that they remember. The history presented in the pages that follow are the facts as best as we can recall and any errors are shortcomings of memory and not of intent.

If I had initially written this book twenty years before rather than in 1995 (and now supplemented by this new edition's input of 2012), much of the information having to do with computer applications and usage would have fallen on deaf ears. Computers were relatively rare in the late 1960's, the applications were somewhat esoteric – some being on the bloody edge of technology (almost literally) - and the jargon almost mysterious as far as day-to-day conversation was concerned. Now, home computers, laptops, tablets and cell-phone technologies are commonplace and that fact should make parts of this book more technically understandable. I hope so. Certain portions of this book are very technical and many readers may wish to skip over those areas. Go ahead. My main purpose for the book is to record a piece of IBM history that has been ignored or forgotten. I hope that the reading of these stories provides even a small fraction of the actual feelings of accomplishment, adventure and excitement as did the actual living of the stories that took place - a long time ago.

# Chapter 1
## Inward Bound

I WAS AWAKENED OUT OF a sound sleep by a tender nudge on my shoulder and a female's soft voice near my ear. I opened my eyes and the stewardess asked, "Can I get you anything, sir? We are about two hours out of Hong Kong and are starting to serve breakfast."

I mumbled a thank you and stretched my aching back and legs. Over previous years of air travel, I had learned to sleep pretty well on commercial jets and rarely experienced the malady of jet lag. Maybe the trick of downing a couple of mai-tai cocktails at the terminal bar for these mid-night departures out of Honolulu also assisted me in falling asleep. (It wasn't really passing out if it were planned for the ten-hour flight across the Pacific, was it?) Maybe it was also the fact that I really enjoyed air travel and had done a lot of it. I thought better of having a wake-me-up Bloody Mary - I had a busy schedule ahead - so I tried to strike up a conversation with the good looking stew by saying that I would love to spend time in Hong Kong with her between flights.

She smiled, ignored my offer and asked, "On holiday or are you bound for Nam?"

I had noticed her shortly after boarding. I was 34, a confirmed bachelor, but always enjoyed female companionship, and the challenge of establishing that relationship. I tried again, handed her my business card and said that I was on a business trip and could she at least join me for lunch.

She said, "I wish I could. That might be fun, but this flight lays over in Bangkok, not Hong Kong, and I'd better get you that breakfast."

*Good try Dan!* I thought stewardesses were really great and had dated more than a few back in Honolulu in recent years.

During the rest of the flight, I had time to reflect on some of the events that had led to the adventure ahead. It was February 1969 and I had volunteered for a two-year assignment in South Vietnam in the service of the IBM Corporation. Was I doing the right thing or was I completely out of my mind? Why would a happy, healthy, carefree bachelor leave a Honolulu paradise in exchange for a life in a war zone? Being a hero for one's corporation was one thing, but was I laying my life on the line? The past five years in Hawaii working for IBM had been the best years of my life. I had a good job, good friends, surfing and sailing, social and athletic club memberships and an abundance of good looking, fun loving wahinis for casual dating. Why push a corporate mission to the extreme? Why trade a comfortable lifestyle for the danger and stress of living in Saigon's unknown chaos? It was a wild and crazy thing to do, and I was really excited and looking forward to any new prospects for high adventure. I also seriously thought that I was about to do something patriotic for my country. I was sure that the other IBMers who had preceded me to Southeast Asia had similar in-flight thoughts. I had been classified 4-F due to a serious history of youthful debilitating bronchial asthma and also went through college with a 2-S deferment during my draftable years in the mid 1950's. I had just missed the Korean War, and this was perhaps my way of serving an overdue military obligation.

Maybe living in Hawaii in the 1960's had been too easy, too much fun and I wanted something more serious to sink my teeth into. Rather than the distractions of where the best surf was, or what local girl or mainland malahini I should be dating, or when the next catamaran race and yacht club party was, what I needed was a tough unique challenge combined with increased business responsibilities. The new job held a promotion and hopefully promised additional professional opportunities after the assignment - or so I had been lead to believe by upper IBM management. I was energetic and in great physical condition (six foot one, 185 pounds) from all my swimming, surfing and sailing, but I had no serious long range plans at all - nothing to keep me from doing whatever I wanted to do or from seeing more of the world. There was also the mercenary aspect of the job, since IBM offered hazardous duty pay on top of a regular salary for working in the war zone. In retrospect and many years later, I believe that I would make the same decision again. I have never regretted that Vietnam decision; it was one of the most exhilarating periods of my life.

I had become heavily involved with the U. S. military in Hawaii during the 1967-1968 time frame as the result of an IBM career change. I moved from being a technically oriented Systems Engineer supporting commercial customers into Federal Marketing. My new marketing responsibilities became the selling and installation requirements for data processing equipment utilized by Pacific Air Force Headquarters (PACAF) located at Hickam Air Force Base; by U.S. Army Pacific Headquarters (USARPAC) at Fort Shafter; occasionally by the Commander in Chief Pacific Headquarters (CINCPAC); by Strategic Communications Pacific Headquarters (STRATCOMPAC) out at Schofield Barracks and by Fleet Marine Force Headquarters (FMFPAC) at Camp Smith, which was co-located with CINCPAC on a strategic hill overlooking Pearl Harbor. These were my primary customers, but I also called on the Marines at the Kaneohe Air Station, at the Army's Security Agency located in the center of an Oahu pineapple field, at the Naval Shipyard at Pearl Harbor, at an Information Data Handling System security installation at PACAF and occasional calls at CINCPAC's alternate headquarters secret underground site at Kunia.

When time and responsibilities permitted, I also flew to Kwajalein Atoll in the Marshall Islands in order to market our products to MIT's Lincoln Laboratories and Bell Telephone Laboratories, both of which had complex computer installations at that far end of the Pacific Missile Test Range. I was extremely busy with this set of customers and gradually became more involved in IBM's business relationship with the Vietnam conflict. Data processing was still in its infancy by today's standards, but it was growing quickly. IBM had just started volume deliveries of the, now almost forgotten, System/360 line of computers, and the military was taking delivery as fast as the procurement process in Washington D.C. would allow. I suppose I was a valuable commodity with an in-depth technical background, computer programming capability, and systems knowledge coupled with a growing understanding of the military's data processing procedures, requirements and organizations. I had even learned almost all the ranks and insignias of the main branches of the services (no simple chore since I had never been in the military) and I had a total respect for their lifestyle and protocol. My agreement to the two-year assignment in Saigon almost seemed like it was preordained. I accepted the dual position of Marketing/Systems Engineering Manager for IBM's Southeast Asia Operation (Branch Office 562) with eager enthusiasm. I was following much of the equipment I had helped sell and now I was going to have to help make it work in the war zone!

Breakfast, and the good looking stew brought me back to reality and I began looking forward to an overnight stay in Hong Kong and the follow-on second leg of my journey to Saigon. We started the descent from 31,000 feet into Kai Tak Airport. This would be my first experience in the orient and since I did not know what to expect, I spent the remaining half hour looking out the port at the fascinatingly beautiful approach to Hong Kong Harbor and thinking about what the IBM Corporation was doing with its employees and their operational status in the Southeast Asia war zone.

In the early 1960's, little was publicly known about American involvement in Southeast Asia. There were the "Green Berets heros" and some covert military operations, but Vietnam wasn't really big news yet. Actually, the U.S. military had considerable presence in South Vietnam, Cambodia and Laos, and there were seasonal battle reports from Vientiane, Laos about fighting in some vague place called the Plains du Jars. In the early 1950s our country deployed military advisors to what was then called French Indo-China and increased their presence throughout the area in the early 1960s. One source states that in 1963 there were 16,000 American military personnel in South Vietnam acting as 'Advisors'. Up until then, Air America had been doing much more than just flying routine supply missions in the area. Marines were the first <u>combat</u> troops to enter Vietnam at China Beach near Da Nang on March 8, 1965. By May our troop presence had increased to 50,000 men. The first B-52 air strikes took place that June.

During these early build-up years, the various military services took a certain number of IBM punched card machines into Vietnam to be used in behind-the-lines administrative applications. This unit record equipment consisted of 026 keypunches, 056 verifiers, 082 and 083 sorters, 514 and 557 collating and card reproducing machines and some 403 and 407 tabulating machines. They were either owned outright by our government, so they were free to take and use them wherever they wished, or they were leased from IBM and probably assigned to stateside bases but were "on loan" to foreign areas. As the fighting escalations began and the headquarters reliance on punched card automation increased, more and more machines were shipped to Vietnam. A few of the early IBM computers (1401s and 1410s) began arriving at various bases. Consequently, the rationale for an IBM personnel presence within the war zone was established and requested.

Southeast Asia was a long way from any major IBM parts depot and there was a serious lack of computer maintenance expertise within the military. The machines broke from time to time and the outages became lengthy while a military or IBM maintenance man was flown in from far away support areas. These outages became too lengthy for the reporting frequency that was being demanded by the various military command headquarters in Honolulu and the U.S. mainland. I was all too aware of this increase in equipment since one of my sales coordinating functions back at IBM's Honolulu Branch Office was to fill orders and arrange shipment for groups of unit record equipment from IBM plants to a pre-arranged holding location in San Francisco's huge Neptune Warehouse. As Army bases were being established and permanent data processing facilities were brought on-line in Vietnam, pre-ordered equipment would be called out by an office at Schofield Barracks by type and by serial number and would be moved to an air shipment point like McClellan AFB or Travis AFB in California for transfer to places like Bien Hoa, DaNang, Cam Ranh Bay in Vietnam or Korat, Udorn or Sattahip in Thailand. As I remember, I helped ship close to 1000 unit record machines from Neptune to Southeast Asia in 1967 and 1968 in addition to a few 1400 and smaller model S/360 computer systems. I used a large accounting-type spread sheet which completely covered my Honolulu desk and which listed military ship-to addresses, planned ship dates and quantities of machines destined for air transportation. There were four Federal Marketing Representatives supported by an excellent IBM Administrative staff in the Honolulu Branch Office handling this military equipment buildup. Our Pacific business requirements were quite adequately supported by the Army, Navy, Air Force and other Federal program offices within IBM at Bethesda, Maryland, headquartered in a large IBM building fondly later known as the "Rusty Bucket" on the outskirts of Washington, D.C.

As I stated above, some of these machines were purchased by the government, while others were rented. The government purchase orders were issued under the auspices of the General Services Administration (GSA) in Washington and given DO and DX priority ratings to insure prompt delivery. These ratings allowed IBM to break the company's sacred sequential delivery policy and expedite shipment. Special contractual provisions were agreed upon between IBM and GSA as to how these machines would be paid for, serviced, replaced if damaged by the war, and then ultimately either returned to the U.S.A. or in some cases purposely destroyed after the war. A few years later I was asked to go to Washington, D.C. to brief GSA on our Southeast Asia operation, and I was able to help negotiate better terms of military support for our personnel in the war zone.

We four marketing reps, Mike, Dave, Jeff and me, in Honolulu (1240 Ala Moana Boulevard) qualified for IBM's prestigious 100 Percent Club during this period but our attainment was carefully engineered by mainland management so that we did not achieve much more than the required 100% of assigned sales quota and did not receive much in sales commissions. At the 1968 100 Percent Club recognition event at the Fontainebleau Hotel in Miami Beach, the four of us Hawaiian Reps sat in the audience and irritably watched as eight other "best of the best" IBM commercial marketing representatives from all over the United States receive recognition awards and big bonus money on stage. The combined sales achievement of the eight winners was considerably less than what we four had worked hard to achieve in the one small Honolulu branch office. Clearly, IBM was not interested in hearing accusations of war profiteering and they maintained that posture throughout the years of the company's wartime involvement.

As punched card data processing transitioned to "information processing" and the military's reliance on this information increased, the need for more sophisticated systems increased. A few of the 1401 computer systems were replaced by the more powerful 1410 and 7010 systems and rudimentary teleprocessing networks were installed using IBM's 1050 family of terminals. In 1964, IBM had taken a five or six billion-dollar gamble and announced its highly successful System/360 series. By 1967 and 1968 IBM was shipping them in quantity (as a Systems Engineer, I had the privilege of helping to install the first two System/360s in the State of Hawaii). Naturally our military wanted the newer S/360 models rather than the older less powerful less reliable technology. The question became, "How can we - the military - support all this new sophisticated equipment in the war zone, equipment that no-one in the military had yet been trained on?" The military asked IBM for more help; they needed IBM Customer Engineers (CEs) in Vietnam as well as better availability of spare parts. It was agreed that a few IBMers would go to Vietnam (on a trial basis) and work in-country part time, rotating in and out as needed. They would initially be based out of Kadena AFB in Okinawa or Camp Zama, Japan and/or Clark AFB or Subic Bay in the Philippines. That worked well - for awhile - during 1966, and we were soon asked by CINCPAC for a more permanent presence in Vietnam. In July 1967, the IBM Honolulu branch office took over the management responsibility for a federal sub-branch at Camp Zama, Japan (Branch Office 560 known as Pac Ops North) and about the same time established what would soon become Branch Office 562 (Pac Ops South) based in Saigon. What followed is the story told in this book.

Landing at Kai Tak Airport in 1969 was an exciting experience in its own right. The approach past Hong Kong Island and magnificent Victoria Harbor is unrivaled in physical beauty (flying into San Francisco International might come close if from certain directions). The outer islands and Chinese mainland together with the twin cities of Kowloon and Victoria frame the central jewel of the harbor. Then comes the landing (hopefully), and in those days the runway was much shorter than the new one at present. Touchdown was at sea level plus about ten feet with harbor waters on three sides of the runway and was followed by almost deafening reverse engine thrusts and heavy aircraft breaking in order to avoid a final crash into the terminal building, hotels, and mountainside just beyond. Flying has never normally bothered me, especially after having flown hundreds of thousands of miles during previous overseas assignments and working a few years earlier for an aerial survey company. However, I have to admit that old Kai Tak really made the adrenaline flow. Later, I was to experience the extra thrill of landing at Kai Tak in the opposite direction - a heart stopping steep descent over mountains and buildings to touchdown and again the noise and breaking to avoid splashing into the harbor at the far end of the short runway. Landing from that direction was just about as gentle as landing a large boulder. Those of you that traveled to Hong Kong in those days will understand.

I was to meet my boss, Bob Tanner, at the Peninsula Hotel, so I processed rapidly through immigration, baggage claim and customs on the way to hail a taxi. The first things I noticed as I emerged from the busy terminal was the hustle and bustle of the Chinese, the riotous colors of the street signs and then my taxi driver speaking perfect English, "Where can I take you sir?" One's first impressions of the Orient are long lasting, and over the next several years they became more and more fascinating. There are several capital cities in the Orient that have been heavily influenced by British colonialism, and one of the most questionable idiosyncrasies to an American's point of view upon first visit is the strange and initially disturbing custom of driving on the left (wrong?) side of the road. (I have often wondered how that all started - left side versus right side - and why? It would make a great college thesis, "eh what?" if written without overly offending the English). Somehow, we maneuvered through the congested traffic. In those days, men traveled in business suits, so my dark blue IBM pin stripe, conservative tie and wing tip black shoes were not out of the ordinary and I was comfortable in the brisk February weather. Hong Kong in the hot and humid summer months would be far more uncomfortable. In a few minutes we pulled up in front of the huge facade of the Peninsula Hotel, one of the most famous hotels in the Orient. My first stop would be a stylish one!

The grandeur of the hotel lobby and polite hospitality of the Chinese made me realize why Bob had insisted that I stay at the Peninsula. The oversized hotel room with its eighteen-foot ceilings and plush furnishings emphasized his good taste. (Was this symbolically like the gladiator's feast before being thrown to the lions in a Roman arena the next day?). I rang Bob, and we met in the lobby a few minutes later, his smiling face and warm handshake provided a nice welcome in those strange sophisticated surroundings.

He gestured across the immense lobby and said, "It is commonly believed that if you sit in this lobby long enough, you will eventually meet every traveler in the world."

I didn't doubt it. We did not have time to wait just then, but over the next few years, the Peninsula lobby, and the lobby at the Hong Kong Hilton across the harbor, became the primary meeting places for IBMers working in Southeast Asia.

"Come on Dan, I've much to show you before the day is out," and we headed for the nearby Hong Kong Star Ferry Terminal, one of the world's most entertaining and colorful rides. The harbor traffic was an extension of the busy city streets and each ferry crossed the scenic waterway in about ten minutes. The next few hours were filled with the sights, sounds and fragrance of a Chinese Disneyland with the real Disneyland in second place. It is almost impossible to do justice to this fascinating harbor and city by writing about it. You had to be there to experience the harbor's crowded shipping, strange harbor craft (junks, sampans and walla-wallas), the hotels and towering business buildings, the smells and street scenes and traffic and perhaps especially the deeply etched facial characteristics of the Chinese people, to say nothing of the many beautiful Eurasian women. All the new sights dazzled my mind. I would learn more about the nightclubs, bars and back streets of the city on subsequent visits.

Bob had some shopping to do - art galleries and jewelry shops were his weakness - but we eventually discussed the serious subject of my upcoming responsibilities in Southeast Asia. Tanner was the Federal Senior Marketing Manager in our Honolulu office, and had accepted the responsibility of organizing the IBM military support team of which I was a part. Bob had briefed IBM CEO Tom Watson Jr. twice on the Vietnam plan and had Watson's full blessings on the organizational and policy changes that had to take place*. Bob was smart, dedicated, experienced and, perhaps most important, a great guy to work for and whom I respected. We had been working together in Honolulu since early 1964 and I trusted his direction and advice. He was on his way back to Honolulu after a trip to Saigon and Bangkok, so was able to give me the latest status of our personnel and business situation there. We walked the streets, rode the ferries and stretched a fine dinner at "Jimmy's Kitchen" into many hours of conversation about Vietnam - and shopping in Hong Kong.

With evening came new sights and sounds - the main streets of Kowloon were lit up like a huge Christmas tree - and at eleven p.m., the Chinese nightlife was just swinging into high gear. I wasn't ready for any more experiences and decided a good night's sleep was wiser than night crawling so as to be fresh for the flight to Saigon the next morning. The comforts of my Peninsula room made sleep come easily and the next thing I knew the bedside telephone was announcing my wakeup call. Shower, dress, repack and meet Tanner in the lobby for coffee and croissants. We both checked out and shared a taxi to the airport. Bob had a flight back to "paradise" and I had my orders and was headed for the war zone. Bob reminded me of the importance of good communications with his office in Honolulu. We exchanged "Aloha's" and headed for our respective departure gates.

The China Airlines flight followed a straight line south southeast for about a 1000 miles, across the South China Sea to the Indochina mainland of South Vietnam. As I remember, the flight crossed the shoreline in the vicinity of Cam Ranh Bay so that the last 120 miles or so took us over much of the battlefield areas on the approach into Saigon. With my face pressed to the starboard port, I could see lush green countryside, shimmering rivers and miles of rice paddies, all of which could easily have been mistaken for a peaceful agrarian countryside. However, as the steeply descending jet approached our Saigon destination I began to notice lines of pockmark like scars (what was later called pot hole topography), small stockades in haphazardly cleared areas and many low flying helicopters. The effects of our B-52 bombing raids and the evidences of war were rapidly coming into view. It was time to start getting serious! We soon touched down at Tan Son Nhut International Airport.

\* Bob Tanner once told me, "The thing that is unique about IBM's (Vietnam) operation is that <u>everything</u> is unique - the special pay plan, the R&Rs, the cars, the radios, the villas, etc. Every time a new accounting type moves into a new job in Washington, D.C., I have to go back there and explain why we are changing long standing IBM rules and why we don't follow the standard procedures as laid out in the Branch Office Manual." Bob, also once told me, "When I briefed Tom Watson (IBM CEO), I told him that the three principal objectives out there were: 1. To guarantee the utmost safety of our people; 2. To assure the military knew IBM was there with them (and this was the reason for the white shirts) and to support them in such a way that they would remember us for many years; and 3. To insure our profit was less than what the operation actually cost the IBM Corporation."

# Chapter 2
## Welcome Home

In 1969 Tan Son Nhut Airport was the busiest airport in the world. In fact, in those days Vietnam could boast the five busiest airports in the world thanks to our U. S. air power and the commercial jet services feeding the war with manpower and supplies. Chicago's O'Hare ranked number six and I soon learned why. After the required steep descent over the crater-marked countryside, we touched down and taxied by an amazing assortment of commercial and military aircraft. I stared out the port at many of the world's best airlines - United, Pan American, TWA, Qantas, Air Vietnam, China Airlines, Thai Airlines, World Airways, and Lufthansa to name just a few, but these aircraft were insignificant when compared to the number of camouflaged C-124s, C-130s and the various fighter bombers of the 7th and 13th Air Force and the Vietnam Air Force (VNAF) aircraft. Our China Airlines flight rolled to a stop a few hundred yards from a relatively small white two story terminal building, and as we de-planed the heat hit me (at approximately 11 degrees north latitude, it was hot even in February) and the surrounding jet and turboprop noises were all but deafening and probably added to the heat. We single filed toward a building that had been meant for easier times, when Saigon was just a tourist destination. I began to notice throngs of black pajama clad Vietnamese, local police and security guards dressed more formally in white uniforms, military personnel of various nations and a few civilians identifiable by their casual western dress. Immigration and customs went surprisingly smooth and I began to look for the IBMers in white shirts and ties that were scheduled to meet me. There was a great deal of pushing and shouting by competing Vietnamese porters and taxi drivers, but I was quickly rescued by two old friends, Bruce Tomson and Larry Pulliam. Both men had already been in country for over a year.

Strong, warm handshakes and a necessarily loud, "Hi Dan. Welcome to your new home. Grab your bags before somebody else does," and "Come-on, let's go, Better hang onto those bags real tight on the way to the car."

Bruce and Larry knew their way around the hot crowded terminal area, and we were quickly on our way to the parking lot through the unruly crowd. Near the car, Bruce showed me his Motorola handy-talky that he said all the IBMers carried. He then contacted home base saying that I had arrived and that we would be back at the IBM main office soon, traffic permitting. He explained that every IBMer kept the main office informed as to their location at all times - whether it might be in Saigon or throughout South Vietnam. Larry added, with a smile, that the compact, heavy handy-talky was also useful for bashing 'cowboys' in case one was trying to steal your watch or wallet. I did not yet understand this unique but useful aspect of the handy-talky. Whatever? I would have to see that in action. After months of anticipation, I was finally 'in-country' and about to begin my grand adventure.

We climbed into Bruce's white diesel Mercedes sedan , drove out the guarded gates of the bustling Tan Son Nhut (TSN) complex and passed a series of buildings which Bruce said were the Military Assistance Command Headquarters (HQ MACV) and where we had an introductory meeting the next day. We headed toward Saigon driving southwest down Cach Mang Street. Once again, I was amazed by all the new sights and sounds of a completely different type of Asian cacophony. First impressions remain stuck in one's brain. Cach Mang was a main traffic artery into Saigon from the military bases to the northwest portion of the city. Our IBM office was located halfway between TSN and downtown Saigon near the busy intersection of Cach Mang and Truong Tan Buu Streets. The traffic along our route was almost indescribable. There were no fixed painted lanes for traffic to move along in. Eight or ten lanes worth of two way traffic filled the width normally required at home for four lanes and the lines of slow moving vehicles jockeyed for position back and forth across the one painted center line whenever space permitted and depending on who could out bluff who. A sort of tonnage rule seemed to prevail; whichever vehicle might do the most damage had the right of way. The vehicles varied from smoke belching Honda motorcycles, to bicycles, to Lambretta jitneys, to military jeeps and trucks, police cars, civilian cars and work-trucks of all makes including black French Citroens, pedicabs (rick-shaw type manpowered three wheel cyclos) to the blue and cream colored Renault taxi cabs and even a few donkeys pulling wagons.

The carbon monoxide from the Hondas was so thick it made your eyes water and the noise made normal conversation difficult. There was also a slight but unmistakable stench of raw sewage. A great deal of honking was taking place and somehow the whole mass managed to move down the street at about fifteen or twenty miles per hour. There was the inevitable minor accident every few blocks but things moved so slowly there didn't seem to be a cause for serious injury. The motor scooters were probably the most interesting because the Vietnamese had learned how to balance an entire family on one scooter. I was told that three on a bike was commonplace and months later I was to claim that I had seen seven on one motorbike (I do have a photograph taken during a lunar new year holiday showing a family of six on one motor scooter composed of a well dressed Vietnamese couple and their four children)! I wondered how I would ever learn to drive in such chaos. Bruce and Larry said I would get used to it, and I did, in time.

We arrived at the IBM office within fifteen minutes after leaving Tan Son Nhat, a distance of only two miles. We turned left off Cach Mang onto Truong Tan Buu Street and then right into a dirt alleyway. This turn was marked by a large blue and white sign attached high on a telephone pole pointing the way to IBM-GEM. For some unknown reason to me, IBM stateside management had grouped Government, Education and Medical into one large U.S.A. marketing unit, thus the acronym GEM, and I never did understand the relationship - especially in Saigon - but there we were for all to see, at least the Government portion. The location was certainly a misnomer as far as any type of gem was concerned. Bruce and MACV had managed to obtain the lease on a grand old Saigon villa that had more recently been used as a Red Cross Headquarters just prior to our occupancy. Its official street address was 115 Minh Mang Alley. The office was across the alley from the Milan Hotel, which was a place where I would later spend time enjoying my free evenings. The Milan

14

served us well over the years as a convenient combination restaurant, bar, dance hall, and bordello with a sixth floor roof-top bar sometimes best used for watching the not too distant war.

We drove through a gated entryway with large steel doors. I could see a white stucco single-story farmhouse-like building in the background. The grounds of our office compound were about a half-acre in size surrounded by a six-foot cement wall, which was topped by barbed wire. The only entrance was through the gate we had just entered. Just inside the gate, on the left, was a small open-faced shack complete with an on duty Vietnamese armed guard (something new with respect to the standard stateside IBM Branch Office). I was informed that we employed two retired Vietnamese guards who shared the duty of protecting the compound. They were trusted veterans of previous Vietnamese wars. The old guard came to a tired attention, saluted Bruce's Mercedes as we drove past and went back to sleep. We pulled up in front of the building that would be my workplace for the next two and a half years. Near the door was a bronzed plaque that again said IBM-GEM. (As of this writing, this bronze plaque is presently in the custody of a retired IBM Customer Engineer who lives in California.) There were a number of civilian cars partially filling the parking area at the side of the building - a mud covered Range Rover, a blue VW bug (with a bumper sticker that said 'Think Snow'), two or three Toyota sedans and a couple of Toyota 4-wheel drive Land Cruisers. There were nice trees and a flower garden and the surrounding high walls gave the compound a strong, private and secure feeling – a refuge from the outside street chaos of Saigon.

Bruce and Larry led me into what had once been a large living room, now converted to a reception area and administrative business office. Several of the salesmen, systems engineers and field engineers were there to meet me and I was introduced all around to Bill Fidler, Grant Giske, John Smith, Bob Curtis, Bill Shugg, Bruce Roth, Bob Kimmerly, Fred Hodder and others. I was also introduced to the beautiful and talented Madame Nam Phoung, our Vietnamese receptionist and secretary who dressed in the traditional form-fitting "ao dai" and whom I soon found was most helpful whenever it became necessary to translate English into either the French language or Vietnamese. I also met the intriguing Carrie "Ming Chi" Lam who was sort of our girl Friday and who could accomplish any number of unusual administrative tasks. I looked through the offices, which Bruce and the others had managed to convert from the various rooms of a villa, all filled with locally procured and somewhat substandard office furniture. There were the sales/SE bullpen, several management offices, two bathrooms (a strange looking large round brass gong occupied much of the space in one bathroom), a small coffee/kitchenette area, and an archaic looking Japanese made telephone switchboard (complete with operating instructions written in undecipherable Japanese) taking up space in the main hallway.

Two outbuildings housed the Customer Engineering parts room, where I met Frank Smith, parts expert extraordinaire, and also the Collins Single Sideband (SSB) radio room that was topped by a massive transceiving antenna. Out back was a gray 10 by 20 foot steel 'conex' container that served as secure storage for the all-important additional computer spare parts. Near that was a huge diesel generator used, quite often, for backup electrical power. The rest of the compound was parking space and the gardens, except for a grassy area at the side of the main building - this was the official IBM Southeast Asia croquette court - which would be put into use almost each day by the IBM athletes after 5 PM. I was told that during the monsoon season, the croquette area contained a half foot of rain water and was called 'Lake Watson' in honor of IBM's CEO. I began to relax and realized that my new office was quite unique from any other IBM facility in the world but that it was going to be a most pleasant environment.

Bruce Tomson filled a couple of coffee cups and we sat down in his Location Manager's Office to begin my indoctrination and discuss how he and I were going to share the dual management responsibilities for marketing and systems engineering for all our military customers in Vietnam, the Philippines and Thailand. I hadn't seen Bruce for at least a year, since we had shared a house and done some sailing together in Honolulu, but we had talked quite often via the TransPacific military phone patch. He looked tanned and healthy but tired and was clearly in need of some time off. He had done a fabulous job in organizing the present operation, and with the growth in computer usage in all three countries, mentioned above, he needed help. Bruce was ideally suited for this job. He had been a Captain in the U.S. Army and had already served an active duty tour in Southeast Asia. From previous conversations I knew that he had been in Cambodia. He knew the territory, as well as the mentality of both the local population and the military. After a couple of hours of talking about how to run a business in a war zone we had nailed down some plans, personnel moves, customer calls, problem resolutions and where I was going to live. I also heard, for the first time and first hand, what really went on in Saigon with these IBMers during the February 1968 TET Offensive. Bruce and the others had holed up for a few days and had some close calls but no one had been injured - just pretty scared and stressed out. While we were talking, there was a loud "blang, blang, blang" sound and a wild scream, which echoed through the offices, and then some laughing.

"What the heck is that?" I asked.

"Well", said Bruce, "That's the SEAWA gong that you saw in one of the bathrooms. SEAWA stands for Southeast Asia Wins Again, and every time one of the guys becomes frustrated or foiled by the crazy traffic or illogical things that happen here in Saigon, he has the opportunity to go bang the hell out of the gong. My guess is that one of the guys just drove back from Long Binh. It's a great way to release some tension."

I opined, "Gee, what a great idea. All IBM business offices should have one!"

We talked some more and then sure enough, right at five o'clock there was some yelling down the hall and I was invited to participate in my first game of cutthroat croquette.

I moved into a walled, gated compound and two-story stucco villa about three blocks from the office and across from a graveyard. For the next couple of months I shared that house with two IBM Customer Engineers (CEs). Both of my new housemates had been in "Nam" for almost two years and I was able to learn a great deal from them on how to get around Saigon and the various military bases. That first night, around midnight, I heard the not too distant "thud, thud, thud" sounds that no one else had mentioned or much noticed any more. The house vibrated slightly and the windows rattled, like a mild Southern California earthquake, but then the sounds and shaking kept repeating on a regular basis. The B-52s were doing their special thing - rolling thunder - which explained to me the numerous strings of craters I had seen on the flight into Saigon. As the nights and weeks progressed, the B-52 bombing runs became almost comforting in their regularity. The bombing runs laid a large mental security blanket over the residents of Saigon. It was when they stopped many months later that the absence of the nightly bombardment really bothered me. Another noise and vibration that I gradually became used to was the "thump, thump, thump" of the helicopters constantly passing overhead, both day and night. To this day, whenever I hear that familiar beat of nearby rotor blades, I am reminded of Saigon. Those are sounds and memories that will never fade away.

Neither my CE housemates nor I spent much time at the villa. The CEs were all overworked and traveling locally or upcountry on service calls, or they were on R & R trips away from Vietnam. I spent a good deal of those early months traveling from computer installation to installation in Vietnam, as well as to customer sites in the Philippines and Thailand. Nevertheless, my villa mates became close and dependable friends in keeping with the bonding that takes place when men are pressed together under extreme and sometimes hazardous conditions. That particular house has two rather funny memories that taught me lessons. One night I wanted something to drink. It was dark in the kitchen and I had to reach up to a top cupboard shelf to get a glass. As I did so, a very large rat ran straight down my arm, jumped to the top of my head and just as quickly disappeared to some other hiding place in the house. I screamed and shuddered and decided I would turn on the lights next time. Another evening, while reading before going to sleep, I mistakenly set a can of cola I was drinking on the bedside table. I woke up later that night and was thirsty, so I took a drink from the unfinished cola and quickly spat the large wiggling and disgusting cockroach that had been sharing my drink out of my mouth. I never left a drink out unfinished after that, and still don't to this day out of respect for the memory of that cockroach.

At that time, IBM had about fifty men in South Vietnam in support of the U.S. military. IBM World Trade Corporation also had a separate company headquarters on Gia Long Street in downtown Saigon that supported the Vietnamese private sector and the Vietnamese government data processing installations. Our two organizations operated completely independent of one another and ultimately reported to Armouk, N.Y. HQ, through totally different IBM organizations. Our IBM-GEM volunteers were all bachelors from the U.S.A. and had been carefully selected for this unique assignment. It was required that we all be unmarried for the duration of the assignment because it was thought that there was some risk of either enemy capture or loss of life. Bachelor status simply made things easier by eliminating immediate family ties at home or trying to maintain separate housing and personnel plans for families in the war zone. However, our single status did lead to a certain amount of promiscuity with the local members of the opposite sex. Most of us had normal sex drives and the real or imagined dangers of war amplified the horniness and provided ample excuse for doing things that we might not have otherwise done at home.

We all had different levels of Security Clearances (i.e. - Secret, Top Secret, or Special clearances above TS) dependent on job responsibilities, and we carried a 'non-combatants' card that stated that if we were captured we were civilians and not involved politically or militarily with the war effort. In retrospect, it was certainly naive to think that this little card would have had any protective effect if captured and interrogated by the VC or North Vietnamese. We also had different levels of Government Service (GS) equivalency depending on our level of IBM responsibility, education and pay scale. For instance, I had a U.S. Government GS-15 ranking, which was equal in theory to an Army or Air Force Colonel. It carried with it certain military officer privileges, which, by the way, we were more than careful never to take advantage of or abuse, unless absolutely necessary.

The way that the GS equivalency levels were determined is an interesting story. Sometime around 1967 when our planned presence in Vietnam was still being negotiated, the liaison between the Federal marketing unit in Honolulu and CINCPAC HQ was through an Air Force Command and Control office at Hickam AFB. A protocol officer there initially tried to establish the GS levels at GS-7, which meant that no IBMer would have accepted an assignment in Southeast Asia. The protocol officer had obtained an IBM Corporate organization chart and equated Tom Watson, IBM CEO, to CINCPAC and then worked downward from there to the GS-7 for branch office personnel. Our Federal Senior Marketing Manager, Bob Tanner, took the protocol officer a chart which showed CINCPAC as a 19 level equal to himself and then the managers in Vietnam to be GS-18s and so on. That too was unacceptable and a compromise was established then and there at the GS-11 through GS-15 levels for our Vietnam personnel.

Groups of IBMers shared villas, rented and paid for by IBM, which were generally located on the outskirts of Saigon between "Stinky Creek" and Tan Son Nhut along the Cach Mang corridor in a suburb named Gia Dinh. The rent was paid to the Vietnamese landlords in piasters, and since there were no large denomination piaster notes (at least not large enough to handle inflation and the black market rates), we would fill a fairly large paper sack with money and carefully hand deliver the rent. The villas ranged from three bedroom homes to the "ten man villa" which was more a dormitory type building of three floors with one common shared kitchen and living area. Extra rooms were always kept available for IBM transients. The villas were of classic tropical French architecture with cement tile floors, high ceilings with powerful ceiling fans, cement stairways, window mounted air conditioners and an emphasis on ways to stay cool. There was usually a stairway to the flat rooftop that was an excellent place to either sunbathe during a day off or watch the war at night. Each villa usually had a high wall around the property and some of the walls had either concertina razor wire or glass shards imbedded in tar along the top. The wire and glass served as added security from unwelcome visitors in addition to the lockable driveway gates. There was usually space inside these walls for several cars. Any car left unattended outside walls would either be stolen within hours or completely dismantled (similar to our large U.S. inner cities of today).

IBM required that we buy used, import or somehow obtain our own cars while on assignment and those cars constituted a serious and temporary investment. Most of the IBMers sold the cars on the economy at the end of their assignments and some were sold at a nice profit. A local Vietnamese driver's license was required and local car insurance was available through several companies. The driver's license could be obtained legitimately after a lot of red tape or could be bought through the use of a local expediter who knew how to do it and who would bribe the right official. I remember that I paid someone in our office, provided a photograph and a few days later a license just showed up on my desk. Cooking and cleaning at many of the villas was done through the services of excellent Vietnamese maids. They would shop, prepare meals, clean, wash, iron and manage the running of a household so that most of our time could be devoted to IBM business and longer than normal hours servicing our military customers. Besides, we bachelors had more important things to do than clean house after work hours.

Life in Saigon was fairly comfortable from a physical point of view. We all received extra pay and had few financial cares or responsibilities. The extra pay was called the International Adjustment Allowance (IAA) and for those living in Saigon it was 60% above one's base salary and for those men upcountry it was 75% extra because of isolation and hardship. In fact, the opportunity to "save money" was perhaps one of the primary reasons that many of our volunteers accepted the war zone assignment. The day I arrived in Vietnam, I began making an extra $1020.00 per month (which was a considerable sum of money back in 1969) and that increased accordingly when I received a raise in base salary. We did not realize that the immediate opportunity to save money might cost us professionally in the long run. We were taken out of IBM's mainstream career paths and given subtle Vietnam War stigmas upon our return to the 'real' IBM world. Many of these mercenary IBMers quit "Big Blue" out of frustration upon their return to tamer assignments at home. There was no room for or acceptance within mainstream IBM for anyone who had been trained to be or continued to act so independent.

My first few weeks were busy ones. I had to meet our MACV sponsors and other key customers and at the same time settle into my new environment and learn my way around a city designed for half a million and now grown to three or four million people (including the section of Saigon called Cholon). The sights and sounds on the streets constantly amazed me. It was so crowded that it took every acquired driving skill to go from point A to point B without being involved in some form of accident. Just driving a car was going to be a major challenge but, for the first few days until I bought a car, I was more than happy to let Bruce, Larry, Grant and the others chauffer me around to meetings or meals.

The day after I arrived, we called on Headquarters, Military Assistance Command Vietnam (HQ MACV) which served as the direct extension of Commander-in-Chief Pacific (CINCPAC) in Honolulu and was in charge of the Allied war effort. This was the domain of the American General Staff that called the shots - literally - and answered to our President and Pentagon in Washington D.C. Our personnel were in-country under the sponsorship and protection of this organization. Our principal interface was with a bird Colonel at MACV, who was also the MACV data processing manager. The relationship was one of mutual assistance. If we had any IBM operational problems we could ask the Colonel or his staff for assistance, and in return the MACV computer installation received excellent service and also probably received first priority if there was a conflict in scheduling manpower, spare parts or technical assistance. Bruce introduced me to the then Colonel in charge and it was immediately obvious that Bruce had established excellent rapport with the Colonel and his staff (The fact that Bruce was an ex Army officer may have helped in this regard). The Colonel was pleased that IBM had finally brought in a technically experienced SE Manager (me) to help advise and interface with his technical staff, manage the growing number of IBM Systems Engineers and help plan future computer upgrades for his data processing systems. I knew immediately that I would be welcome around the MACV installation. At that time MACV had a 1410 computer system housed in a fairly modern computer room with space to grow. They also had a rudimentary 1050 terminal network spread throughout the MACV building complex. Those were still the days when the punched card was king, and there were keypunch machines, verifiers and other unit record equipment spread throughout the many hallways and special areas of the MACV complex. I was pleased with what I saw technically, proud to meet the officers and enlisted personnel and knew that we were working with a competent group of professionals.

Our next stop that first day was the computing center that supported the Headquarters, 7th Air Force. It was just across the street from MACV, but not an easy transition by the time one passed out through MACV security, drove through the MACV parking areas and streets, out the MACV main gate to busy Cach Mang, through the checks and guards at 7th AF and down busy air base roads to the data processing buildings, found a parking spot, walked down several long hallways past guards to a door with a cipher lock and finally into another air conditioned room which housed another IBM 1410 computer installation (twenty minutes to cross the street!). We went through the same introductory procedures and shook hands with Colonel Jack Hawley, Chief of data processing and a man who I was to learn was a well seasoned data processing manager and who became a close friend. He was in his early forties, in good shape but had snow white hair, which I was to learn later had turned white almost overnight during an earlier jungle escape from an enemy tiger cage in Laos. He was a man of experience and appetites! Colonel Hawley was friendly and candid about his operation, said he was glad to see me, and also said that he would need additional Systems Engineers to support the upcoming computer upgrade to a S/360 Model 50. He bragged about the IBM maintenance support he had been receiving and said he expected it to continue in light of the increasing complexities of the air war and increases in new applications and data. This was an account that I would pay very close attention to over the next couple of years, and justifiably so.

After the MACV and 7th AF meetings, we headed for BOQ 1, a nearby officers' mess, for an early lunch and I was introduced to military dining. One of the things that the headquarters based military personnel did in Vietnam was eat well, and our officer level privileges gave us access to all of the dining halls throughout Vietnam. After loading up on a trayfull of roast beef sandwich, vegetables, soup, salad and milk, we found a table and watched the military relax for a short period in their stateside-like cafeteria environment. Bruce asked me what I thought so far and jokingly whether I planned to stay. Based on my limited exposure, I knew that there was going to be plenty of work. I switched subjects and said, "It appears that the military really needs us here and heavily relies on our computer expertise. Tanner told me that IBM management in the U.S. had several more bachelors ready for this assignment, so do we have adequate housing to handle them?" Bruce admitted that was one of the challenges that he was working on and as soon as he could line up a few more villas in town he would let Bob know when to send the new men onward. We talked about the

MACV and 7th AF account plans and whether the S/360 upgrades would provide adequate computing capacity. When we drove back to the IBM office compound, I told Bruce, " Don't worry about me staying; I thrive in these kinds of environments", and my old friend knew that some of my unique experiences as an exploration geologist a few years earlier in Morocco, Libya, Iran and Saudi Arabia would probably come in handy.

At the office, I spent some time listening and talking to some of the IBMers assigned to our permanent 'up-country' locations - Da Nang, Cam Ranh Bay, Nha Trang and Qui Nhon - via our Collins single side-band radio network. Each location had an identical SSB transceiver, and in addition each IBMer carried a handy-talky strapped to his belt, on his desk or in his car. The office base stations were monitored 24 hours a day and the standing order was that every IBMer would keep either his own base station or the Saigon headquarters station apprised of his whereabouts at all times. At night, the handy-talkies sat in their charging units and were kept 'On'. This system proved invaluable, not only for personnel safety and communications but also for ordering supplies needed by the remote customer sites as well as coordinating computer and unit record spare parts.

Later in my assignment, I would occasionally hear a jibber-jabber sing song Vietnamese female voice come through to the base station and would understand that one of our guys was probably in a Saigon tea bar somewhere letting one of the 'hostesses' at least play with his handy-talky, if nothing more. One afternoon I heard a high lilting voice saying, "I love you, I love you" and our Vietnamese base operator quickly returned the message with, "I don't have any money, please sign off." Our Collins network also extended to multiple locations in Thailand and theoretically could enable us (on a clear day!) to talk to a transceiver installed in the Honolulu Branch office. This network was also respected by various military units. From time to time some GIs would show up asking if they could use our network because their phone system was inoperative. We would gladly comply. There was a radio-talk protocol and we all learned the "Saigon base calling so-and-so, do you read, roger, over-and out" jargon of the day. Later that same day, I probably played croquette again, ate a good meal at a downtown French restaurant and slept well to the tune of the B52s' nightly 'thud, thud, thud'.

The majority of the IBMers in the war zone were the Customer Engineers (CEs) who were our well trained data processing maintenance men. The military possessed a certain amount of programming skills but they could not repair most of the equipment, handle the upgrades or perform the necessary preventive maintenance on the hundreds of different types of machines at all the bases. Our operation thus provided these skills for almost every IBM installation in Vietnam, Thailand and the Philippines. Where the military had larger, permanent and more secure upcountry or remote data processing installations, we had one or more CEs in residence. The CEs lived either in villas in cities near the bases, if available, or in Portacamps (large trailers) on base, which were purchased by IBM and imported from the U.S. mainland. Small administrative offices with the Collins SSB equipment and parts storage areas were set up in the upcountry CE villas, or in some cases at a military facility. As an example, our Da Nang sub-office was a centrally located rented villa that was used as an office and as sleeping quarters for visiting IBMers. Providing parts and repair service on a timely basis was key to the success of our IBM mission. All the stories of heroics and brushes with danger by these CEs, while performing their duties, go beyond the scope of this book, but some will be passed along and intertwined within or featured in following chapters. Suffice it to say that data processing during the Vietnam War could not have existed without the services of our hard working IBM Customer Engineers and the efficiency of our multi-country parts supply system.

The map of Southeast Asia below shows where the principal military data processing installations were located and consequently shows where IBM had resident personnel and office facilities.

The main office in Saigon housed most of the sales, Systems Engineers, Field Engineering personnel (same as CEs), administration and management. It was also the main parts depot since we tried to keep enough parts in country to meet almost all short term requirements. The next level of the parts supply system was a depot in Okinawa that had ready access to daily flights into Saigon or Da Nang. Beyond Okinawa, the parts came from Honolulu and the U.S. mainland.

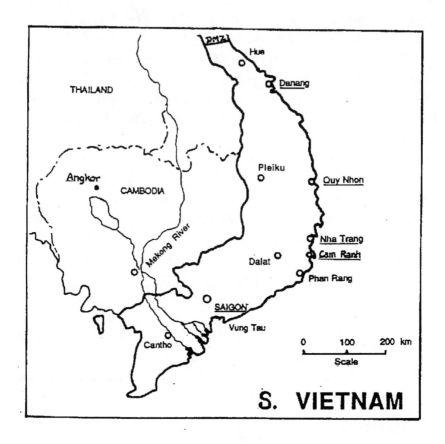

The system worked well! As an example: if a part were needed for a system in Qui Nhon, let's say a 1401 memory board, and it was not in stock in Saigon or we could not borrow it from another 1401, a call would be placed to Okinawa and/or Honolulu. The board would be placed on the next available military or commercial flight out of 'Oki' or 'Hono' and arrive at either Da Nang or Saigon within 24 hours of the outage. The part would then be either hand carried by an IBMer or by a military volunteer (an aircraft pilot would sometimes personally carry the part) via C124 or courier jet to Qui Nhon, where the plane would be met by a CE on his way to the needy system. The SSB network helped coordinate all of this supply system. Machine outages were not tolerated for long and as a result of this type of IBM/military cooperation the repair service at all Vietnam locations was probably as efficient as anywhere in the U.S.A. at that time.

There were a few locations that only used punched card machines, such as: 026s, 029s, 056s, 083s, 504s, 407s, etc. These were generally smaller more remote sites and when they experienced an outage our nearest IBM office would be contacted and a CE would be dispatched with tool kit, handy-talky, a 4-wheel drive Toyota Landcruiser, and sometimes an overnight bag. Pleiku Air Base was one such location that was serviced out of Qui Nhon. Our friendly troops controlled the roads in that area during the day, but often the Viet Cong controlled them at night and a trip during night hours for an IBM CE was simply not safe. One story goes that a CE had a flat tire on one of these day trips and needed help to get to Pleiku to have the tire repaired and the machines serviced. The CE reportedly flagged down a passing local on a Honda and did, in fact, persuade him at gunpoint to take him and the tire into town. The CE retained the local and Honda during the tire repair and they drove back to the waiting Toyota. The CE put his gun away, paid the Vietnamese, replaced the tire and completed his drive to Pleiku and the repair mission.

Yes, some IBMers did carry fire arms, but more on that later. Sometimes the military provided a jeep escort for a CE if the area was generally not secure or if it was late at night and considered unsafe. Other travel alternatives included riding with or joining a military convoy or using hastily obtained flight orders for the next helicopter or other aircraft heading in the right direction. The military always accommodated and respected our people during these service trips, and I do not know of any instance wherein an IBMer was not treated as well as possible. I think most U.S. soldiers thought we were crazy for being there in the first place, but they knew we were needed and always went out of their way to help.

Bob Dillon tells the following story. "I received a call one afternoon from a Lt. Bruner at Chu Chi, an Army camp west of Saigon. He wanted me to come right away to repair a 407 listing machine that was giving them trouble. I said it was too late in the afternoon, by the time I got there it would be 4 or 4:30 and that I had plans that evening in Saigon; could the 407 wait until the next morning? Lt. Bruner said, "No, Bob, you have to come this afternoon; there's a Chu Chi bound helicopter out at Hotel One that you can still make and I'll take care of you tonight. You can eat well in our mess, drink my booze and even sleep in my hooch." I said there was no way for tonight, "That place scares me," and that I wanted to stay in my own villa and not stay overnight under potential VC attacks if I could help it and went on to say that I just didn't feel safe in Chu Chi at night. There had been too many recent attacks, etc., etc. After much discussion, Lt Bruner finally relented and I promised him I would be at Hotel One (the TSN helicopter terminal) at eight the next morning and see him soon after that.

The twenty-minute helicopter ride was uneventful and there was a short walk to the data processing building and Lt. Bruner's hooch. The lieutenant had built himself a private one-man specialized sleeping quarters complete with sitting area, comfortable bed and well stocked bar. It was hexagonal in shape and made out of scrap wood and metal and somewhat set apart from the regular BOQ sleeping dorm. I walked past some palm trees that shielded my destination and when I turned a corner and looked to see Lt. Bruner's hooch, it just wasn't there. The hooch had been completely leveled in the night. It was just a pile of rubble. The whole side of the data processing building had been blown out too. Oh, boy! I hustled over to some GIs who were cleaning up the mess and they said that Bruner's hooch had taken a direct hit from a 122mm rocket just after midnight. The machines looked like they were OK, but I was afraid to ask about the lieutenant. Just then Lt. Bruner walked in another door and said, "Welcome Bob, I guess you saved my life! I haven't slept in the regular BOQ since I built the hooch, but after talking with you yesterday afternoon and listening to all your arguments about not wanting to be here last night, I decided I would sack with the rest of the guys." He shook my hand and said, "I owe ya one; let's get to work."

I was to learn this whole CE/parts/maintenance procedure very quickly and took my turns at the single side band stations whenever possible. The Collins equipment worked flawlessly and needed little maintenance. We also employed a few Vietnamese civilians and two hard working western women (an Australian and an American) to help operate and monitor the Collins system at the Saigon home base. The two women had remained in Vietnam during the hostilities because one had a serious ongoing relationship with a news photographer and the other was married to a civilian contractor in Saigon. The single Australian gal was a young, good looking blond by the name of Robin and received much attention from our bachelors. She managed to remain independently aloof and faithful to her own interests, but she made an excellent radio operator anyway. The American woman, Gloria, presently lives in Las Vegas and has contributed to this book. Her story is told in a later chapter. Our radio operator team worked diligently and kept our communications nerve center working night and day.

One of my early familiarization duties was to visit a number of our remote locations, so I set up trips for Cam Ranh Bay, Nha Trang, Qui Nhon and Da Nang. The purpose was to learn the problems and needs of both our IBMers and customers at these locations and then to produce a manager's status report for Bob Tanner in Honolulu. Stateside management needed to know whether we were doing the right thing and what the personnel needs and business forecasts might be for future military data processing. To do this, I had to call on appropriate military officers and try to determine whether the war and data processing volumes were escalating or de-escalating (in actuality, it was doing both). The travel procedure for a civilian was to first obtain MACV permission and flight orders; this was done fairly routinely and provided us with a flight status and a reservation on either a helicopter, C-124, C-130 or in some cases a small prop-driven courier aircraft. We would catch the flights at the Hotel One helicopter pad or the Tan Son Nhut military terminal and usually wear our standard IBM white shirt and tie garb in stark contrast to military blues, fatigues or khaki.

My first trip was to Cam Ranh Bay, where we maintained a couple of 1401 systems and considerable numbers of unit record equipment used by the Navy, Air Force and 'Sea Land' shipping. The resident CEs lived in two portacamps on base and the Air Force provided office space for our CE work desks, telephones and Collins equipment, plus a storage area for that coastal area's spare parts inventory. The CE living quarters were hot and dusty, and despite their heavy workload and somewhat Spartan living conditions they were in excellent spirits and were glad to see me and hear fresh civilian news from our Saigon headquarters. They appreciated my perspective on the status of our overall IBM mission and enjoyed the compliments I was able to pass along as a result of calling on a few high level Data Processing officers. One CE had just returned from his R&R holiday in Hong Kong and Taiwan and another was in the process of planning a R&R to Australia. Naturally the non-business conversation that afternoon centered on these trips - and the qualities and availability of the various women indigenous to those countries.

*Cam Ranh Bay CE Living Quarters – Home Sweet Home*

Our upcountry personnel were paid the extra hazardous duty pay, and they also enjoyed a generous vacation plan, paid for by IBM, which caused a constant shuffling of men back and forth to keep each location properly staffed. Without some excellent corporate benefits, why else would a civilian live an overworked, lonely and semi-dangerous life on a military base? The R&R trips and paid vacations at the end of a two-year assignment were what the upcountry CEs really looked forward to. In some respects, our CEs lived no different from many of the military personnel, except that they were better paid and had a bit more freedom. However, they had signed on for at least two years rather than the one-year hitches of the military.

That first night upcountry, I ate and slept in Air Force Bachelor Offices' Quarters (BOQ) Quonset huts, and after turning in I either hadn't noticed or was too tired or naive to appreciate the location of my bunk with respect to the nearby airstrip. About midnight, there was such a roar that I was sure that a freight train was ready to roll right over me. I jumped up and ran to a window in time to see the fiery tail pipes of a couple of F-4 Phantom jets in takeoff on a late night sortie. I think I was probably assigned 'the bunk' properly positioned for the neophytes in country. Not being able to fall back to sleep, I wandered up to the cafeteria for coffee and suddenly realized that the war did not slow down just because the sun went down. The cafeteria was full, and pilots and crews were arriving and departing in full combat gear as the night battles continued. Some were hollow-eyed, dog-tired, solitary figures sipping coffee and others were in animated conversation explaining their recent flight experience. Cam Ranh Bay was one of those five busiest airports in the world and it functioned at full pace 24 hours a day. I think I probably matured a bit more that night.

During the next few weeks, I made similar trips to our other remote locations, learning the ropes, talking with the military, visiting our data processing sites, assimilating knowledge and forming a basis for war zone computing and business requirements that was to serve me for the next few years. I learned quite a bit about the flow of the war while waiting for a ride on a military aircraft at the various air bases. Sometimes the wait for 'space available' was many hours and I would lean against a fence watching C-124s and C-130s load and unload, AC-47 gunships come and go, combat ready helicopters fill and takeoff and wounded GIs returning on stretchers being carried to waiting red cross vehicles. Once, at Da Nang, I waited all night for a morning flight, my briefcase for a pillow, sleeping on a wooden bench.

*The author on his way up country, first class*

Some of the travel was exhilarating and some morbid. Once the C-124 I was flying on could not lower it's landing gear until the very last minute (I watched as the flight crew manually lowered the gear with a large wrench just before touchdown) and we were put into head down crash landing mode on final approach. We made it and I was reminded of an old mathematical formula that stated, "if the number of landings equaled the number of takeoffs, you were probably OK." Another time, the courier aircraft in which I was flying had to suddenly abort a landing at a remote airstrip because the control tower informed our pilot that we did not "own" the runway at that particular moment. We flew on. During another C-124 flight, I was one of only a few living passengers on board; the remainder of the cargo deck was filled with rows of body bags on the first sad leg of their return trip back to the U.S.A. I thought of the newly popularized song, *Where Have All the Flowers Gone,* and the words of some of the verses like: *"Where have all the soldiers gone, Gone to graveyards every one, When will they ever learn, When will they ever learn?"*

My early weeks and months in Saigon were equally educational. When not calling on customers, working with my Systems Engineers, traveling upcountry, developing business plans, writing personnel appraisals and preparing requirements and financial reports for Honolulu, I was trying to become familiar with Saigon proper and any of the surrounding 'safe' environments. Saigon had truly been a beautiful city and at one time was called the 'Paris of the East'. It had been a city where wealthy Thais and other Southeast Asians went for vacations. What a change! Sandbagged gun emplacements, concertina wire, traffic congestion, clouds of blue exhaust from the two-cycle Lambrettas and cyclos, extreme overcrowding, shantytowns, the smell and evidence of raw sewage, battle scars and rubble. The omnipresent military had converted the wide tree-lined boulevards and fine buildings of years past into a besieged ugliness which hid its romantic past. Many fine buildings of colonial French architecture had become black mildew stained ugly structures and there was no time or funds for architectural pride. The accelerating pace of the war was taking its toll on Saigon. The city served as a huge refugee center for all of South Vietnam. Saigon also served as the political and business center for supplying and trying to manage a major war (the war was being called a "conflict" in the States - bullpucky!) and served as the commercial center for military and civilians alike. The people could buy and sell everything and anything - and I mean "anything". The black marketing trade was rampant, and anyone who spent time in Saigon in the late 1960's and early 1970's can bear testament to that fact.

I carried a small 35mm Rolie 35 camera wherever I went and literally took hundreds of photo slides of the scenes along the majestic tamarind, teak and kapok tree lined streets of Saigon. Physical places of interest included the Government Palace and beautiful park across the street, the new U.S. Embassy, the large classic Notre Dame Cathedral, several now famous downtown hotels such as the Continental, Rex and Caravelle, the impressive statue of the Unknown Soldier (since purposely destroyed by the Communists), the huge open air food market, the National Bank and Post Office buildings, the Circle Sportif swimming and tennis club which was the domain of the remaining French, many excellent French restaurants, scenes along the Saigon River, the flower market on Nguyen Hue Street - especially each year at TET (Lunar New Year), and, of course, the activities along the infamous Tu Do Street where much of the lower forms of commercial exchange took place.

Tu Do Street was where one went for Saigon entertainment, sex and action, in the form of poor to very good music, girls for hire, drugs, black market items and the rumored "contracts" on sanctioned individuals. Popular 'tea bars' on either side of the street were hopping every afternoon and evening until curfew; they were full of contractors, military men off limits, news reporters, and Vietnamese business persons trying to sell whatever they could to the rich Americans. I went there from time to time to enjoy the sights and the music (the Vietnamese singers and musicians had practiced and practiced so that they could almost perfectly mimic the many popular American entertainers of the day and many were truly talented). We IBMers had been counseled, pleaded with, threatened mildly and warned not to get involved with Saigon bar girls or illegal trafficking of anything, and to my knowledge none of our men did, to any serious degree. It was fun to have a drink or two and watch. Tu Do Street was also where one went to buy the well known Vietnamese ceramic elephants and other products from these talented and artistic people. We then mailed the ceramics home via the courtesy of APO 96309. My favorite shop was the Thanh Le store that sold exquisite art, Vietnamese scenes made of inlaid mother-of-pearl or lacquered, tiny egg shell pieces, and all colors and sizes of the famous elephants. Literally, thousands of those elephants - some of which weighed over fifty pounds each - were shipped home by American military and civilians alike. The APO instructed everyone to simply tie an address tag around the trunk of each elephant, rather than try to package them in crates or boxes. Most reached the U.S. unbroken.

While driving around the streets of wartime Saigon, one could experience and smell the rawness of life. The humid weather enhanced the stench of a population who for the most part used no soap or perfume and saw nothing wrong with urinating or defecating street side, in public view or perhaps behind an available tree or small bush. The city's public services were sadly lacking for such a swollen population, the trash and garbage continued to pile up and the rat population prospered.

There was a nightly curfew throughout Saigon, which varied in time depending on the immediate threat of enemy attack, general military tension or even just rumors. If anyone remained on the streets after what was usually 9 p.m. or 10 p.m., they were subject to arrest by the Quan Canh (Vietnamese Police who were called "white mice" because of their white uniforms and apathetic demeanor) under suspicion of collaborating with or actually being an enemy. We tried to respect this curfew diligently and if one were not home on time, one simply remained where one happened to be when curfew began (girls of the night included if they happened to be making house calls). The bars and restaurants all closed early, parties and social gatherings around town broke up early and unless one was on official business and carried orders, one was home by curfew! In those instances when an IBM machine would break down after curfew and it was serious enough to warrant repair that night, a military jeep escort would be called, and it would pick up and return the IBM CE to his home in order to guarantee safe passage and avoid any possibility of attack or arrest. The well known black pajamas of the VC blended well with the night, things happened at night around Saigon, buildings got blown up at night, and people got killed at night. It was best to be home in your own secure villa, at night!

There was an active social scene around Saigon too. It may have been that the frustrations and mental fatigue of the constant warring resulted in more American and French Vietnamese social gatherings than were otherwise necessary. These were well attended by our active IBMers, whenever we could find out where the party would be held. Keep in mind – we were probably all between the ages of 25 and 35 years - with energies to spare. The parties gave us an opportunity to blow off some steam as well as size up which American or the more exotic French Vietnamese young women were still available. It was also an opportunity to exchange 'unofficial' information about the war or for lining up weekend dates if the ladies could be so enticed. There would be good food, music, some dancing and the booze would be provided by the American civilians and military, courtesy of the local base's PX. Certain aspects of life had to go on, even in a war zone, and the girls were friendly and beautiful. Yes, I was beginning to understand some of the finer nuances of my new home. I learned to take advantage of the benefits and to be wary of the hazards. It was wise to learn quickly or else suffer the consequences!

# Chapter 3
## Keep A Low Profile, But Experience Everything

### Everything

DEPENDABLE TRANSPORTATION WAS A NECESSARY evil and IBM wanted us to purchase our own transportation if assigned to the Saigon area. I bought a light blue 1965 Volkswagen Bug from Graham Seibert who was moving upcountry for a few months prior to rotating home. Graham would be using an IBM owned Toyota Jeep in Da Nang so could release his car. I figured the VW would just about take me anywhere I wanted to go, even during the approaching wet season, be reliable and be relatively obscure among all the other vehicles on the road and therefore be somewhat safer. I guess my theory proved out, because I never had any trouble with the car or with any 'unfriendlies'. I had no reason to impress anyone and did not want a car that would attract undue attention. My plan was to keep a low profile and still confidently get around Saigon and the nearby military bases.

The VW had a sunroof. By standing on a seat and emerging up through the open roof area, while someone else was driving, I was able to take many movies and photos around the city. The VW also turned out to be a great mudder during the summer monsoons. I had leased a couple of VW Bugs in North Africa in the '60s and I knew that in sand or mud the VW was the next best thing to 4-wheel drive. I became adept at driving in the wild Saigon traffic and somehow completed my 2 ½+ year assignment accident free - maybe this was more luck than skill (even though I had been well trained on the busy streets of Southern California). Some of the other guys were not so lucky and ended up with bent fenders and payoffs to Vietnamese opportunists when involved in an accident where fault was either questionable or contrived.

For lunch and dinner, a bunch of us would usually pile into several cars and either head out to the nearby bases or risk the drive into downtown Saigon or nearby Cholon. We usually ate at a half dozen French or Vietnamese restaurants in downtown Saigon. One favorite was called the International House or simply 'I House'. The 'I House' was administered and operated in some obscure way by the U.S. Embassy and a membership was required but easily acquired. It was almost 100% American (or our allies) during lunch, and later at dinner was attended not only by Americans but also by a few high ranking Vietnamese officials, escorting a mix of their Vietnamese girlfriends (concubines). It was always crowded, the food was excellent and the prices quite reasonable. The 'I House' also had a band during lunch and dinner and a great open buffet on Sunday featuring prime rib, pork chops, fresh garden salads and various deserts. We often wondered how they could consistently serve such great food at those prices, and rumor had it that a few American supply sergeants were supplying more than just their own base mess halls. In Saigon, there was always some background scheme in process. There were slot machines on the ground floor, as well as a nice coffee shop. The main restaurant was up a broad staircase that led to what could have been called a grand ballroom in better days. It was filled with round white cloth covered tables, dining patrons and busy waiters. We stopped going to the 'I House' in 1970 after a serious upstairs plastique bomb explosion, that either seriously injured or killed a couple of American GIs (I don't know which).

You didn't want to be in the wrong place at the wrong time. On separate occasion, I was to meet the manager of IBM World Trade Vietnam at a certain restaurant in town. We both happened to be about twenty minutes late. As we walked from his downtown office, toward our restaurant destination, we were met by smoke and flames. The general area was cordoned off by both American and Vietnamese MPs. Lunch on those two bombing occasions could have been my last.

Parking a car in downtown Saigon was also something of an experience, even if and when a parking space could be found near a restaurant or popular bar or store. There were always the ubiquitous

'I-Watch Boys'. As soon as the car was parked, a group of boys between the ages of eight and fourteen would materialize out of no-where and begin shouting "I watch, I watch". You then had to pick one. These street waifs were one level above the beggars and one professional level below the Cowboys and too young to be drafted into the Vietnamese army. They had devised a whole new industry based on a simple scare tactic - "I watch for you so nothing happen you car, you pay when come back, OK Joe?" Sometimes the car would be broken into anyway, by a Cowboy, and the I-Watch Boy would still want to be paid because he had remained on station and watched exactly what had happened. I once came out of a restaurant just in time to see a man relieving himself on the front tire of my VW. It was too late to intervene, nor did I want to, and my I-Watch Boy insisted on payment. If you tried to drive away without paying, it would invite shouts of "You number 10 cheap Charlie" and/or a barrage of rocks well aimed toward your car.

I once drove to a less desirable section of Saigon to visit a shop that was known for its ceramic elephants, temple dogs and elegantly painted oriental vases. The workmanship was superb. I didn't buy anything, but when I emerged from the store, I was met by two young street urchins asking for candy or money. That seemed innocent enough so I gave them each some piaster, the equivalent of about ten cents U.S. That was my big mistake because suddenly from no-where there were ten more young beggar kids yelling for a handout. I couldn't help them all and I tried to explain with hands up and open that there would be no more money. With growing concern I began to walk faster through the increasing number of children, but the scene became worse. Soon there were twenty and then about thirty or more little Vietnamese urchins all jumping, pushing, yelling and shoving against me wanting something from the rich American. I knew I was in trouble and may have knocked one or two down in my concerned haste (I don't remember), but began to run to my car, which was about a block away - and it was a good thing that I was in good shape - I had to run fast. It was mob hysteria from the very young and very deprived. I reached the car, jumped in, re-locked the doors and drove away shocked and trembling. How could I be afraid of a bunch of kids? The streets of Saigon were full of surprises – many of them bad.

In a lighter vane, the trips into Saigon proper presented us with some visual pleasures. It was most enjoyable to watch and photograph the shapely young Vietnamese women gracefully strolling through town wearing their traditional dress, the 'ao dai'. They often carried sun umbrellas to shield their delicate features (it was said that they didn't want to look like the darker skinned Cambodians). Many were extremely well endowed in feminine features. Their watchful and flashing dark eyes, straight posture, shiny long black hair and loosely fitted black pajamas were in contrast to the flowing butterfly-like silk dresses of bright yellow, greens, blues or patterned silken material. We captured many of these good-looking women, but only on Kodak film. They were Catholic, proud of their bearing, aloof in public and not to be fooled with - in public!

On many evenings we would eat at the Club Nautique du Saigon and Monsieur 'T' would serve us steak and salad on the open-air top deck of that riverside yacht club. The group usually consisted of Bruce, Larry, Conrad, three Bills, Bob and myself. A leisurely dinner would sometimes be highlighted by gun-ship firefights a mile or so directly across the river - U.S. helicopters firing on VC rocket launching positions. Alternate entertainment was provided for us during dinner by a large quantity of geckos running around the ceiling and somewhat fewer mice running around under the tables. Several of us belonged to the yacht club and the group owned three small wooden ski boats (of dubious seaworthiness) that we jokingly referred to as our IBM 'Emergency Escape Plan' naval vessels. Nearby was the floating My Canh restaurant, which was blown up a year or so after I left Vietnam.

There was always some strange event in progress. Bruce Roth, our Field Engineering Manager, had his new imported Mazda sedan stolen from in front of his villa. He reported it to the local Saigon police with the help of an interpreter and a strange thing happened-- the car was actually found about two weeks later, in a field, out of gas and undamaged. The thief, a teenage Vietnamese, was also captured. Bruce was called by the police and with the translating help of our secretary Madame Phoung was told what had happened and to come pick up his car. When he arrived at the police station he identified the car and signed some papers and then was taken into a back room. There was the teenager, tied hand and foot and secured to a chair. Bruce was told he could do anything he wanted to him to retaliate for the theft. He was encouraged to pound away at him with fists. Bruce had no stomach for that sort of thing and declined the invitation, but he did come away feeling better about the Vietnamese Police and their 'eye-for-an-eye' legal system. He didn't know what happened to the boy and we all thought that their immediate system of justice was possibly better than that in New York or Los Angeles.

Driving the roads, streets and highways of Vietnam was probably a greater danger to our well being than any VC incursion, random plastique bombings or cowboy street attacks. One of the busiest highways was the road north, over the Newport Bridge, to Long Binh and Bien Hoa. These two were the locations of U.S. Army Vietnam Headquarters, with its sprawling supply depot, and yet another very busy USAF air base. We serviced several data processing installations at both bases, including a couple of IBM 7010 systems used for Army supply applications. We were also in the process of designing and installing a fairly extensive 1050 type terminal teleprocessing network, used to gather data from around the large Long Binh campus. The Air Force used unit record equipment and there was also a 360 Model 20

AUTODIN tributary installation at the 1st Signal Brigade (for you historians, Auto-Di-N equals Automatic Digital Network. This was a very very early equivalent of today's e-mail).

Long Binh was only about a fifteen-mile drive from the Saigon office and although we had a couple of Customer Engineers resident at the big army base (see Chapter 9), the installations also required additional IBMers from Saigon on an almost daily basis. The highway had been properly financed and properly built with a 35 million dollar grant from USAID, but the drive was like running a gauntlet, with tanks, huge trucks some towing howitzers, personnel carriers, taxis, Honda motorcycles, bicycles, ox carts and Vietnamese farm equipment all jammed on four unmarked lanes and all in a rush. The roadsides were also busy with Vietnamese vendors and service stations selling food and watered down bottled gasoline. Any IBMer, after a day's work at Long Binh and the frightening return trip, was a nervous wreck. The monsoon seasons made the trip all that more hazardous and in those summer months Grant Giske's Land Rover always won the most muddy car award.

Occasionally, some of the guys would also drive the 30 odd miles down Highway 51 to the beaches at Vung Tau, southeast of the Saigon/Dong Nai River delta. A constant stream of U.S. Navy ships could usually be seen, carrying men, supplies and weapons up river to the bases around Saigon. Vung Tau was a great place to take a girl friend for the day and the beaches seemed at the time to be almost the equal of our Southern California beaches – more river mud than sand however. Our men could relax there and it made a good day off-- providing they all returned safely. Vung Tau provided a good romantic getaway – away from Saigon's streets of chaos and war.

One day in 1970, John Moss and Cary Campbell came into the office and said that they had just returned from a drive, with their Vietnamese girlfriends, northwest out of Saigon (Highway 1 west) and had reached the Cambodian border without incident. On the way, they passed a few burned out villages and stopped their car to watch helicopter gun ships firing on an enemy position a mile or so away. I know this is so, because I have seen the photographs taken that day. This area was the famous "Parrot's Beak" and was a main VC/North

Vietnamese incursion route throughout the war's duration. Their trip was sheer foolishness! In a later chapter, Stu Schmidt talks about making that same drive, but he was smart enough to turn around early.

On another occasion, I was on an inspection trip to Nha Trang and had spent a day reviewing customer installations and future data processing requirements. I had flown there via a C-124. Two of the Nha Trang CEs said that they planned to drive to Cam Ranh Bay the next day (Bob Dillon and Ed Baker I think) and asked whether I would like to go along.

"Is it safe?" I asked. "Sure is," said Ed, "as long as we don't have a problem with the Toyota jeep and we arrive before sundown. After dark our fighting side friendlies no longer own the road."

Well, it turned out to be a beautiful trip! Vietnam has some pretty nice weather during the dry winter months and it was a cloudless but cool day – maybe 80 degrees. We fell in behind a U.S. Army truck convoy for part of the way down Highway 1 (also known on another stretch as the 'Street Without Joy') that runs the length of the South Vietnam coast. We then turned off the main road for a few clicks in order to see an abandoned French rubber plantation. At one time Vietnam had been the world's fifth largest rubber producing country. There appeared to be no-one living on the property, but the sprawling old two story main house looked quite livable and it was obvious that this had once been a thriving and profitable family enterprise. It reminded me of some of our old cotton plantations in Georgia but was probably a VC controlled night meeting location.

We then continued south through some beautiful farming areas and an occasional small village punctuated by the spire of a Catholic church's bell tower - and passed by a 1000 year old ruin left by the 'Chams', the same generations of people that built the Anchor Wat complex in Cambodia (see Chapter 8). I reflected that there was some ancient history here trying to preserve itself in spite of the war. During that drive we passed many rice paddies being actively farmed. I thought the peaceful scenes were in direct contrast to the nightly TV news stories about firefights and bombings in that same area; that is, until one of my companions pointed out that the general feeling was that the black pajama clad farmers in their cone shaped hats that we were driving by were most probably VC during the night.

*Rice Farmers or VC Activists?*

After a few hours, we reached the sand dunes around Cam Ranh Bay, drove through some guarded gates to view a long blue natural harbor and watched a 'Sealand' cargo ship approach a dock where it would off load tons of war supplies. The drive seemed to have transgressed time.

Driving through the war zone was a form of entertainment, a way to see Vietnam, but in retrospect was probably very stupid. There was more unauthorized travel going on than I realized, and we couldn't keep track of everyone as well as we supposed. Some of the other Systems Engineers and CEs drove their civilian vehicles to such places as Hue and the DMZ in the north from their assignment location of Da Nang, or to My Tho down Highway 4 out of Saigon where the idea was to visit a well known 'mad monk' on an island in the middle of the Mekong River delta. Two of our CEs took a taxi from Saigon to the Vietnam/Cambodian border, walked across the border, and took another taxi from there to Phnom Penh. Two other CEs flew to Phnom Penh for a weekend and changed their flight plans on Sunday so they could hitchhike back to Saigon (see

Ed Baker's story in Chapter 11). This happened just one week before the joint ARVN and U.S. Army invasion of Cambodia overran that same area. Another SE drove west on Route 1 through Cu Chi, then to the border and on to Tay Ninh near the Black Virgin Mountain. Others would occasionally drive to what was called the summer capital of South Vietnam and visit the beautiful mountain city of Dalat in the central highlands. I knew I shouldn't, but wished I had.

These and a few other side trips made us realize what a potentially beautiful country South Vietnam could be - and would be again some day, but the bomb craters, grave yards, defoliation and huge piles of junked and rusting instruments of war were certainly taking their toll. The beaches and offshore islands around Nha Trang appeared to me to be a future vacation play land and potentially something like today's gold coast of western Mexico. The beaches of Da Nang, like China Beach, looked to be similar to those at Surfer's Paradise on the central east coast of Australia - after removing all the Marine barracks, concertina wire and trash of a foreign military occupation force. As I write this portion of the book (mid 1990s), more and more vacation packages are being offered to those interested in rediscovering "Indo China" and it is hoped that this author will someday have the opportunity to again see Vietnam as it should be seen. (Author's Note: This 1990 forecast of future vacation packages to the coast of South Vietnam has come true. Unfortunately, I have not had the opportunity to return and view the progress of a pseudo communist country now steeped in capitalism. Other IBMers have made the return trip - some multiple times).

Our IBM mission in Southeast Asia included the installation and servicing of data processing equipment in Thailand and the Philippines at U.S. military locations that supported the Vietnam War. We had more than a few resident IBMers at Army, Navy and Air Force bases in both countries and my responsibilities required that I schedule trips to these sites outside Vietnam. Once in Thailand or the Philippines, the normal routine consisted of driving or catching a military flight to a military base, making a polite protocol visit to the base commander's office, visiting the equipment installation site to discuss any problems about the machines, software, maintenance or personnel with the data processing staff, updating the commanding officer about any new IBM products or recommendations and generally exchanging data processing knowledge as it pertained to improving the applications and service to military requirements. In Thailand and the Philippines, these trips were based out of Bangkok and Manila and I would usually be absent from Vietnam for a week. I became familiar with all the Air Vietnam and Thai International flights out of Tan Son Nhut; with the attractive hotels and nightlife of the two beautiful capital cities; and with the follow-up ways to travel to almost all of the bases in Southeast Asia. During the departure routine, as the 727 or Caravel lifted out of Vietnam and over the Mekong, there was always an intense sense of relief as I realized I was being taken away from the noise, chaos, dangers and constant stress of working in the war zone.

Like Hong Kong, Bangkok is a very interesting and exotic city and our many U.S. movies, travelogues and photographs cannot do justice to the sights, sounds, smells and daily life in and around the capital of Thailand. If at all possible, everyone who enjoys travel should, at one time or another in their lifetime, see and experience Bangkok (and the rest of Thailand for that matter). Ignore the heat and humidity, the insects and snakes, the traffic and impatient taxi drivers, the crowds, the smells and the noise. Instead concentrate on the shopping, the fascinations of the river and klongs (canals), the temples and palaces, the enchanting effects and idiosyncrasies of the Buddhist religion (like the ever present tiny ghost houses), the open day to day raw life in the streets and waterways, the fine hotels and restaurants, the night life and massage parlors, and most of all the friendly fascinating and talented Thai people themselves.

The city was a kaleidoscope of sensory pleasures. In 1970, Bangkok was fun, dangerous, erotic, crowded, dirty, fantastically exciting and busy with a booming war based economy. Our IBMers, to a man, tried to spend as much time in Bangkok as possible; one of them said, "Going to Bangkok was like sinking slowly and peacefully into a warm bath, cocktail in hand, with a stereo blasting at full volume and a riotous party next door." The American presence, in support of the Vietnam War effort, was an unprecedented economic boost that finally and forever removed the traditional isolationism, dignity and mystery of the earlier days of the Kingdom of Siam.

Favorite leisurely things to do in 1970 while in Thailand and not on IBM or military business:

1. Take a cyclo ride to the old Oriental Hotel by the banks of the Chao Phraya River; lunch with drinks in the outdoor courtyard while watching traditional Thai dancers with the river scenes in the background; then hop into a riverboat taxi and spend a couple hours on the klongs zooming past golden pagodas, rustic river homes, outdoor markets, floating vendors and whole families bathing, playing and swimming in the river waters as your boat races other high speed water taxis; then back to the Oriental Hotel for late afternoon drinks, conversation and more scenes along the passing river. This was a photographer's paradise.

2. Visits to the jewelry shops, art galleries or weekend open-air markets - what wonderful bargains and more great photography opportunities.

3. Dining out in any of the many fine restaurants of Bangkok. I believe that the consensus among our group was that a restaurant by the name of "Nick's Number One" was the best. It was set inside an old run-down mansion, the food was excellent and the atmosphere quiet and pleasing. A few years later, two IBM FSD employees completed their assignments at Nakhon Phanom (NKP), quit the company and went into the restaurant business in Bangkok. They bought an old wooden rice barge and converted it into a fancy restaurant that sailed out of a riverside dock near the Oriental Hotel. A Thai style dinner on the Chao Phaya River was very romantic and for many a tourist must. There is a story about an IBMer who took his fiancee to Bangkok for an R&R. One evening, in an effort to impress his lady, he took her to the well known 'Two Vikings' restaurant. They ordered drinks before dinner that were prepared at the table from a drink cart; their appetizer (shrimp flambeau) and Caesar salad were also prepared at the table; the main course of roast beef was served at the table again from a cart and silver platter; and, of course, the dessert of crepe suzettes was also prepared and served at the table. The IBMer was sure he was making a big impression, but his unimpressed lady turned to him and innocently asked, "What's the matter with this restaurant; doesn't it have a kitchen?"

4. A trip to the now famous resort of Pattaya for swimming, water skiing, fishing and sailing, Thai food and other more exotic forms of total, sex for sale, relaxation.

5. An hour or two at one of the many Thai massage parlors with the girl of your choice. This needs some explaining: first of all let me state that the younger Thai women are extremely good looking, in fact, most of them are beautiful and to have one or more of them massage one's entire body was a most enjoyable pastime for male civilians or military alike. The parlors usually had appropriate sounding names like "The Happy Hand", "Birds of Paradise" or "The Lotus Blossom" on the outside ground floor marquis. One entered into a pleasant hallway or up stairs to a second floor and into a sort of welcoming lobby, where you were met by a polite supervisor, offered tea or a soft drink and invited to look through a very large internal glass window and select a massage girl. There were usually 15 to 20 slightly clad – usually bra and panties - dark haired beauties sitting on benches reading, watching TV or doing their nails while waiting for customers. Each wore a number. I believe that the window glass was one way so that the girls could not see who was watching (or maybe they just got used to men studying them?), but I was never invited to the other side of the glass to find out.

After selecting the right girl (or girls if one preferred?), she would emerge with soap, bubble bath and a towel and lead you down another long hall to a large private massage room with bathtub, low lights and a clean narrow bed. She would strip down to her skimpy underwear, if not already, and tell or motion you to completely undress while she would fill the tub with warm water and fragrant bubbles. There would be soft background music and incense burning. She would kneel next to the tub and unabashedly soap your <u>entire</u> body and if she spoke some English, she would answer questions about her life in Thailand as you became more relaxed - and very clean. She would then rinse you off, dry you, temporarily wrap you in a towel and lead you to the sheet covered massage bed. This all took about half an hour and the next half hour would consist of either an amateurish or totally professional body massage - from toes to head - depending on their mood, how much they liked you or how long they had been employed.

These girls were skillful at popping toes and fingers, walking on your back (if not too heavy and they usually were not) and finding sore muscles that didn't know they were sore. They had soft manipulative hands and available passion. If time and extra money permitted, they could and would offer additional special sexual favors, but that was not what it was supposed to be all about. However, if a gentleman would, for some reason, temporarily fall in love, he could offer added financial incentives and "buy" the girl out (out of the massage parlor) for the rest of the evening or for the next day or two. There were many couples enjoying this arrangement on the Pattaya beaches or in hotel bedrooms during short vacations and happy weekends.

Normally, though, the delightful experience would end at the parlor, a tip would be given to the girl depending on one's satisfaction, the girl would leave for her next appointment or viewing room, and after dressing, the gentleman would float down the hall and out to the hot steamy streets of Bangkok, satiated and probably looking forward to the next massage. I might add that this was an excellent way to learn the rudiments of the Thai language (a variation on the old "sleeping dictionary"). From time to time, during these years, certain high level executives from IBM headquarters in the U.S. would make 'business' trips to Southeast Asia. It was noted that when in Bangkok, they would announce during the day that they had to do some serious shopping for their wives at home. They would disappear for a few hours and re-appear looking very relaxed with some sketchy statement about jewels or art. The massage parlors didn't discriminate between military, contractors or IBM executives. I sincerely hope that these massage parlors are still operating in Bangkok!

6. A visit to the King's Palace with a friend to see golden pagodas, many different Buddhas, snake charmers, saffroned monks, Thais kneeling in prayer with incense sticks, and to learn a bit about Thailand's religious beliefs and heritage.

7. A trip to the more remote and fascinating town of Chiang Mai - by railroad or commercial air - where the local mountain artisans had mastered many handicrafts which are valued and collected by the western world: teak wood carvings, celedon porcelain, brightly woven silk brocade material and their woven products, hand painted umbrellas, teak furniture and much more. Mountains surrounded the rice fields and jungles on the outskirts of Chiang Mai, and the scenery was spectacular and apparently peaceful, in spite of the nearby opium trading trails of the Golden Triangle and probable refugee camps - then and perhaps even now?

IBM World Trade Corporation was capitalizing on the booming

Thai economy and bringing state-of-the-art computer technology to this somewhat technically unsophisticated country The main office was on narrow but popular Pat Pong Road, in the heart of Bangkok's hotel and entertainment district (if memory serves me correctly, there were at least a dozen massage parlors within a five minute walk - and, no, I did not try them all!). Pat Pong Road was privately owned, so the authorities did not show up often to enforce any morality laws, if there were any! Our organization, IBM-GEM, occupied a couple of desks in the multi-storied IBM Building, and used certain World Trade services such as airline ticketing, check cashing and banking, help with Thai automobile usage, housing and document translation when necessary. Here, as in Vietnam, our respective customers were separate and distinct, yet World Trade personnel were able to benefit in some ways by receiving technical assistance and education from the two or three very talented American Systems Engineers we had assigned to the Bangkok location. This barter system - office space and services for technical assistance - worked well and both IBM-GEM and IBM Thailand were the winners.

Whenever I think of that IBM Thailand office, I think of a unique method of moving a heavy IBM machine that I once saw progressing along a sidewalk from the office to a waiting truck. Thai men are fairly small in stature, and I came upon three IBM Thais moving a machine that may have weighed 800 pounds. Two of the men would hold, balance and roll the machine (an IBM 407 Accounting Machine, I believe) and the third man would run from behind their charge to the front of the machine with a fresh round log and then back again for another log so that the whole group moved smoothly along rolling the machine on logs. It got the job done.

The General Manager and his beautiful wife were Americans on "assignment" and ran the growing Thai data processing expansion as an independent business, but reported to the IBM Far East Company in Hong Kong - as did the American General Manager of IBM Vietnam. Our IBM-GEM military operation maintained a close relationship with both of these World Trade offices and considered them an added layer of safety in the war zone, an unofficial caring sponsor for our presence there and an alternate means for getting things done diplomatically. Another way of saying this is that the IBM WTC offices were "licensed" to do business in their respective countries by the appropriate government offices of those countries. We, on the other hand, were not licensed at all but were instead attached to the U.S. Military. We sort of felt the World Trade offices could provide a possible safe haven, should the need ever arise, and we welcomed their friendship and cooperation. IBM Headquarters personnel in Hong Kong, Tokyo, Honolulu, Los Angeles, New York and Washington, D.C. communicated somewhat, across IBM dotted or more established reporting lines, and were generally all aware of our unique presence and distinctive mission in Southeast Asia.

Occasionally, I could plan a few days of real vacation if: the workload was somehow finished, IBM reports completed (business books closed for the month and forecasts done), installations in three countries running well and on schedule, no personnel problems and someone to back me up in Saigon. This actually happened a couple of times and the best place to spend a few days was definitely Thailand. I once spent three days in Pattaya with a very good-looking American girl whom I had never met prior to our weekend introduction. It turned out to be a romantic liaison, graciously set up by a mutual friend. We stayed at the World Trade beachside villa, courtesy of IBM Thailand. I had not seen a "round eye" woman in almost a year and apparently she also had reason for what turned out to be a short but warm and loving vacation. We swam, water skied, and even rented a 25-foot trimaran sailboat for two days and sailed to a remote and almost uninhabited island south of Pattaya with another couple and temporarily forgot that there was a war somewhere nearby. The days were fun and the nights were passionate, just what I needed. I never saw her again.

Another all too short holiday was spent in Bangkok and Chiang Mai with a former UCLA college sweetheart with whom I had continued to correspond years after our school day's romance had ended, and she had married. We arranged to meet at the Bangkok International Airport and stayed for two days and nights at the Oriental Hotel and another two days in Chiang Mai, shopping and enjoying each other and the unique countryside. To have and to hold a special loved one in that fascinating country is a memory to have and to hold for a lifetime! I still occasionally look at the photographs taken during that vacation and wish for a time machine. Saying good-bye that time was especially tough, but I was becoming used to 'good-bys'. The return to the realities of Saigon was sad after such holidays.

Our IBM responsibilities in the Philippines included minor data processing installations at the U.S. Embassy in Manila, at the Sangley Point Naval Station (submarine base) at Cavite partway across beautiful Manila Bay, Mactan Air Field near Cebu Island, at Clark Air Base and at a few other out-of-the-way places. We had a major installation at our Navy's Subic Bay location where a computer application called 'Stock Points' handled supply for our western Pacific Fleet. Two Systems Engineers and four Customer Engineers were resident at Subic and they supported the System/360 computer systems operated by the Navy. The SEs helped install software and instruct Navy personnel in the COBOL programming language and OS/360 operating system. The CEs maintained the Subic complex and also took calls at the more remote unit record sites. These IBMers worked and lived with the Navy, but had a bit more freedom that led some of them into the evening fleshpots of notorious Olongapo. I visited a few of the Olongapo bars (which were within walking distance of the Navy's main gate) just once, and that was enough for me. Wow, what an education for a young innocent.

I made calls at Clark and Subic and both were impressive U.S. bases in size, personnel and activity. I did not call on the intelligence customers because I did not have the requisite 'need to know' and they were fairly remote from the main installations. At Clark and Subic, I talked with the various data processing officers gathering information about their needs and problems, suggesting better ways, and informing them of planned upgrades coming out of their headquarters in Honolulu and Washington, D.C. These officers often learned more about what was being planned for them from my visits than through their own chains of command, since computer upgrades in those days took months of scheduling and planning.

In 1970 the Navy Supply System at Subic was upgraded from a 1410/1710 computer system to a System/360 Model 50 and it was my job, and that of my two SEs, to insure a smooth and successful transition. Not long after that upgrade, the computer installation ran into a unique "glitch" that caused some changes. The S/360 was located in a large building fairly close to the ship docks and bay waters. The computer equipment suffered a series of outages which were difficult to explain, but after a few too many outages, we were able to correlate the outages with the arrival of a few of the light cruisers, destroyers, supply and intelligence ships which usually docked with their side scanning radar still operating. The scan pattern included the computer building and the radar signals would knock out the computer systems, thus causing the possible loss of the application that was running, as well as a lengthy recovery process. We couldn't move the computer building, so orders were given to change the docking procedures. I am sure there was a certain amount of grumbling at the Navy ship Captain level but the radars were turned off and the computers won that line of command battle – IBM = 1. Navy Captains = 0.

Perhaps I should not tell the following story, but I believe that it will serve a purpose by explaining the environment in which we were working. In the middle '60s, IBM sent the first American salesman to Southeast Asia to call on and work with our military in Thailand and the Philippines. I will say that his name was Dave. He was an excellent salesman and a uniquely talented individual who was good at his job. However, in time he became good at too many other things that tended to interfere with his job. Dave needed supervision, but his manager was resident in Japan and later even farther away in Honolulu. He was on his own. He had a beautiful oriental wife and a fine home in Bangkok, was on an expense account, and also had a Filipino girl friend in Manila. Gradually he began justifying more and more IBM business trips to the Philippines. I first met Dave on a 'familiarization' sales trip to the Philippines. We called on a few customers, made what were called 'turn-over calls', and spent the evenings seeing Manila - with his girl friend and with his girl friend's younger sister as my date. I enjoyed seeing Manila with people who really knew the city and I have to admit that I enjoyed seeing the younger sister after business hours, on a subsequent business trip.

Bob Tanner, our Honolulu manager, was worried about Dave's conduct and knew that he was spending too much time on non-IBM activities. Bob made two special trips to SEA to spend considerable time with Dave trying to re-establish some professional respectability, but he finally concluded that Dave should go back to the 'States' to rejoin the IBM mainstream. It was too late; Dave did not want to go back to the U.S. He had become Southeast Asia-ized and had too many business contacts in the non-computer world and had become a serious personnel problem. As an example, I believe that he was making good money trading precious cut gems, possibly for his military contacts. Dave had become what was known as a "China Trader". He refused Bob's offer, moved his personal effects out of his Thailand home and promptly disappeared, leaving his wife and young son high and dry in a foreign country. One of our Bangkok based IBMers helped Dave's wife pack and move, and she was given a good job with IBM in Los Angeles where she became a successful professional for many years that followed.

Dave showed up one day in 1973 during the closing of the Saigon office. He was overweight and according to another IBMer, looked like a 'lost soul'. He said he was working for a Hong Kong trading company. The last I heard of Dave was that he was roaming the streets of Hong Kong and was pretty much down and out. Maybe he found what he was looking for in the Orient? The temptations and attractions for a Westerner were and are certainly there, and I do not think anyone knows the ending to his story. And that is the point to this story: it could have been all too easy to lose track of why we were sent to Southeast Asia if adequate supervision, hard work, dedication and performance objectives were ignored. The times were potentially rewarding and potentially distracting from the main mission. Many years ago, Rudyard Kipling probably said it best:

"It is not good for the Christian health
    to hustle the Asian brown,
    for the Christian riles
    and the Asian smiles
    and he weareth the Christian down.

And the end of the fight
    is a tombstone white
    with the name of the late deceased,
    and the epitaph drear
    a fool lies here,
    Who tried to hustle the East."

# Chapter 4
## Processing The Information Of War

As far as I know, Vietnam was the first and only war in which data processing was extensively used by all branches of the U.S. military involved in that conflict. I can only guess that the American and United Nations Forces which took part in 'Desert Storm' and the past ten years in Iraq and Afghanistan also used sophisticated computer applications, but the major room-size equipment installations were very probably not placed within the war zone bases - as in Vietnam - nor were the machines maintained or applications developed on site. I leave this as an open question, as I have no information sources about our modern wars.

IBM provided the hardware and software for literally hundreds of small to large data processing installations throughout Southeast Asia in the 1965 to 1973 time frame and thousands of Army, Navy, Marine and Air Force enlisted men and officers were assigned to these installations. We worked with them all. Data Processing had become a career path in the military, and the men who brought their training and expertise from the U.S.A. were skilled professionals who in most cases were already familiar with IBM products prior to arriving at their Vietnam duty stations. Our job was to hone their skills, keep them updated, teach the computer languages of the day (COBOL, FORTRAN, Assembly Language and some PL/1), assist with new software releases and hardware upgrades, take part in their planning process, answer technical questions about hardware and software and in the end, when it was all over, help send the equipment home. These military men became our friends and best supporters as well as our valued customers.

When trying to categorize the many battlefield computer applications into a generic few, I have always classified them as follows: a) Command and Control, b) Intelligence, c) Communications, d) Supply, and finally e) Miscellaneous. This somewhat simplifies the type of work being done, but certainly does not give due credit to the level of sophistication of each type of application or even the individual jobs within them. Let me simply say that the effectiveness and efficiency with which the work was produced was for the most part equal to anything being done 'Stateside' for that late 1960s early 1970s time period and in a few cases probably exceeded 'Stateside' capabilities. There was one prevalent application common to all of the classifications named above, and that was - a weekly, or even daily, listing of men, by name and serial number, and their scheduled departure date from Vietnam (DEROS), which was always posted in some conspicuous hallway location around the base or camp headquarters. It was done for information and morale purposes and chewed up quite a few computer cycles. This chapter is intended to give a general overview of how data processing was used by the various commands within the first four categories mentioned above. Chapter 5 will address some additional special situations.

Command & Control concerned both the availability of and either real or possible deployment of men and material within the areas affected by the war as well as the planning and decision process of what to do about the assembled information. The 7th Air Force installation on Tan Son Nhut Air Base consisted of an early IBM 1410 system later upgraded to two S/360 Model 50 Central Processing Units (CPUs), which were IBM's next to largest processors of the S/360 family of computers, and a balanced component of 2400 magnetic tape drives, disk drives, high speed printers and an assortment of Punched Card Accounting Machines (The Air Force called this PCAM). The 360 systems ran under the OS/360 operating system and were installed in a large, secure, raised floor, air conditioned, state-of-the-art computer room.

The installation was staffed and operated 24 hours 7 days a week by Air Force personnel who, for the most part, were data processing career professionals and had been trained in the U.S.A. The Chief Data Processing Officer was full 'Bird' Colonel, Jack Hawley, whom we advised and answered to. He was a good guy, but when the Colonel said, "Jump!" we would think, "How high?" His staff included both officer level and enlisted men with whom we worked on an almost hourly basis. The site included a fully stocked parts room and Customer Engineering (CE) repair room and we tried to keep two IBM CEs on site on a 24 hour rotating schedule to insure immediate availability for problem resolution, especially during red alert periods. Two IBM Systems Engineers (SEs) were also assigned full time to this account and they were generally present during prime shift. In my role as SE Manager, I tried to be at the installation once or twice a week or as emergencies and equipment upgrades demanded. This was truly a key account in that it supported the air war in and 'around' Vietnam.

One of our major computer replacements (late 1969 or early 1970) was the change from the 1410 system, mentioned above, to the first 360/50 system at 7th AF. A great deal of planning went into computer replacements in those days and there was no margin for equipment configuration ordering errors or other screw-ups because of the shipping distances involved. The General Services Agreement (GSA) Contract based purchase and delivery order was coordinated at PACAF HQ in Hawaii, approved at AF Headquarters in Washington, D.C., given a DX Priority rating by an Air Force contracting officer and given an "In Support of Southeast Asia" priority by the IBM plant in Poughkeepsie, New York. A DX Priority meant that the Air Force would have the very next 360/50 coming off IBM's assembly line after receipt of the purchase order – thus breaking IBM's sacred policy of sequential delivery, in support of the war effort. Prior to installation in Saigon, we conducted new hardware and software training for Air Force personnel, checked and re-checked our Systems Assurance Review and installations plans, took early delivery of the system's under floor cables, recommended operational procedures and hoped for the best.

*7ᵗʰ Air Force – S/360 Model 50 Unpacking*

The system arrived via C130 transport out of McClellen AFB, California early one Friday morning - 18 large wooden crates all boldly marked "THIS SIDE UP', 'FRAGILE' and 'IBM CORP'. The old 1410 had been disassembled and pushed aside on the machine room floor earlier that same morning. Extra CEs had been assigned for the installation and they all went to work - even before the crates arrived on the machine room floor. Our objective was to have the 360/50 physically up and running in 36 hours, plus all the diagnostic and test runs completed by Sunday noon and well ready for the next week's processing. 7th Air Force could not tolerate a longer outage so everyone pitched in and it went well. In fact, most of the command and control applications were back on-line by 0800 Sunday morning. A few days later, I received a letter of commendation from the DP CO that at one point said, "Your team of Customer Engineers and Systems Engineers exceeded all targets and are either the best in the world at their jobs, or the luckiest!" I was glad to be either one and quickly made sure that the letter went to our management and personnel folders back in the States. The AF commendation was followed by return IBM congratulatory letters, and IBM performance awards given to various members of the installation team.

A few days after the above installation took place, some of our IBMers were driving down a busy Saigon street not far from Tan Son Nhut. They saw a number of newly constructed shacks in a previously empty roadside lot. Each house had several large blue "IBM" stenciled letters on a wall, roof or doorway, as well as various machine type numbers like 360/50, 2400, 2305 and 1401. We were glad to have contributed to a few homeless refugee families and pleasantly happy to see that our computer crates made such fine houses.

In the 1960's, IBM always asked one of the technical managers to fill out a System/360 post installation review report - what went right and what, if anything, went wrong – and on this occasion I was able to respond quite positively. As I completed the report for the 7th AF installation, I recalled the report I had turned in a few years earlier from Honolulu. There had been a six-month delay after shipment for the installation of a System/360, and IBM HQ wanted to know why! My customer had been the Government of Guam. They had ordered a small 360 Model 20 to do some accounting and handle the growth from their existing

1401 applications. The Model 20 shipped on time from the U.S. plant, but during the transportation days in route to Guam's capital city of Agana, the Mariana Islands were hit by a devastating hurricane with winds over 150 mph. Much of Guam was leveled, including the intended 360/20 computer site. I had to hold the Model 20 in a warehouse in Hawaii until a new site could be prepared. Alas, I had not met the target installation date and IBM HQ wanted a detailed explanation of what I was doing about the delay and how I would meet targets the next time. I wrote a long (facetious) report on the pre-printed Systems Assurance Review forms recommending that a complex wind monitoring system be installed throughout the western Pacific Ocean (floating sensors anchored to the 10,000 foot deep bottom plus manned island stations which would continuously report on typhoon conditions to over-flying satellites) so that a Typhoon Early Warning System could be tied directly into the IBM ordering and manufacturing process and thus avoid any future computer installation delays in that area of the Pacific Ocean. I pointed out that the system could be adapted to the Caribbean area as well. For some reason there was no reply from HQ on that report.

The 7th AF account was one of my favorites. I had been IBM's Marketing Representative to PACAF at Hickam AFB in Hawaii during 1967 and 1968, and I understood the operation better than most IBMers. Two of the principal applications were referred to by their acronym or code name - PIACCS (Pacific Interim Air Force Command & Control System) and Seek Data II. PIACCS ran on the 360/50 computer system. It gathered data by debriefing Air Force pilots after every sortie and tied that data to a similar system in Hawaii via a high speed communications line between two IBM 7740 programmable Communications Controllers (initially this was via a trans-Pacific sub-seabed line and later became a satellite link-up; I remember this because a Colonel once told me that the new satellite link cost the Air Force $72,000 a month – a heady amount for those days). The pilot data was first transceived from all Vietnam and Thailand air bases via a fairly sophisticated IBM 1050 terminal network over slow speed lines (1200 and 2400 bps were state-of-the-art line speeds). This was a leading edge application and was developed and continually improved upon while we were in Vietnam. I never did learn what the "Interim" part was interim to, but the Air Force was proud of what they were accomplishing with the system. The software package for Seek Data II was written and developed in Vietnam by Control Data Corporation (CDC) under special contract to the Air Force. CDC had quite a few programmers who worked at Tan Son Nhut and lived on the economy like we IBMers. The previous year, in a meeting at Hickam AFB with Colonel Ernest Saliba, Director of PACAF Data Automation, the Colonel asked me which half of the Seek Data II project I wanted, hardware or software?

I said, "Colonel, IBM wants both halves."

The Colonel replied, "Dan, I can't give you both, our procurement guidelines won't let me; now which half do you want?"

I said, "If that's the way it has to be, then I'll take the hardware."

And that is how IBM installed the two 360/50 systems (a very significant hardware order) and CDC received the contract for the Seek Data II software development. The mission of Seek Data II was threefold: There was 'FRAG Prep', the preparation of mission orders to be sent via PIACCS to the appropriate air base. The orders included date and time of attacks, what kind and how many planes to fly, targeting information, ordinance requirements, etc. The 'frags' (short for fragmentary orders) were stored on the 360/50 System and were modified and transmitted based on intelligence reports. There was 'CREST', or combat reporting system. After each mission, the pilots would submit the results of each individual sortie to their base intelligence center. These results would then be fed through 1050 data terminals and be transmitted by PIACCS to the computer center at TSN and also on to PACAF HQ in Hawaii. These reports would then be compiled into a master report that would be used for top level briefings and to create subsequent frags. And last, there was 'Airlift Management'. This was the planning and coordination of the massive movement of men and materiel by air throughout Southeast Asia. Each flight manifest was created and stored on the 360/50 and then dispatched to the appropriate supply or personnel center. The tracking of all these movements was also coordinated by this part of Seek Data II. These applications represented the Air Force's version of Command and Control.

*7th Air Force IBM System 360/50 at TSN*

The Air Force also had several IBM 1130/2250 installations at various bases in Vietnam and Thailand. The 1130 was a small but powerful scientific computer and had been accepted by the Air Force as one of their standards. The large-screen cathode ray tube (CRT) of the 2250 was one of IBM's first products which would allow interactivity via a light pen and keyboard, and Air Force personnel could display, change and re-enter command & control data via this large remote terminal. The first 1130/2250 system was sold to PACAF in Honolulu as the result of a computer demonstration at the Honolulu branch office. IBM had provided demo software for a 'Pong' type game (remember pong?) using attacking aircraft and tanks that would shoot at each other on the screen upon operator command. After a few effective demos at the Honolulu Branch Office, the game captured the imagination of Air Force officers and they bought the system. Soon after, I was called out to Hickam Air Force Base, again by the same Colonel Saliba in charge of Data Automation.

He was upset and said, "Feltham, I want the latest version of the operating system for my 1130/2250!"

I said, "Colonel, you have the latest version" and he replied, "Well then, get that damn tank and airplane game off my system. My staff Captains and Majors aren't getting their work done around here because they are always playing silly war games with each other at the computer."

I always thought that maybe the colonel himself had also become addicted to one of the world's first computer driven arcade games.

The following year, one of the 1130/2250 systems was installed in a small upstairs room near a Tan Son Nhut main aircraft runway. Upon delivery, the equipment had to be raised by forklift and moved through a large hole cut in a second floor wall and then re-sealed into a secure environment. Soon after the system was put into use, intermittent glitches and outages (known more appropriately as core parity checks) began to occur. These parity checks shut down whatever program the 1130 was running and the system then had to be restarted. This occurred every few minutes and was certainly not acceptable for a computer anywhere, much less for one in the war zone. IBM called for 'expert' help from the states and two of our top 1130 specialists were flown out from California within the next two days. They worked for 48 hours straight trying to resolve the problem. The account Systems Engineer even wrote a small program that would cycle the 1130 memory in an effort to help the specialists isolate which memory bit was failing. The failures continued to be random and there seemed to be no solution. The specialists gave up and went home. We were in deep trouble.

A day or so later the account SE and CE were sitting in the 1130 computer room discussing the problem. They noticed that every once in awhile the CE's Motorola handy-talky emitted a "beep". They analyzed the frequency of the beep and after a couple of hours found that the beeps had an interval of some multiple of 12 seconds. This beep frequency was discussed with some of the air force officers and one of them remembered that the side scanning radar at the end of the TSN runway had a 12 second interval. He also said that the radar's power was varied to minimize enemy jamming. This explained the 1130 outages. We called IBM Honolulu immediately and asked them to buy, at the nearest supermarket, all the 3-mil tin foil rolls that they could package up that day and send to Vietnam – asap! Our Honolulu people thought this was a strange request, but the tin foil arrived within 24 hours and several of us went to work inside that computer room and completely tin foiled the walls and ceiling.

This blocked the radar signals, and the 1130/2250 system ran flawlessly from that day on.

There was an excellent spirit of cooperation between our IBM professionals and the Air Force. It was generally recognized that both IBM and Air Force personnel were working hard toward a common goal. Whenever IBM management and/or visiting corporate executives made General Officer level calls, compliments regarding Air Force staff performance were passed along, as deserved. In like manner, IBMers sometimes received complimentary letters regarding our performances. I will quote most of a Headquarters Pacific Air Force letter (retained in my personal files ever since?) that was sent to our IBM GEM Regional manager in February 1970, regarding a second 7th AF 360/50 system used for Seek Data II:

"Dear Sir,

I returned from Saigon on 20 February and would like to take this opportunity to bring to your attention one of the most outstanding efforts that I have witnessed in over 20 years of participating in an Air Force/contractor environment. The second 360/50 computer and its associated peripherals including an 1130/2250, required in support of Seek Data II, were delivered to 7th AF on 31 January 1970. An IBM team, led by Mr. Feltham and composed of Messrs. Kelly, Martinson and Percox, met the aircraft and participated in the fork-lifting, uncrating and set-up of every piece of equipment delivered that day in support of Seek Data II. This team of extremely skilled and knowledgeable IBM personnel immediately took steps, after properly locating the equipment within Building 538, to bring the system up to operational status. Under Mr. Feltham's direction this group, acting in an extremely professional and orderly manner, proceeded to obtain a fully operational system by 13 February.

By bringing this system up in less than two weeks, (Author's Note: it was actually quite a bit sooner than that, on the order of a few days) and making it available for operational use, within what I consider to be record time, a significant contribution was made toward accelerating implementation of the Seek Data II System in Southeast Asia. Early use of Seek Data II by units in the field will have a marked impact on lessening the reporting workload and improving their responsiveness.

As the Air Force Seek Data II Project Director, I wish to state on behalf of the United States Air Force our sincere appreciation for a magnificent job that must surely reflect credit upon IBM and those individuals directly concerned with this outstanding effort........"

The letter was signed by the appropriate USAF Colonel and represents the level of respect between the two data processing partners. IBMers not mentioned in the letter but who contributed significantly, such as an excellent team of Systems Engineers, were more privately complimented. Many similar letters were received from the various branches of the U.S. military during our stay in Vietnam.

Other command and control applications ran on the computer systems at HQ MACV and at Marine Headquarters in Da Nang. These two systems were also upgraded during my assignment to dual S/360 Model 50 mainframes. They represented a significant piece of business for IBM and needed planning and technical support. The operating systems were OS/MVT and HASP (for those of you who may be computer history buffs, the acronyms need not be defined. You computer dinosaurs will understand).

## Da Nang

The Marine installation on the outskirts of Da Nang was a real showplace for Vietnam. The Marines did things right! A new two-story building was designed and constructed especially for dual 360/50s. There was a tape library area, an isolated printing room for the older 1401/1460 SPOOL process, programmer areas and more than enough room to walk between machines. All machines were painted red, in the Marine tradition. (I remember something about one blue machine or blue machine panel arriving in error and the ensuing trouble within IBM to replace it with the proper red). There was even an entry area where shoes and combat boots had to be exchanged for clean cloth booties prior to entering the sanctity of the machine room. The one thing they forgot with the new building was a restroom, which tended to increase the traffic through the bootie exchange area on the way to outdoor latrines. Oh well, good personal planning and strong bladders became Marine requirements for that installation. There is a story about some of the IBMers obtaining Marine permission and IBM funding to build a special 'civilians only' men's latrine near the new computer building. It was done much to the *relief* of all those concerned, but I do not have the details, and I only used it a couple times.

The Marines were excellent customers and good working partners, except when they became obstinate or angry about some equipment operating procedure. As an example, one Marine had trouble remembering that you shouldn't load tapes on the tape drives with the covers still on and that you shouldn't just rip the tapes off the drives without unlocking the drive spindles first. As a result, our CEs did extra duty there repairing tape drive equipment. I guess our machines were not completely Marine proof. They also believed strongly in Optical Character Readers (OCR) in lieu of keypunching and the OCR machines also caused considerable maintenance problems. Company clerks typed their reports on special typewriters equipped with OCR fonts; they were instructed to use standard phrases and formats. The reports were then optically scanned into the computer system that did eliminate the keypunching phase. This was considered leading edge technology for that time.

Da Nang was not the easiest or safest place for resident American civilians and IBM had considerable presence in the area – usually six CEs and one SE plus other personnel from Saigon as needed. John Leussler covered accounts in Saigon and also served as our IBM marketing representative in the Da Nang area for over three years. He was supported by SEs Curt Maxwell and Graham Seibert – all three technically superior individuals. John tells the following story: "About 3 a.m. on Labor Day 1969, I was awakened by the distant thump thump of incoming rockets. I was in Da Nang, ('Charlie's dartboard' according to Bob Hope) and another nighttime rocket attack was in progress. As I started to go back to sleep, there was a tremendous explosion. The window broke, dirt, plaster and geckos fell off the ceiling and I lost all thoughts of sleep. I grabbed my pants and shoes and ran outside, sure that either the office or the CE's villa next door had taken a direct hit. But all was quiet, nobody running around, all the buildings intact, no bodies or debris in the street. After checking the area, I decided it wasn't my problem and went back to bed, and eventually to sleep. How wrong I was."

"The next morning I went out to visit my U.S. Navy customers. When I arrived I found total destruction: buildings caved in, machines blown over on their faces, and lots of people running around. A quick inquiry and I discovered that the ammunition dump had taken a direct rocket hit. Two of our CEs had been on duty and had been entering the underground shelter when the dump went up. The CEs had actually been blown <u>in</u> to the shelter but suffered only minor cuts and bruises. That morning, the Seabees were already busy jacking up the roofs of the buildings so that we could move the IBM 1401 processor, a 557 repro machine, a 407 tabulating machine and a few other pieces of equipment out and start on their repairs. Once the equipment was removed, the Seabees rebuilt the buildings. In fewer than 72 hours, the buildings were rebuilt, the machines were repaired and reinstalled, and the data processing installation was up and running again, a terrific job by both the Seabees and the IBM Customer Engineers."

*"Hmm. What seems to be the trouble here?"*

John goes on to tell about his U.S. Marine customer: "Computers in Vietnam were used for pretty much the same things that computers were used everywhere, but the Da Nang Marines had at least a couple of unusual applications. One of the problems that the military had was that the tour of duty in Vietnam was only twelve months, and so the people there at any given time had little or no memory of previous problems, or of their solutions. This was almost universally true at all of our accounts and our IBMers, on two and three year tours, often provided that memory. Since the VC and NVA tended to be creatures of habit, the ability to remember what had happened two or three years earlier was a decided advantage. To extend the battlefield memory, the Marines kept track, on the 360/50 system, of the route of each combat patrol and what happened to each patrol. As a result, when a patrol went out, the leader was given a computer printout showing just where on his route previous patrols had encountered ambushes and when. In another application, the Marines were able to locate the launch point of a rocket attack and record it. Some of the enemy's favorite launch sites were then pre-targeted with our artillery, so that when the next attack took place, two or three artillery rounds could immediately be fired onto each of the plotted launch sites, without waiting to do the calculations necessary to determine exactly where the rockets were launched from."

Graham Seibert talks about his experiences in Da Nang with the Marines: "In spite of the insistence on cleanliness at the new computing facility (booties and outdoor latrine?), there was a sand problem with the 2401 magnetic tape drives (remember those?). They got more than their fair share of errors. The Marines had a 'Take that hill mentality' for most solutions to errors. The system's job control language had three options for dealing with errors – 'Abort', 'Retry' or 'Skip'. If 'Skip' were chosen, the program would simply pretend that it never read the block of records containing the error. Since it was their supply system being run, the result was that they ended up with a quantity of orphaned supplies in their warehouses or yards. The computer didn't know about them and couldn't issue them. However, the programmer/operators were not concerned. They had solved their problem."

Graham also volunteered to teach classes in 1401 Autocoder language to Marine programmers. Graham had been taught the correct way to program – first conceive of what the program is supposed to do; then plan the logic of the program using diagrammed flowcharts. Only after doing these two things, should one start to write code. Graham writes that the Marines came to class with pencil and paper ready to write programs. "To hell with the details!" I'm sure they had the same programmers foolish wish, as did I when first with IBM, that if one's perfectly devised code didn't run the first time through the computer, then simply run it again until it worked. It must be the machine's fault, because it couldn't be the logic, right?

Many years later, Graham called on a data processing center in Kaiserstautern, Germany – the Army's postal service. This same 1401 system that had survived the Da Nang warehouse blast was still running smoothly there. He noted that IBM machines were literally bullet proof. The system was being operated by an Army Captain who Graham had befriended in Da Nang. Small world!

Graham also says that one of the most important things he learned from the Da Nang Marines was 'Don't try to out drink a Marine'!

Along with the risks, the hard work and hard play came the ability to appreciate the Vietnamese people as they went about their day-to-day responsibilities while surrounded by the war. We knew we could always leave the country, but the children of Vietnam had to grow up while seeming to ignore the chaos caused by less innocent adults. One bright Da Nang morning as John Leussler was driving to breakfast, he saw a little girl, who looked about four years old but was probably six or seven. She was walking along the road with the family water buffalo, headed out to the fields for the day's work. Her massive but docile buffalo had apparently done something to incur the little girl's wrath. She had a thin switch, longer than her height, and she was beating the buffalo with it - going at him hammer and tongs just as hard as she could. The buffalo, which weighed about 40 times the girl's weight, was plodding along totally oblivious - he barely knew she was there; the flies buzzing around were more of an annoyance than she. John imagined the conversation at the Vietnamese dinner table that night: "But I beat him as hard as I could and he wouldn't pay any attention to me!" There were many such indelible scenes that easily conjure up fond memories of Vietnam.

## Saigon Installations

Back near Saigon, one of the most memorable sights at the MACV installation was the IBM 1403 printer decorated with a "Purple Heart". MACV had several computer systems and each had a 1403 high-speed printer. One of these printers supposedly took a hit during the 1968 TET offensive. There was no damage to the internals of the printer, just a hole in the machine's bottom kick plate. The machine was in a totally enclosed room and there were no bullet holes anywhere else in the room. One rumor explained the wound as being the result of friendly fire and that there had been a nervous Major running around blowing holes in the building with his trusty 45. I was shown the Purple Heart beautifully painted on the front of the machine during my first visit to MACV, but never had a completely adequate explanation. Whatever happened was soon lost as military personnel rotated back home. Several years later, one of our IBMers procured the portion of the machine that was wounded and managed, at considerable trouble, to send it back to the U.S. He offered it to IBM Headquarters, thinking that it might be of interest as a Vietnam memento for display in an IBM museum. IBM HQ said they were not interested, which reflected the prevailing attitude in the United States and within IBM in 1972 about the war and about our exploits. I am sorry to say that same "not interested" attitude has prevailed within IBM ever since.

The Intelligence installations and applications were esoteric to most of us; one had to have a security clearance above Top Secret (TS) for general access to the account facilities. TS took many months of processing for a civilian to obtain and anything above that level required more months of detailed investigation into one's personal history. I didn't need any special clearances and in fact did not want anything above the TS. Persons with anything above that level had to file flight plans whenever they traveled and had to keep a special secret group informed of their activities. Yet, a few IBMers were blessed with the higher level clearance out of necessity so they could service certain intelligence or communications accounts. I remember attending a few military briefing sessions and planning meetings in which all persons without either a special clearance and/or 'need to know' were asked to leave the room, which I readily did. Curiosity was not important and I did not want to be running around with a bunch of really heavy secret information in my head.

There were two Information Data Handling Systems (IDHS) in the Tan Son Nhut area and these computers processed what was considered to be especially sensitive data, which I surmised to be such things as - results from prisoner interrogations, prisoner lists, battle results, casualty details, weapons lost and captured, villages relocated, villages searched and converted to 'friendly', body counts, terrorist activities, VC suspects, VC defector lists of those who chose the South's "chieu hoi" (open arms) program, incursion information into Laos and Cambodia, photo reconnaissance data, secret agent reports and so on. This was a job only a computer could handle. Both accounts upgraded to S/360 Model 40 systems in the 1969/1970 timeframe from older 1400 computers, but I believe they ran the systems in the slower but simpler 1400 emulation mode. I rarely made a call on these accounts, but made sure that our cleared CEs and SEs serviced them as best we could. Additionally, IBM's Federal Systems Division had people assigned to these accounts who were closely involved with the intelligence community (spooks). There was even a rumor that a second level FSD Manager (Wil Derango), dressed in full army fatigues, accompanied military personnel into the delta areas on fact gathering and/or sensor placing missions.

One Air Force IDHS DP Officer had a unique method for holding computer time down to just the critical applications. He would routinely hold back certain daily or weekly computerized reports from their intended distribution, figuring that the stacks and stacks of printer output being produced was never actually read by anyone important or that it was an obsolete application holdover from previous requirements or duty assignments. If the purposeful omission received no complaints, inquiries or urgent report requests for two or three printings in a row, he would then cancel that application and make time for something more important. I always admired this management technique and it allowed that particular IDHS installation to remain within the 360/40's production capacity in spite of application growth in other key areas. There was the obvious need for close cooperation and some exchange of data between the Command and Control systems and the IDHS systems, but nevertheless the IDHS guys were a special breed and probably remain so to this very day, as the saying goes – 'once a spook always a spook'.

## Communications

When I mention Communications as a data processing category in Vietnam, I am mostly talking about the AUTODIN (Automatic Digital Network) installations in Southeast Asia. AUTODIN was a state-of-the-art store and forward message transfer/switching system that could transmit non-voice information to most U.S. military bases in the world in a matter of seconds, or at most minutes - places like MACV in Saigon to CINCPAC in Honolulu to the Pentagon in Washington, D.C. and many other network nodes in between. (Note: there was also a voice-equivalent network called AUTOVON). AUTODIN used the sub-seabed communications cable across the Pacific and later tied into satellites for urgent traffic.

IBM in Bethesda and Gaithersburg, Maryland, had designed special hardware and software for the S/360 Model 20 processor and the 2701 communications adapter which met "mil spec" standards for government encryption/decryption requirements. These Model 20s then tied into larger hardwired, and later programmable, communication switches which, I believe, were manufactured and operated by Philco-Ford and RCA and were located in key locations around the globe. The nearest switch to Saigon was at Phulam, just south of Cholon. The system worked well and we worked hard to support it. By the end of our U.S. interests in the war, there were probably a dozen Model 20 AUTODIN systems in Vietnam and Thailand and many more scattered across the Pacific. The Model 20 installations were all contained within secure environments, with the so-called extra "red - black" RPQ (IBM term for non-standard hardware) interfaces, and required that supporting IBM personnel have special security clearances. They were operated around the clock seven days a week. I have always referred to the AUTODIN system as the cardio-vascular system of the U.S. military body. The volume of messages handled during the war was impressive, even by today's standards.

Soon after the 1968 TET offensive, two of our communications hardware CEs, Bob and Jerry, were at the Phulam STRATCOM switch location working on a 360/20 late one night. They finished their maintenance work and decided to stay the night and sleep in the military barracks. Sometime after midnight, they were awakened by a siren and the "whump, whump" of incoming VC mortar shells. Bob said he looked to his left and saw Jerry scrambling out of bed saying, "Let's get the hell out of here." Bob said he then looked to his right for the military CE but that bunk was already empty, and he realized that he and Jerry were the only ones left in the barracks. "Those 18 year olds can sure move fast when they want too", thought Bob. They dressed rapidly and beat it out to the nearby bunker to join the other troops. Bob wrote the following, "As I was just inside the bunker, I could see the base mortar firing 'illumination flares' and as they drifted with the slight wind, the building's shadows shifted eerily. For some reason, I needed my flashlight and I reached into my pocket to turn it on. Well it wouldn't work, so I stepped to the bunker's entryway to check it out in the light of a flare. I then figured out that it wouldn't work because it was a bar of soap. I also noticed I had two different colored socks, one of them military. Who, me nervous, but at least there was a military guy also out of uniform with one of my socks."

Bob went on to say, "We survived the night and at the crack of dawn, Jerry and I were seated in the back of a deuce and a half (2 and 1/2 ton truck) that had convoy escort duty that day. We sat for a couple of hours until the convoy pulled out and our truck became the lead escort for a fully loaded propane truck on its way to the Esso yard. The GIs were all taking bets as to whether the propane truck would survive the trip through Cholon. The trip was terrifying, first a jeep with an M-60, then us in the deuce with a mounted 50-calibre machine gun, followed way too closely by the propane. We moved at full speed through the narrow Cholon streets, so narrow that the second story balconies seemed to overhang the trucks. With horn blasting and whistle shrieking, we made it OK. Jerry and I put away the M-14 we were sharing and thankfully returned to the quiet of our civilian villas." This was an interesting but not atypical service call to repair a machine.

## Supply

Keeping the U.S. Military machine adequately supplied 12,000 miles from the U.S. mainland was a Herculean task. Staging areas, such as Hawaii, the Philippines, Okinawa and Thailand certainly played a major role, but ultimately the bullets, bombs and boots had to come from the U.S.A. This supply process was a major computer application for all the services and the various programs ran on IBM 1460s, 1410s, 7010s, 360/40s and 360/50s. Most of the supply applications were developed and tested at military installations in Hawaii and when ready were moved to similar computer systems in Southeast Asia. For instance, the Army's 3S supply applications were developed at Fort Shafter, USARPAC HQ in Hawaii and then moved to the 1st Logistics Command, USARV HQ at the mammoth Long Binh Army base north of Saigon. The early computers at Long Binh were twin IBM 7010 mainframe processors - one at the 14th Inventory Control Center and the other at the 506th Field Depot. These two systems processed the Army's materiel requirements and tried to keep track and disperse the in-country inventory.

*USARV HQ – Long Binh*

The base at Long Binh was the largest army base in the world. It served as Headquarters for the U.S. Army's entire operation in Vietnam (USARV HQ), hosted all of the Army's support organizations needed to administer a couple hundred thousand men, and housed the fighting men and equipment being deployed upcountry via ground transportation or out of the nearby Bien Hoa Air Base for airborne deployment. It was a huge busy place and one needed a good map or an experienced escort to avoid becoming lost within the base's perimeter. Our IBM civilian cars definitely looked unique when mixed with tanks, trucks, jeeps and troop carriers. My light blue VW "Bug", Bruce's white Mercedes or George League's bright red Mustang Fastback were definitely out of place among the olive drab army vehicles. Our IBM white shirts and ties were also out of place, but we felt it appropriate while on short visits to wear IBM's official uniform - and, we did not have to salute anybody.

How things actually were requisitioned and processed through our computers I never did know, but I am sure that someone could have explained in detail how a pair of boots or a howitzer or a helmet moved from their place of manufacture in the States all the way to Long Binh. But it was apparent that for the most part the Army was well supplied, that the process was long and complicated and that when the military departed Vietnam, there were probably thousands of tons of excess equipment and supplies left behind, most of which had been processed through those computers.

A few errors were made along the way, for instance, the story of the telephone poles. During my trips upcountry to various bases, I occasionally caught sight of large piles of telephone poles, perhaps hundreds to a pile, and since I saw these piles at multiple locations I was curious about their intended use. I learned that a small requisitioning error had been made in the computerized ordering process - a small error with a large result. Some organization had ordered something like 100,000 FEET (lumber and apparently poles are ordered in board feet) of telephone poles intended, probably, for cross country communication lines. In the ordering process, the FT for 'feet' was changed to EA for 'each' and the computer system did the rest. Remember the quaint computer saying, 'garbage in, garbage out'? Our efficient ocean transports, like SEALAND, carried the order to Vietnam and off-loaded the 100,000 poles (can you visualize 100,000 telephone poles?), which I guess were subsequently spread around the country in order to disguise the screw-up. Sometimes there were excesses and sometimes shortages, but they did their best under always urgent circumstances.

The U.S. Navy also developed a huge automated supply system called "Stock Points", which ran predominately on IBM 1410 Systems and later on new 360/50s. The two main computer locations were at Subic Bay in the Philippines and at Sattahip, Thailand. We serviced both locations with resident CEs as well as SEs assigned to Subic. A serious thing happened when the 360 Model 50 was being delivered to Sattahip. During the transportation off-loading process the $1,000,000 Central Processing Unit (CPU) - mainframe of the Model 50 - was dropped (from a ship's sling?) and damaged beyond repair. IBM scheduling grabbed the very next 360/50 from the Poughkeepsie manufacturing plant's assembly line, which had been scheduled for a commercial customer somewhere in the States (imagine their consternation when told their system was in Thailand!), had it flown to Thailand, and the entire system was up and running with only a one week delay. This reflects the level of commitment with which IBM supported its Federal Government customer.

In addition to the above described computer installations, we supported almost all of IBM's entire product line in Southeast Asia (SEA). There were a few unique products that we would not or could not support or maintain. The approved list of equipment that could be shipped by IBM to SEA appeared in the pages of the GSA Contract. The GSA Contract was our operative bible; it addressed the procurement, use, maintenance duties, and rental, purchase and maintenance fees for all of our equipment. It also addressed how we, as civilians, would be treated by the military in the war zone. In general, if it wasn't in the Contract, we didn't do it.

Sometime in 1970, one of the Army units came to us asking if we could provide them with something on the order of 10,000 IBM 1001 handheld porta-punches. This was a small, hand-held, outdated board upon which a punched card was placed and a stick smaller than a pencil was used to punch holes in the card. The idea was that each soldier could order boots, socks, bullets, grenades and so on while still in the field. The cards could then be collected, sent to a processing center and batch processed into the Army's inventory system. The Army unit wanted to know if the 10,000 little porta-punch machines could be delivered in the next few months. This wasn't an entirely coo-coo idea; how basic could the ordering process get? But, we said "No, it isn't in the GSA Contract and that IBM hasn't made any 1001s for years." Thank goodness, because it would have been a major pain in the butt to manufacture, ship and deliver all those tiny units. We also doubted whether all the punched cards would have arrived at data processing without being folded, spindled, muddied or mutilated.

Other unique machines were not made available either, but hundreds (perhaps thousands?) of IBM Selectric typewriters found their way to Vietnam - which required that we have two IBM Office Products CEs in country to maintain them. These two men were stretched to the very limit by taking maintenance calls on individual typewriters and traveling to most South Vietnam bases. Finally, at the height of our service involvement, we had to say, "No more up country travel. Send the typewriters to our Saigon office and we'll repair them there". At the opposite end of the machine spectrum were two Model 65s used in a secure environment at Nakhon Phanom (NKP) in northeast Thailand near the Mekong River and Laos. The story of these 65s and their code name "Igloo White" application will be told in chapter 5.

## Machine Maintenance

Customer Engineering and System Engineering support was critical, and the GSA Contract promised that IBM would provide at least two hour, or better, response time in the event of a non-expendable machine outage. (Common sense had to prevail at times. If a location was under attack and we considered the situation unsafe, we could refuse to travel.) These were the days prior to micro-electronics and the computer systems still used magnetic core planes as memory boards. The largest IBM S/360 main memory initially available was 512,000 positions of addressable storage (later expended to 1,024,000) and the concept of 'virtual memory' had not yet been introduced. Disk drives were large and slow and most permanent data storage was kept on magnetic tape (remember the 729s and 2400 tape drives?). The fastest line printer was the 1403-N1 rated at 1100 lines per minute, but most printing did not approach that speed.

Spare parts supply and storage in Vietnam was also critical, and since we did not have the space or foreknowledge to keep all possible parts for every machine in Vietnam, we had our own spare parts staging system spread out across the Pacific. If a needed spare part was not on site at a computer location, we would use our handy-talky and single side band radio network to order the part from the Saigon office's supply. If Saigon didn't have the part, we would put through a priority call to a large IBM parts depot on Okinawa. If Okinawa didn't have the part, then the next best source was Hawaii or the U.S. mainland. If a part was slow in arriving, we would occasionally borrow what was needed from a less critical machine or perform some technical magic. As an example, one night a main memory board went kaplooee on the 1410 system at 7th AF. This was a rare event and we did not stock memory boards in country. One of the Senior CEs stayed up all night and actually re-wired 1410 memory using tweezers and a magnifying glass to work copper wires through the tiny magnetic cores. The system was up and running by 1st shift the next morning. That CE should have received some kind of medal, but he simply saw it as his job and something that he should do.

IBM had a policy that if a machine was destroyed, either on purpose due to obsolescence, accident or rocket, an IBM CE or administrative person had to obtain a pencil impression of the machine's type and serial number which appeared on a metal tag behind or under the machine itself. Well, we lost a few machines in Vietnam; one was a 082 card sorter that was destroyed by a rocket at Dong Tam. We reported the loss and the IBM plant at Endicott, New York said that we had to get a pencil impression of the serial number - I guess it was either for some insurance purpose or some bean counter wanted to keep his records straight. We wrote back that the machine had been totally destroyed. The plant wrote back saying that we absolutely had to do the pencil impression thing. It was inferred that our branch office administrative measurements would suffer and we certainly didn't want that in the war zone! Oh, my! This went on for several months until finally two of our innovative office personnel packed all the old machine parts they could find, plus a few other pieces of beat up junk and car parts, into a bag and sent that to the plant with a statement that the bag contained the very machine itself and that they could re-assemble it if they wanted. The plant did not respond.

It seemed like we were always carrying something extra on business or rotational assignment trips in-country - a 1403 print train, diagnostics, a magnetic tape with a new utility or new operating system release, personal mail, a new CE repair kit or a spare part. If we weren't available to carry whatever it was, then we would go out to Tan Son Nhut and ask a military or commercial or Air America pilot to carry the package - everyone cooperated. The CEs were always juggling schedules, locations and responses to outages. We drove all the main roads during the day but usually stayed home at night. If a night repair was required, the CEs could and did call for a military jeep escort if it was considered to be an unsafe situation. They would ride with the military or follow closely behind in a civilian car and sometimes not return until morning. One CE was called to repair some unit record equipment in Pleiku; he was based in Qui Nhon along the central coast and set out one morning, east along Highway 19, in his Toyota Jeep. Half way to Pleiku, the Toyota had a flat tire; the CE removed the tire (I guess the spare was flat too?) and started flagging down passing traffic. A young Vietnamese came by on a Honda and stopped but refused or didn't understand the need for a ride. Our CE convinced the Vietnamese to take him to Pleiku, with the tire, at the point of a .38 revolver. They had the tire repaired and the CE, Vietnamese man, the tire and the trusty .38 returned to the Toyota, and the CE went on to his machine repair job.

Another unusual maintenance call caused us considerable worry. The story as I remember it goes somewhat as follows: A CE, whom I will name Jack, was called in Saigon to go down to the docks along the Saigon River to board a U.S. Navy ship. He took only his tool kit expecting to be gone only a couple of hours. There was a 407 Listing Machine in need of repair somewhere in the bowels of the ship and when the ship pulled out, Jack was still hard at work and unaware of his unplanned departure. Jack finished the repair and went back on deck to return to the office and found he had either been 'shanghaied', or that the Navy had forgotten he was on board. The ship was on its way to the U.S. Well, that wouldn't do, so dispatches were sent and another ship came alongside and Jack was transferred in a swaying basket, with his tool kit, to another ship bound for the Philippines. Jack ended up at Subic Bay without money, passport or clean clothes. This is where the story becomes a bit hazy. One version has Jack adopted for a few days by a benevolent and caring nurse and another version has Jack urgently trying to return to Saigon via any means possible. Eventually, he did catch a military flight into Da Nang and then another flight back to Saigon. He was gone a full week and we at the IBM office had no idea where he was. We kidded him a great deal about taking the whole week to fix just one 407, but were glad that he returned safely. Some CE calls in Vietnam were definitely non-routine.

# Chapter 5
## Special Customer Situations

Our IBM/GEM office had some interesting installations and responsibilities at other than the four application areas described in the previous chapter. Those that follow here are no less important and two of them, USAID and a project called *Igloo White* in Thailand, received special attention due to their high political profile. We were especially proud of IBM's contribution to their successes.

### USAID Saigon

The United States Aid (USAID) Mission was one such special account. USAID appeared to be a concerted, sincere attempt on the part of our government to genuinely help the Vietnamese people, and the computer applications in which we were involved reflected their mission. We had either a 1401 or 1460 computer system installed there in the late 60's, which was later upgraded to a faster S/360 Model 40. The machines themselves were crammed into what had apparently been a couple of makeshift offices within the USAID compound (a compound in Saigon was usually one or more buildings surrounded by a wall with an iron gate and topped by barbed wire). In Vietnam many of the rooms were definitely not designed to house computer systems; rather it was the other way around and we made the systems fit into what was available - perhaps an old house, a hallway, a large closet and in Da Nang the back end of a U.S. Army truck. The USAID computer rooms had water pipes and air ducts running across the low ceilings and early on there was no raised floor that normally covered computer cables. Anyone walking through the area had to duck, bob, and weave as they picked their way around the machines and stepped over the thick cables. Whenever we had to add some new IBM equipment, figuring out where to put it was like solving a large jigsaw puzzle.

There were also other idiosyncrasies. The Vietnamese computer operators and maids used to cook their lunches on small hibachis behind the row of tape drives and the repulsive stench of the aged fish sauce called nouc-mam would permeate the machine room and discourage any western visitor from wanting to ever return. At another nearby machine installation, a 407 tabulating machine suffered an extended outage due to rats chewing through the power cables. The CE repairing that machine had to make up an imaginative outage code for his work report. Computers are said to have "bugs" but they aren't supposed to have rats.

We taught computer programming at USAID, mostly to young Vietnamese and Chinese civilians. USAID originally used American contract programmers, who were very expensive both in salaries and in logistics support. Since there was nothing classified about the work they were doing, it made more sense to use local national programmers. AID asked IBM to develop a program to train locals and they placed advertisements in the Saigon paper looking for new programmers. In addition to fairly attractive pay, the job offered a draft exemption for men – they were flooded with applicants. The students were handpicked by the Mission and it was planned that they would become computer specialists and professional data processors. They were attentive, intelligent and were a pleasure to work with. One of my sources of personal satisfaction during our several years of support, was watching the students grow to professional status under SE Graham Seibert's tutelage. Graham developed the course materials to teach the elements of program design and then how to program in Assembly Language, FORTRAN and COBOL. The course was fairly intensive, all day every day. Graham would lecture in English and one of his Chinese assistants, a Miss Khanh, would translate into Vietnamese. After about four months of training, the new programmers started productive work, and within the year all the American contract programmers were gone. By the end of my own assignment in Vietnam, many of these early students had become the instructors, and good ones too.

Another satisfying result of our mission at USAID was that several of their programmers escaped Vietnam when it fell in 1975 and went to work for IBM in the States. Ms. Khanh escaped a bit later as a boat person. IBM sponsored her to come to America where she worked for IBM until going into her own business.

I assigned two American SEs, Bill Shugg and Graham Seibert, to work almost full time at USAID – Bill responsible for the S/360 equipment upgrade and both SEs completed a flawless conversion from DOS to the OS/360 operating system. After IBM "unbundled" and began charging fees world-wide for SE Services in 1969, we converted the SE work at USAID to service contract format and billed them at $35.00 per hour per man. I then converted, overnight, several of our other technically trained Systems Engineers to the title of Marketing Representative and they continued to assist our customers on-site as before. Consequently, I didn't have to charge for what I felt were inappropriate SE Service charges in the war zone. Fortunately, this went un-noticed at IBM HQ.

Several of the Vietnamese students were beautiful young women and spoke fluent French and English as well as their native language. I had to watch my bachelor SEs carefully and even occasionally gave them some fatherly advice regarding how they should or should not relate to these women. Once, after learning that one of our SEs (not Bill or Graham) and one of the students were spending too much late evening time together, supposedly in tutoring sessions, at his villa, I had to change personnel assignments on the account. This was a sensitive issue and would normally not have been any of my business, but USAID management was aware that business and moral conduct were being compromised and asked that I become involved in the interest of a greater cause. I learned later that a USAID manager was interested in the same young lady and had complained; apparently he had the greater cause.

A major and unique accomplishment at USAID led to the design and development of the "Vietnamese 1403 Print Train", which for the first time enabled the printing of legal documents in the native Vietnamese language. Four IBM SEs worked on the project - Curt Maxwell, Bill Shugg, Graham Seibert and Conrad Selewach. Curt led the design effort and several of the SEs received significant IBM recognition awards as well as praise from the Vietnamese government.

Curt was one of the first IBM Systems Engineers to accept the Vietnam assignment and along the way fell in love and married a young

Vietnamese. Consequently, he learned the language much better than most of us and with his wife's help was able to translate our English language ABCs and alphabetical sort sequence into the graphical shapes and sort sequence for the Vietnamese language. A thorough explanation of Curt Maxwell's design process appears in Curt's Chapter 12.

IBM manufacturing in the U.S.A. (Endicott, New York) converted the SEs' design into the physical train itself and shipped several new print trains to Vietnam in record time. The necessary Vietnamese diacritical overmarks and undermarks* were included on the new print train, but they required a second pass of the train over the printed document. This second pass slowed the 1100 line per minute speed of the printer considerably, but was well worth the effort to the Vietnamese computer applications. The first important use of the Vietnamese Print Train was with a land redistribution program called 'Land-to-the-Tiller'.

*(Footnote - In 1649 a French Catholic priest by the name of Alexandre-de-Rhoades converted Chinese ideograms into the now familiar Vietnamese written language known as "Quoc Ngu". The language has twelve vowels and twenty-seven consonants and he had to use diacritical markings to help distinguish the pronunciation and meaning of the tonal Vietnamese vocabulary).

In 1954, approximately 60% of the Vietnamese peasants were landless and another 20% owned less than two acres of land. Most of the land belonged to wealthy landlords in the same manner of land ownership in feudal Europe during the Middle Ages. Tenant farmers paid an average of 34% of their annual crop to these landlords. In certain areas that they controlled, the Viet Cong (VC) redistributed land and gained stronger peasant following. It was recognized that something had to be done to engender a feeling of patriotism among the South Vietnamese population and persuade them to give allegiance to the authority in Saigon. The premise was that the peasants would not fight to defend land they did not own. USAID was asked to help with that mission. In 1968 and 1969, President Nguyen Van Thieu directed a land reform program that would initially return government land to 50,000 families, and restoration to former land owners was prohibited. On March 26, 1970, the RVN passed the 'Land-to-the-Tiller' Act, which provided for an end to rent payments and began to issue ownership titles to the peasants currently working the land. Huge tracts (measured in hectares) of government or French land holdings were subdivided into small farm-like parcels and the deed or title was printed on USAID's IBM system in Vietnamese, complete with the new owners name in his native language. By 1972, the 'Land-to-the-Tiller' program had distributed land titles to 400,000 formerly landless farmers totaling more than 1,500,000 acres. By 1973, all but 7% of the farmers in South Vietnam owned their own land. This was a great morale booster to the farmers in the countryside (who were being courted by the Viet Cong) and was one of the principle *Vietnamization* government projects. It would have been even more successful if it hadn't been interrupted by the 1975 invasion from the North.

Another program that USAID implemented was the Commodity Import Program modeled on the Marshall Plan that was so successful in rebuilding Western Europe following WW II. This program's purpose was to enable Vietnam to import American goods. It functioned as follows: any Vietnamese wanting to import U.S. goods would apply for a commodity import license which explained what he wanted to import, why, and that he had the necessary local currency (piasters) to pay for the goods. If approved, the order would be placed and when the goods arrived, the Vietnamese importer would pay USAID in piasters and USAID would pay the U.S. exporter in dollars. USAID would then use the piasters to pay for their local expenses such as payroll to their local nationals, rent, utilities, etc. Though no official accounting of this program was ever publicized, rumor had it that USAID never came close to using all the piasters that were paid to them (and it is assumed that the U.S. taxpayer covered the difference in dollars). The program certainly flooded South Vietnam with Yankee goods. The bookkeeping for this program was also a major application for USAID's IBM 360/40 computer system.

I'll briefly touch on one more computer application. It was called the Hamlet Evaluation System and was intended to evaluate the relative safety of the country over time. Every hamlet in South Vietnam was identified by name and province. Periodically, the relative safety was assigned a numerical grade, from one to five. At one extreme a village would be considered safe enough for an American to live there, and at the other extreme a village would not be safe enough to visit even with an armed escort. I don't know how reliable the data was, who made the evaluations or whether the ever changing safety between night and day was considered.

We worked closely with USAID and their Vietnamese employees and students. The following incident was told to me by one of our Systems Engineers. The Vietnamese were sometimes very class conscious and certain families considered themselves better than other families because of wealth, religion, social or professional position. USAID had assigned salary and promotion categories to each Vietnamese employee, which was somewhat similar to our U.S. civil service GS rating structure. It was called a VS rating and was used to indicate the difficulty of an employee's job responsibilities and his or her compensation range. The American head of USAID received recommendations for promotions from his department heads and decided who would actually be promoted to a higher VS rating. His Vietnamese secretary typed these promotional letters for his signature. One day the secretary was typing a promotional letter for a computer programmer who was up for a VS-8 level increase, a level higher than her own. She considered her family socially superior than the family of the programmer and was highly insulted. She screamed and berated her USAID manager and ran through the USAID offices letting anyone and everyone know how she and her family had been affronted by this unacceptable and unthinkable act. The head of USAID had to use his best diplomatic tactfulness to calm his secretary and may even have had to also promote her too.

## Other U.S. Contractors

IBM wasn't the only American company in Vietnam. Control Data Corporation (CDC) had several important programming contracts with 7th Air Force as described in Chapter 4, and there were Control Data 3100 computer systems installed at the RMK-BRJ offices in downtown Saigon. The CDC programmers were housed in a three-story villa on Phan Ton Street near the RMK offices. I really never came into contact with the CDC personnel or equipment and had no reason to. The RMK-BRJ Company was responsible for building ports, naval bases, airfields, hospitals, storage facilities, camps and military housing. As an example, I believe they built the huge army base at Long Binh. They were called "The

Vietnam Builders" and was said to have been awarded 2 billion dollars in no bid contracts to establish the military infrastructure that was needed to conduct the war. As a guess, RMK-BRJ was probably the only group of companies in the world, at that time, which could handle the huge amount of workload required.

The Vinnell Corporation was responsible for military equipment repair, for construction of power plants and also had a relationship with CIA activities. Philco Ford was the contractor for the large communication switches in country, such as the one at Phu Lam. Univac and NCR equipment was also in use, but I don't know if these companies had personnel in country. I assume they did. I'm sure there were other companies and their civilian employees in Vietnam, but not mentioned on these pages. Any omission is not intentional.

## PA&E Saigon

Pacific Architects and Engineers (PA&E) was another unique customer account. PA&E arrived in Vietnam in 1963 with 274 men located at six sites and expanded to over 24,000 workers in more than 120 locations by 1968. The work force they used was made up of 5% Americans, 15% from assorted countries, and 80% from Vietnam itself. PA&E's main responsibility was to provide all the facilities engineering support for the Army in Vietnam. The government's responsibility was to provide the equipment, repair parts, tools, materials as well as living facilities. PA&E provided the labor, organization, and management. They also provided for pest eradication throughout the country.

PA&E was responsible for organizing the labor to build the CIA's newly designed interrogation chambers in each of South Vietnam's 44 provinces. These new buildings provided the South Vietnam government with the internal security they needed to carry out the Province Interrogation Program through out the villages and towns across Southern Vietnam.

PA&E was an excellent IBM customer and initially installed a System/360 Model 25 later upgraded to a Model 30 with disk, tape drives and the rest of a neat little system. Their offices were located on a back road near Tan Son Nhut Airport and close to the golf course. They operated fairly independently, had good data processing people and only needed occasional IBM support during hardware and software upgrades. They ran a mixture of accounting and engineering applications and employed two of our Systems Engineers on a part time basis via a services contract. The PA&E computer people were civilian contractors like ourselves and lived on the local economy, also like us.

The most memorable incident involving PA&E (and probably the most stupid and least important) indicated the level of tension and corporate hysteria within IBM stateside with regard to our in-country American assignees and equipment. As I recall, PA&E took delivery of some new 7330 magnetic tape drives sometime in 1970 and returned the older 729 drives in the same crates back to IBM's plant in Boulder, Colorado. When the 729 drives were unpacked back at the plant, a technician saw a thin red stick which looked to him like 'plastique' explosive laying at the back of the crate. Local IBM management was called and the panic began. Soon afterward, we in Saigon received a telephone call via the Honolulu Branch saying that "IBM manufacturing plants were being subject to possible VC sabotage and we should halt any and all machine shipments planned or already in route to the U.S.A." Honolulu management added that we in Vietnam should stop all Customer Engineering service calls until the all clear signal was given by them. (The tail was certainly wagging the dog at this point.) The conjecture by Corporate IBM, 5000 and 10,000 miles away, was that a possible VC sympathizer organization might be trying to blow up multiple IBM plant sites and thereby slow or halt computer equipment being shipped to the U.S. military in Southeast Asia.

The IBM Saigon location manager on duty at the time (my predecessor) knuckled under to poor logic and called PA&E with the story, as well as several other major customers like MACV, 7th Air Force and the Da Nang Marines and told them we could not work on their equipment until given the all clear because the safety of our stateside personnel might be in jeopardy. At the same time, our Saigon and Honolulu administrative personnel went to work on compiling information about equipment shipments in route to the States so that other potentially explosive crates could be identified. At the Boulder plant an Army SDI bomb squad was called to handle the threat, to identify and then defuse the explosive. Phone calls were flying back and forth from the U.S. mainland to Honolulu to Saigon and it was two days before we received the "all clear" and permission to return to normal operations. The bomb squad in Boulder had handled the hazardous situation with the suspected plastique in a professional manner and after looking at the red stick culprit for a second or two, they declared to the IBM plant supervisor that the danger was over and they had in fact "disarmed" a common stick of rat poison!

IBM stateside never admitted to any embarrassment, but we in Saigon had to wipe the egg from our faces and explain the embarrassing circumstances to several key accounts, while our CEs returned to work. Later we learned from PA&E that one of the Vietnamese cleaning men had accidentally swept the rat poison into the IBM crate, and I learned at the time that PA&E had a large contract in Vietnam for rat eradication on all military bases. Things soon returned to normal, our U.S. plants were safe again, we could continue shipping older machines from Vietnam and what became known as *"The Great Rat Poison Caper"* passed into history.

## Okinawa

A primary IBM customer on Okinawa was the Marine tank repair facility. After being beat up in Vietnam, tanks were shipped to Okinawa for body work and a tune up. They used an IBM 360/50, primarily for inventory control and scheduling, but had no resident systems programmers. From time to time, we would dispatch a Systems Engineer to Okinawa to help with software maintenance. Our Okinawa customers were covered by both the Saigon and Camp Zama, Japan based IBM offices (offices 562 and 560).

One strange incident involved the local Okinawan utility company. At that time, Okinawa was still under U.S. administration and the U.S. military was expected to provide guidance for various quasi-government organizations. IBM was asked to bid on a new computer system needed by the electric company. Two SEs were assigned to the project and although they knew very little about accounting practices, they went to Okinawa willingly. The financial manager for the utility ran his operation from his desk drawer and did so quite honestly. The two SEs spent a month trying to systematize a seat-of-the-pants desk drawer operation but finally gave up. (The result was that the utility was not automated until years later when Okinawa reverted to Japanese sovereignty). IBM owned a house on Okinawa that was nicely located on a small hill with ocean views in two directions. No one lived in the house and IBM was unable to sell it because the deed had been lost. Our Saigon based SEs learned of the house and stayed there on every business trip. The house was partly furnished and the plumbing worked well. Electricity was always disconnected, but could be reconnected by pushing the meter back into its socket. We never learned who paid the utilities or occasional maid service. Okinawa was bizarre.

## Philippines

Once every few months I would make a sales trip to the Philippines, and although my principal reason for the trip would be to visit our large computer installation at Subic Bay and spend managerial time with some of IBM's personnel assigned there, I would also stop by other IBM customer sites, such as the Cubi Point Submarine Base on Manila Bay and Clark Air Force Base near the town of Angeles. The unit record installation at Cubi was one of the largest card machine (no computer) installations in Southeast Asia. We felt that an upgrade to a small System/360 was well justified, but during my assignment they just kept adding more and more unit record equipment. Cubi Point is a promontory that juts out into Manila Bay and rather than take the long circuitous drive along the shoreline, it seemed more expedient to obtain transportation orders from the U.S. Embassy and take a navy craft directly across that portion of the beautiful bay. I don't know whether Cubi ever did replace of all those sorters, interpreters and tabulating machines, but it was an interesting location and a good IBM customer. Maintenance service for Cubi Point was provided by our CEs located at Clark or Subic, who would travel there, many miles distant, via military transportation whenever schedules permitted. Our Air Force had a couple of small IBM installations at Clark; I only made a couple of visits but I gained an appreciation for the massive size of that base and size of our U.S. investment – now gone - in the Philippines.

Driving through the town of Angeles made everyone somewhat nervous, since there were stories of too many unsolved murders; we knew that it was a home to bandits who occasionally ambushed military convoys for cigarettes, alcohol or other U.S. goods. One of our IBM CEs was once trapped in some Philippine cross fire during an Angeles shoot-out and simply hid behind his car until the gunfire subsided before continuing on to his account.

I once drove to Subic Bay with a CE who was returning to his account and then returned to Manila a few days later on a local bus. The bus was called the Victory Express. My memory of that bus ride places it right at the top of my all time most fascinating rides. Somewhere along the bus route, the thirty passenger recommended load limit grew to at least 60 people plus their accompanying live pigs and chickens. It was stiflingly hot and the ride was noisy, bumpy, dusty, smelly, and dirty. Street vendors were allowed to board the bus via the front door as we entered a village, then during the multiple stops and slower progress through town, the vendor would climb over and around the passengers and animals hawking his wares, and then disembark at the last stop before the bus re-entered the countryside. The same vendor would then wait awhile and repeat his selling technique on a bus going the other way.

I reached Manila sweaty and dirty after that trip, but am glad to have had that experience. Trips to the Philippines were always interesting for their potential variety of things to see, do and buy. There were great shopping opportunities, excellent hotels (most hotels were accommodating should a bachelor invite a local unregistered female guest for the evening), monsoon rains, fine restaurants and night life, frightening and colorful traffic and beautiful scenery, all of which helped me escape the stress of life in Vietnam.

## Nakhon Phanom, Thailand and the Automated battle Field

My responsibilities also took me to exotic Thailand that also had a unique set of customers and locations. Nakhon Phanom, better known as NKP, is a town on the west bank of the Mekong River in northeastern Thailand. A bridge crosses the Mekong there today, but in the late 1960's there was no official need for a bridge - to cross into Laos. It was enough for most of us to look at Laos across the river, and although there was a limited amount of boat traffic between the two countries, most of which carried either foodstuffs or infiltrating communists, the Thai side was supposedly safe. Our U.S. 13th Air Force operated a military airfield as guests of the Royal Thai Air Force Base. The base was nine miles to the west of NKP town and placed our aircraft within easy flying distance of the Ho Chi Minh Trail or other North Vietnam and Laotian targets (and just 230 miles to Hanoi). Our NKP Air Force's Task Force Alpha (TFA) operated a sophisticated computer installation that attempted to play a key role in the war by reducing the volume of truck traffic carrying men, materiel, guns and ammunition down 'The Trail' to the Communist aggression in South Vietnam. Little was known outside of Southeast Asia at that time about the TFA complex and the mission of Igloo White, but the computers were IBM's most powerful S/360s then available and the installation was serviced on site for several years by IBM personnel on a 24 hour, seven days a week basis.

Prior to my departure the initial time for Vietnam (late 1968), I arranged a visit for myself to the Neptune Warehouse in South San Francisco. As previously stated, this warehouse was the staging point for hundreds of IBM machines destined for Southeast Asia military sites. I wanted to take a partial inventory of the machines under my marketing responsibility as well as see first hand how the machines were being prepared for their Trans-Pacific air shipments. While walking through the huge warehouse, I noticed quite a few large wooden crates marked 'Igloo White' that were destined for Southeast Asia (SEA). Since I thought I knew everything about what IBM was doing in SEA, I asked where exactly the crates were going and what 'Igloo White' meant. I was told to mind my own business and that I did not have a 'need to know'. Well, this was quite a surprise and a shock to my ego. I decided I should shut up because I would probably find out soon enough. Sure enough, a few months later those "Igloo White" machines became my Thailand marketing responsibility and suddenly I had 'A Need To Know'.

Before getting into the Igloo White application let me describe a perhaps too simplistic scene along the Ho Chi Minh Trail. Sometime in 1959, or before, work began by the North Vietnamese Army to reconstruct an old supply trail that ran from North Vietnam through the western portion of the Laotian panhandle southward to various exit points into central South Vietnam. During the next few years, under the political ruse of Laotian neutrality, the old foot trails became a network of two lane highways, some of it paved, complete with parking and staging areas for on and off loading supplies as well as maintenance, equipment and ammunition storage depots. By 1964, when U.S. and ARVN combat troops began escalating the war, the 'Trail' had become North Vietnam's principal supply route south. Ocean traffic down the coast of Vietnam had been stopped by our Navy, and north/south routes across the DMZ were also closed. U.S. political restrictions did not allow a ground invasion across Vietnam's western border that might have halted the enemy flow of traffic south and by 1967, the Ho Chi Minh Trail had extended into neutralist eastern Cambodia with spurs branching off in the direction of all major South Vietnam cities and our military bases. One source said that there were possibly up to 10,000 trucks using the entire length of the trail at any one time and that in 1967 there were 60,000 tons of military stuff a day being delivered down the trail to various destinations. (TV documentary film, 'Vietnam, the 10,000 Day War').

By 1968 North Vietnam was able to send up to an estimated 10,000 NVA troops a month to South Vietnam along with enough food and weapons to feed and equip them. Since our politicians at home successfully kept our ground troops from halting this flow, there was only one other way to stop the enemy and his supplies from reaching the Vietcong positions in the South - air strikes guided by an effective intelligence system. An electronic warfare operation was devised by a top-secret group of American scientists called the Defense Communications Planning Group (DCPG) and implemented by the U.S. Air Force. It was code named 'Igloo White'. IBM's Federal Systems Division (FSD), headquartered in Gaithersburg, Maryland, was selected as the prime contractor to provide the computers and help program and operate the system in Thailand. I believe that FSD also helped Parsons, Inc. design and build the computer facility with the construction and site maintenance activities under the supervision of the U.S. Army Corps of Engineers. FSD and a Florida company designed and manufactured thousands of unique sensing devices that were used to monitor the Trail. Our IBM-GEM office in Saigon was given the responsibility of maintaining the computer systems with on-site CEs and of providing sales and systems engineering assistance whenever needed. I learned about my responsibilities after arriving in SEA and during my first trip to NKP in the summer of 1969. I also learned how our military was, at last, attacking the supply routes that were fueling the enemy war machine in the South.

The secret electronic sensors came in three or more flavors - those that contained a microphone and responded to sound called acoubouys (acoustic sensors); those that responded to seismic vibrations in the ground (ADSIDs – Air Delivered Seismic Intrusion Detector); and those responding to heat from passing bodies and vehicles. Another magnetic variety responded to nearby metal. The acoubouys and their small parachutes were camouflaged with mottled jungle colors and when dropped from planes were intended to hang in trees and appear to be part of the foliage. The seismic sensors were the workhorses of the system and could detect heavy movement for a distance of approximately 100 feet. The sensors that I saw were quite large, were built like fat lawn darts and designed to look like large green weeds, pointed at one end with a thick cylindrical body containing the sensor electronics and with loose foliage appendages at the top to resemble leaves. They must have been waterproofed and were probably made of rubber and/or plastic (I don't know). I assume the sensing portion was shock mounted because these weed-type sensors were sown from low flying aircraft so that they formed patterns or strings at predetermined geographic locations along and across the Trail segments that were to be monitored. Some of the seismic sensors undoubtedly lodged in trees or brush as they fell, but it was intended that they hit the ground thus burying the pointed end with the foliage end sticking up to resemble the natural vegetation of the area. It is reported that over the life of the Igloo White project, something on the order of 20,000 to 30,000 sensors were deployed at an estimated cost of between $600 and $3,000 each – depending on the type and sophistication of the device.

Once in place, the sensors were activated and began transmitting any noises, vibrations or heat from passing North Vietnamese traffic. If the sensors were picked up or handled in any way they were designed to self-destruct to keep the enemy from learning how they worked. Circling U.S. aircraft (EC-121 highly modified Constellations?) would then receive the sensor transmissions and in turn relay the signals to large dish shaped receivers on top of the TFA computer building back at NKP. These signals would then be permanently recorded and analyzed on the IBM equipment. The small sensors' radio transmitters were battery powered and only good for 30 to 40 days before they eventually wore out, but FSD was working on a next generation sensor which could be turned on and off remotely as needed in order to save the batteries.

The Air Force had divided the entire trail up into large square map segments that were identified by a geographic coordinate system. I do not know how accurately the sensor positions could be mapped (our present day Global Positioning System GPS would certainly have been much more accurate), but at least the relative position of each sensor string was known and could be identified by some characteristic of the transmitted VHF signal. By timing the transmissions from the estimated sensor locations, the direction and speed of a truck could be fairly well determined. Once the sensors were activated and transmitting data, the NKP listening stations and computer system could, in theory, begin analyzing all the information about each Vietnamese truck convoy and then discriminate traffic patterns, such as: speed, direction, duration of travel, quantity and estimated size or load for each truck. Statistical reports printed on IBM 1403 printers would track and record convoy activity, night by night, and there would be approximately 1000 to 2000 trucks being monitored each night. One could sit in the NKP computer complex, put on a set of earphones and, during periods of movement down the trail, listen to the drone or roar of truck engines and even hear Vietnamese soldiers in conversation.

I once heard some banging on a sensor device with some kind of metallic object (a soldier's curiosity?) and after some audible Vietnamese jibber jabber conversation the banging stopped and the sensor had either self-destructed as designed or had been tossed aside. I have been told, a third or forth hand story, that some NVA troops came across one of the audio sensors, apparently did not know what it was and presented it to their battalion commander as a souvenir. The commander put it in the back of his command tent and forgot about it. For some short time afterward everything his battalion did was anticipated by our U.S. forces, thus causing him heavy casualties. This definitely could have happened because the audio I heard was clearly discernable. As a curiosity, I was told more recently by an IBMer that he discovered one of the FSD sensors in a war surplus store in Tennessee; he didn't tell me the price.

NKP became the site of the largest and probably the most sophisticated computer installation in Southeast Asia. In 1968, the TFA building was said to be the largest single building in Southeast Asia. Two System/360 Model 65 processors were installed with associated banks of disk and tape drives, many terminals and a large number of radio and sensing devices used as signal transceiver computer 'front ends'. It was thought initially that two Model 65 processors would be needed, one for primary processing and the second as a back up system. The second processor was eventually returned to IBM because of the excellent reliability of the Model 65. The entire project was initially very "Top-Secret" for a variety of political, technological, tactical and strategic reasons, but not too many years later it was declassified and explained to the general public. A more detailed description of Igloo White can be read online on various Google articles.

Security at 'Igloo White' seemed to me to be surprisingly lax, but perhaps I did not appreciate the unseen extra precautions taken to protect this high profile installation. There were high chain-link perimeter fences with razor wire around the 200,000 square foot facility and guard dogs were used on patrols. Large barriers and massive walls of the main building protected against mortars or rockets that might explode nearby. However, the single guard shack at the open-gated front entrance seemed insufficient. When you arrived at the guard shack you were required to sign in and were given a badge, and that was all. You did not have to show any identification to prove that you were an American citizen or much less that you needed to enter the complex. Perhaps my white shirt, tie, dark slacks and wingtip leather shoes were sufficient? Once through the front airlock entrance you could go anywhere in the building with easy access to the command center or computer room. There have been many long discussions and speculation about why no effort was made by the enemy to bomb or sabotage the project. One conclusion that many arrived at was that all the technology and bombing was not hurting the North Vietnamese to any serious extent and that it acted as an enormous diversion in tying up American resources in a futile effort. I guess we will never know.

The early objective was to only monitor the Ho Chi Minh Trail, but it became evident that the system might be well utilized to attempt to slow the truck traffic. The trucks initially always moved at night, since daylight traffic would make easier U.S. aircraft targets. In the early 1970s the North Vietnamese began camouflaging thousands of kilometers of the trail and were able to move unseen from the air during the day. By extrapolating the traffic patterns (it was possible in theory to predict within a minute or two when a truck would be arriving at a known point) a pilot on the ground at NKP would watch sensor activity on IBM display terminals and attempt to talk F-4D Phantom and A-6E Intruder jet pilots already airborne into effective high speed bombing runs so that he would release his ordinance at the right time and location. The estimated right location was determined by using LORAN (Long Range Aid to Navigation) coordinates, which was fairly loose control for a jet moving at over 1,000 miles per hour and at several thousand feet in the air; consequently the truck "kill" count was problematical or even disappointing. Hitting moving targets on serpentine mountain roads through heavy jungle foliage at night using target identification information in real time was a very tall order. Lower and slower aircraft such as the Gruman C-1A and the B-57 Canberra were tried and were more effective, but they made easier targets for North Vietnamese anti-aircraft guns and some were shot down. Trading a 1A or Canberra and pilot for one or two trucks was not a good wartime trade. Later on in the project, C-130 cargo planes were transformed into AC-130 gunships and they became a much more effective truck killer.

One other weapon was used. The computers, through a variety of statistical processes combined with manual deductions and other intelligence sources, could identify probable enemy truck parks where convoys were held during the day awaiting the next night's move. The NKP center could then direct high level (30,000+ feet) B-52 strikes, out of Anderson AFB, Guam and U Tapao, Thailand against the suspected truck park. (Against all rules, some of the IBMers would try their luck at selecting targets and partially controlling the strikes and some operators referred to the entire system as a large pinball game). Results were not known until the next day after analyzing the recon photographs. Occasionally our U.S. bombs would set off secondary explosions giving immediate indication of success.

There was a formal briefing for the Commanding General every morning that we IBMers were allowed to attend. A Captain would stand behind a huge transparent Plexiglas map of the trail complex, divided into sectors, and either use a pointer or write in mirror image so that the viewing audience, including the General, could watch the recreated truck movement along the Trail that had taken place during the previous night. It was probably the most condensed and accurate briefing available on the overall tactical situation, and although it mainly concentrated on the night's activity along the Ho Chi Minh Trail, it also provided a continuous update on the effectiveness of the NKP mission. The Air Force felt that they could quantify with reasonable accuracy the percent of traffic being destroyed by indicating how many trucks were still active after a raid, which in turn continued to justify the NKP mission. Certain portions of the Ho Chi Minh Trail were miles wide and although the Igloo White project was partially effective, the ingenuity of the North Vietnamese still managed to supply a remote war machine, via a labyrinth of trails through mountainous jungle terrain, many many miles from their homeland. After deploying the estimated 20,000+ sensors (mentioned above), Igloo White was terminated in early 1973 because of the high cost (reportedly, an unsubstantiated one billion dollars per year), because too many trucks were still making successful trips south and because prospects for peace at the Paris talks were supposedly going well.

Project Igloo White became a political football in Washington DC. A great number of enemy trucks were reportedly destroyed: 5,500 in 1969, 6,000 in 1970, 12,000 in 1971 and 12,000 1972, the last full year of its operation. One estimate was that in 1971 only 20 percent of the supplies that entered the trail system made it to their destination (comment: no way to prove any of these figures). The last bombing raid on the Ho Chi Minh Trail was a B-52 strike in April 1973.

The NKP air base played host to a variety of surveillance and relatively slow fighter aircraft. Alternately, the EC-121s (with their load of IBM developed radio relay equipment and mini-command centers) were based at Ubon two hundred miles to the south and the F-4s flew out of Udorn, one hundred and forty miles to the west. NKP was also host to a variety of "spooks" (intelligence personnel); some were uniquely interesting people, but it was strongly suggested that IBMers should pretend that they did not exist. One such spook did us a special favor by shooting a large cobra snake found crawling in the computer room. There was a periodic Top Secret briefing by the CIA agent resident in Laos. These briefings were reported to be so hilarious (unintentionally) because of their obscure references to nothing, meaningless rumors, pointless speculations, name-dropping and obvious uselessness that briefing attendance was always high.

One of the IBMers told me that he crossed the Mekong River on several occasions (unauthorized) and joined a U.S. agent for casual drives in Laos. He said that they once drove north for quite some distance and decided to stop and turn around when they observed that there were nearby gun emplacements - all pointed south! The town of Thaket was just across the Mekong from NKP and since Laos was off limits, several other IBMers wanted to "try it once" and so they also took the small boat rides to "see what was on the other side of the river". This was considered pretty dumb but fortunately there was never a problem; dumb luck I think, since Laos had no political distinction and there would have been literally no help from any source if any problem had arisen with our personnel.

In such a computer dependent operation, IBM support was considered critical. Whatever the Commanding General wanted, within reason, the General got! I rotated our best and most knowledgeable System Engineers to the site as needed and in 1970 and 1971 the on-site Customer Engineers performed their preventive maintenance and repair duties on a 24 hour 7 days a week basis. During critical tactical missions, at least one CE was assigned a sleeping cot in the nearby CE parts room to be present immediately throughout the night, if needed (this was done at a General Officers firm and specific request to IBM management). Living conditions on the NKP air base for the IBMers were rather simple. Home was a shared room in a 'hutch', a cross between a barracks and a dormitory. Meals were taken at the officer's club (not as grand as it sounds) or at the NCO Club or enlisted men's mess (which, reportedly had better food). The hutches had maid service, but absolutely no 'live-in' girls (that I ever knew about anyway). A few CEs elected to live in town. Most of the IBM people stayed for two to three years and life in Thailand, on and off base, was indeed fascinating. More than just a few of the IBM CEs succumbed to the many fascinations of Thailand – the easy economy, the beautiful women, cheap booze and housing and the freedom of the "farangi" living over-seas – and they remained beyond their assignments.

It was at NKP in 1973 that one of our CEs surprised a thief as he returned to his hutch late in the evening. The thief was armed with a bayonet. After the CE hit him in the head with his hand-held two-way radio the IBMer was stabbed five times in the chest, face and legs. One wound punctured his lung and he was quickly drowning in his own blood. Fortunately that particular hutch was the only one that had a telephone so that our CE was able to call for help, just in time, and that clearly saved his life. He was medevac'd to the U.S. military hospital at Udorn where they were able to treat his then collapsed lung and other punctures. The stab wound to his face just missed his eyeball but did permanent damage to his eye muscles. The thief was apprehended and he turned out to be Thai soldier stationed at Udorn, but even after being identified by our CE, he was never prosecuted - a typical example of Thai injustice.

One interesting subject was the IBM 'recreation room'. This was a self-help project built with surplus materials (permitted by Air Force rules) and constructed by IBMers with considerable help from other construction contractors. This 'rec room' was easily the nicest place on the base. It was air-conditioned, had a ping pong table, a good pool table, a paperback book library, comfortable lounge chairs, and a well stocked bar. It was later expanded to have two bars. One of the IBM drivers (a local Thai) doubled as a bartender. The bar defied written IBM policy since drinking on IBM premises or during work hours was strictly taboo everywhere else in the world in those days. Any visiting IBM management consistently gave orders to close the bar (there were not too many IBM management visits because the local IBM staff, to some extent, could deny permission for 'civilian' IBMers to fly to NKP). The bar closure orders were uniformly ignored and this continued until Arthur K. Watson (the brother of Tom Watson, IBM's CEO) visited the site. A.K. was in Thailand to visit the King, who was a yachting friend, and the IBM Manager at NKP went to Bangkok and insisted that Mr. Watson visit his operation. Mr. Watson was given a tour of NKP, including the recreation room and bar, "built from surplus materials by IBMers in their spare time." The remoteness of the location and stressful day-to-day hardships were, perhaps, overemphasized, and Mr. Watson sincerely praised all concerned and returned to Bangkok that night. Thereafter, visiting IBM managers were informed that Mr. Watson had personally approved the recreation room and all its contents. Toward the end of the war, most of the U.S. General Officers in the theater were based at NKP. The

IBM people had left and the Air Force had taken over all aspects of the operation, including computer maintenance. The IBM recreation room became the Generals' own club.

*Ho Chi Minh Clock Tower, NKP (courtesy, Tom Camargo)*

IBM provided a minibus to take our people into town in the evenings - a 20-minute ride. The city of Nakon Phanom was interesting. The town's clock tower (so it was said) had been a gift from local Vietnamese in honor of Ho Chi Minh and built many years earlier. There were a number of restaurants that served good water buffalo steaks, many souvenir stands, a number of massage parlors and quite a few bars. The local economy had been drastically enhanced by the nearby American air base. The bars were well populated with girls, and a few of the bars were declared "off limits" for health reasons. If the VD rate went above twenty or thirty percent, the particular bar which had been the alleged source of the problem, was temporarily placed off limits to military personnel. Base personnel who contracted VD too often were reported to their commanding officer, or manager for civilians. Only one IBMer was known to have earned this dubious distinction.

One of our more conservative Systems Engineers told the following story:

"I took advantage of the bus service in to town one evening and found the ladies in the dance halls to be surprisingly well mannered and refined.

They were young, well dressed, polite, and demanded good behavior from the clientele. They were also very pretty, as were most Thai women.

Late one afternoon, I was relaxing with some of the base staff and listening to an Armed Forces radio station announcer reciting a list of numbers. Everyone had pulled out cards from their wallets and watched carefully as the list was read. I asked if this was some kind of radio bingo game and I was treated with whoops of laughter. The numbers were ID cards of the dance hall girls who upon their weekly medical examination were found to have contracted VD!

I had difficulty resolving the two concepts of quiet refinement with weekly medical examinations for venereal disease. My Midwestern, bible-belt upbringing could just not process this dichotomy! Apparently my narrow understanding of human nature had much to learn. I do believe that the Thai culture did not hold prostitution as such an evil occupation as it was in Kansas."

Travel to and from NKP was awkward and haphazard. The standard method was to ride on a C-130 (configured as a cargo carrier with extremely uncomfortable webbed seats for passengers). An alternate method was a small courier jet, named 'Scatback', which flew from Saigon to NKP every morning and stopped at a number of places in route to pick up photoreconnaissance film. These flights were not secret, but were little known and a passenger needed a Top Secret clearance in order to obtain orders and flight reservations. There were only a few seats and they were often full. One of our Saigon based Systems Engineer used the Scatback flights to NKP quite frequently, which helped cut down on his travel time. Another travel option was to 'thumb a ride' on a 'Jolly Green Giant' to Udorn and then there were a number of options from there. The SEs reported that the biggest danger in flying with the big choppers was 'deafness'. Even with earmuffs, they were incredibly loud. As a last alternative method to reach NKP, one could charter a private plane out of Bangkok for the 350-mile flight with an American pilot (Air America).

One of the most frightening flights I have ever experienced in my life was via a chartered Cessna 172 return flight one late afternoon after a management meeting with the NKP Commanding General. Bob Tanner, Larry Pulliam and I had really enjoyed the early morning 365-mile flight from Bangkok's Don Muang Airport across Thailand to NKP, but we departed NKP too late to avoid a huge expanding cumulous cloud buildup in central Thailand. At one time, with sleet, thunder and lightning buffeting our little aircraft, I looked at the altimeter, which was indicating 14,000 feet. We had no artificial oxygen supply and it was very cold. I asked the pilot what the maximum altitude the aircraft was rated for and he said 13,500 feet but not to worry, he was sure that he could fly over or around the weather. I began to wonder about our future. Another complication was the fact that the plane's radio was inoperative, and the pilot did not help our confidence level by constantly tapping on the fuel gauge and compass. I hadn't even bought flight insurance. A full hour overdue, we finally broke free from the storm clouds in the vicinity of Bangkok but had no radio with which to contact the control tower for landing instructions. We three passengers were told by the pilot to keep a sharp eye out for incoming 747s while he landed the plane. Our number of landings again equaled number of takeoffs that day, but I was positive that I would not use that method of transportation to or from NKP again. Our IBM mission at NKP always seemed to expand one's sense of adventure.

## A Special CE's Special Story

Tom Camargo was a highly skilled Customer Engineer and remained on assignment at Nakon Phanom for five years, 1970 to 1975. Tom was also a true 'wild duck' and enjoyed everything that Thailand had to offer. His condensed story follows:

Tom had almost five year's experience with IBM Field Engineering in the Los Angeles area when he got the call to go to Southeast Asia. He had spent some time in SEA with the Navy and jumped at the opportunity to return. Tom thrived in an environment where he had to live by his wits. He would spend the better part of his IBM assignment servicing the big S/360 installations at NKP, and he loved it. In fact, Tom loved everything about his assignment – the technical challenges and ingenuity needed to repair complex equipment, even when there wasn't the same level of spare parts needed or when called upon to fix equipment that he had not been directly trained on. Tom could probably repair just about every piece of IBM equipment at NKP. Tom also loved the freedom and adventure that living in northeast Thailand afforded an energetic bachelor, including the opportunity to travel throughout the region (mostly at IBM's expense) and to sample the watering holes and exotic women of the area.

Tom initially lived directly on the NKP Air Base, in a hutch with other IBM CEs, and had the use of both the officer's club and the famous, bootlegged IBM 'Rec' room. However, he later chose to live in the town of NKP, near the Mekong River, enjoying a two-story Thai style bungalow. Living in town afforded more freedom, plus a houseboy, a live-in maid and space for pets, multiple cars and motorcycles and multiple guests. He was on call 24/7 and could respond to a machine outage back at the TFA complex within twenty or so minutes. IBM staffed the NKP installation with excellent maintenance personnel and the equipment was, for the most part, very reliable. The personnel rotation system gave the IBMers time enough off for R&Rs and weekend trips. As we in Saigon, Tom became an expert at world travel.

Tom and other IBM CEs, traveled extensively throughout Thailand, using military transport, public buses or his personal car or bike (e.g. Honda 350 or Kawasaki 500). Tom enjoyed many visits to Chiang Mai and U-Dorn and made many friends with his personality and photography, an avocation that he still pursues. He was fond of driving the back roads of Thailand and stopping in small villages and making friends with the locals. On one such trip he met and drank with a Peace Corp volunteer and two GIs that were operating a remote military communications outpost in the middle of a thick forest; their exact purpose went unstated. Another memorable trip was made with two other CEs on motorcycles from NKP to the interesting city of Penang in Northern Malaysia (a trip of probably 1500 miles). The return trip was by train with the bikes on board, and Tom says, "I marvel now at how naive we were in dealing with the officials at the Thai/Malaysian border, trying to get the motorcycles back into Thailand. The paperwork had all been correctly done well beforehand, but the process took hours – until the proper bribe was placed into the hands of the proper official."

When Saigon fell in 1975, Tom was still on assignment at NKP – the last IBMer remaining there. Much of the IBM computer equipment had been returned to the US and down-sized from the original dual 360/65s to a single 360/50 system and a single 1130/2250 system. Suddenly, there was no longer a need for an IBM presence and Tom was asked to pack up the IBM equipment and supplies and either ship it all back to the 'States' or give the remainder to IBM Thailand. The TFA installation was de-activated on June 30, 1975.

At the end of his assignment, Tom went on an IBM paid R&R around the world. When he returned to Thailand, he submitted his resignation. He had not really gone 'native'; he just wasn't ready to go home yet. Tom and a Thai IBMer invested in a tourist hotel in the River Kwai area in western Thailand. Tom ran the bar and restaurant and helped purchase the facility. The hotel eventually failed and Tom returned to the USA in 1978 where he was re-hired by IBM to maintain large IBM System/360 hardware. He told me once that years later he had taken a maintenance call at Camp Pendleton in Southern California and actually worked on the same 360/65 mainframe (Idled by serial number) that had been his responsibility at NKP. He eventually left IBM and worked in computer maintenance with several other hardware firms as well as formed his own company that maintained computer equipment at White Sands, New Mexico. Tom is now semi-retired and living happily in California. He traveled back to Thailand on vacation in 2003 and was amazed at the progress and development made in the area near his old hotel near the River Kwai.

Tom states, "To say that my SEA assignment seriously altered the course of my life is no over-statement. Every now and then, I think about how things might have been had I not volunteered for that assignment and I am sure I would not have wanted the boring (stateside) alternative. I would do the whole thing over again without hesitation."

## Tales of Laos

In 1969 one of our marketing representatives and a Systems Engineer attempted to sell a small computing system at the request of the U.S. Aid Mission in Vientiane, Laos (Laos was definitely outside of our military support jurisdiction). The SE made several follow-up calls. No system was sold, but his experiences were memorable. That SE has passed along the following anecdote: "The air service was erratic in quality and timing and after a year or two in the area, we were all rather blasé about an aircraft's condition or safety. However, rather than chance it, we once decided to forego flying and try another means to return to our assigned location.

We hired a fisherman to take us across the Mekong, found a Thai official to stamp our passports and then took a train from northern Thailand to Bangkok". He went on to say that Vientiane was very interesting,

"At that time there was no effective Laotian government and one could purchase anything. It was said to be the most active gold market in the world and one could buy pure 24 carat gold in any quantity or form. One popular form was in the shape of an egg. It was also one of the most active drug markets in Asia, with anything available in any quantity, for cash. The major tourist attraction in Vientiane (there were no real tourists, of course, just a mixed pack of war related or embassy related adventure seekers) was the White Rose Bar that featured a troupe of young attractive female entertainers. These Laotian beauties performed in a large open bar area and were usually totally nude. They would entertain during the day in accordance with the size of an extracted fee. The entertainment there became more personal at night. It has been said that, one way to divide the world is between those who experienced the White Rose Bar and those who did not."

Laos held a fascination for certain adventurous types of people and although our office had been discouraged by upper IBM management from extending any marketing or services into Laos, an occasional and unauthorized trip by our personnel somehow became self justified. John Leussler enjoyed taking side trips to out-of-the-way places and he has contributed the following story:

"In February of 1970 I decided to take a trip into Laos before the Communists seized control. I boarded a Royal Air Lao DC-3 at Tan Son Nhut. My fellow passengers were twenty or so Laotians who took with them a great deal of food and some live pigs and chickens. The DC-3 seemed lacking in maintenance but flew its sweaty, noisy, smelly cargo without falling apart. Our first stop was at Pakse, a provincial capital, just north of Cambodia in the Laotian panhandle. We had a one-hour wait, so while the rest of the passengers and their animals huddled in the shade of the plane's wings, I took a walk down the road heading toward town. I'd gone only a short distance when I came to a Laotian boy, perhaps eight years old, playing in an empty field. He was wearing a yellow tee shirt that said 'Apollo 11, First Men on the Moon'. The Apollo landing had occurred only the previous July, and I wondered at either the efficiency of the

Asian consumer goods distribution system, or perhaps some American had given the boy the shirt in that strange and remote place. The moon landing had given our country tremendous worldwide prestige and even here was an eight-year old Laotian in tiny Pakse wearing a coveted symbol of American success."

"When I arrived in Vientiane, Laos, I checked into the 80 room Hotel Lane Xang, which is in the center of the city across a riverfront street from the mighty Mekong. The riverbed of the Mekong at Vientiane is extremely wide - perhaps 3/4 of a mile across, and in February is mostly dry. The river itself hugged the far Thai shore leaving a wide area in front of the city used for parking cars and soccer games. Clouds of dust caused by racing cars, soccer games or anything else that moved rose from the riverbed. Vientiane in February was hot, dry, dusty and sleepy. The next day after some sightseeing, I found a bar full of Americans and spent a couple of hours drinking beer and talking with Air America pilots. That evening I made the recommended stop at the White Rose Bar, and it definitely lived up to the reputation so well celebrated in song, story and the front page of an issue of the *Wall Street Journal*. It was populated by rowdy Americans and some of the best looking and least restrained young women in the world. It was an enjoyable place to stop."

"The next morning I caught another DC-3 flight almost due north to Luang Prabang, the old royal capital and the oldest city in Laos that dates back 1200 years. If Laos is shaped like the side view of an elephant's head and trunk, Luang Prabang is about where the eye should be. It sits astride a much narrower Mekong River, in the middle of verdant mountains made smoky by small fires that dotted the slopes. I hired a taxi for the day and explored a few of the 30 or so temples (wats) in the city and a few outside of town, one of which involved climbing a small mountain. This made my driver happy; he could sit near his taxi and talk to his friends while being paid. The views from the top and the picture taking opportunities were superb. There was much more to see but the next day I reluctantly returned to my responsibilities in Saigon. The general ambience of the area made Luang Prabang one of my favorite stopping places in all of Southeast Asia."

The customer accounts and adventures described above represent some of what we IBMers did in Southeast Asia. It was frequently dangerous (sometimes the danger was self imposed) and depending on where one was, there was usually a great deal of tension. Life, and the possibility of death, was so very real that memories for most of us can still be vividly recalled to this day. We made and kept appointments across the boundaries of three separate nations. We traveled however we could - commercially, with military orders via C-130s, jets, helicopters or Army jeeps, or with our own cars and jeeps. We lived on the economy off base in villas or with the military in hot crowded portakamps, Quonset huts and occasionally in bunkers during enemy attacks. We worked hard and long and when we were not working, we played hard. We had some fun. We advised the military on how to improve their data processing effectiveness. We kept the military computers and punched card machines humming and provided service to our accounts 24 hours a day on a par with or better than most data processing facilities in Los Angeles, Dallas or Boston! The conditions and logistics were simply more challenging and extreme, and every man one of us loved it!

# Chapter 6
## White Shirts And Ties

Between 1967 and 1973, IBM sent approximately 250 bachelor data processing professionals to Southeast Asia. They came from all over the United States, but were predominantly from the West Coast. The average age was probably under 30 years and each man had particular hand picked skills and training designed to mesh with the needs of the overall support mission. Each man also had to have a spirit of adventure and personal independence as well as a positive opinion as to why the United States was involved in the Vietnam conflict (or at least keep his opinion to himself in the interest of good collective morale). Each volunteer passed through Honolulu on his way west where he was given a Vietnam briefing at the IBM Branch Office and a few last days on the beach. Much of the input for this book has come from those IBMers who are proud of the role they played in the Vietnam War and are still enthralled to this day by what they experienced there. This book is written by and about IBM professionals who voluntarily left the normal course of careers in 'stateside' data processing and took some Time Out For War (the original title of this book).

I believe that we were selected or that we volunteered for the two-year overseas assignment because we were what Tom Watson (IBM CEO Emeritus) referred to as "wild ducks" -- an IBMer who perhaps did not quite fit the cloned corporate headquarters image or life style pattern of a typical IBMer. Most of us adapted well to living in such a strange and tension filled country. However, a few of our assignees arrived in Saigon, saw what was going on, freaked out and went home after a few weeks or months. One CE (Customer Engineer) was sent home with what was at the time diagnosed as 'shell shock'. He had literally been blown out of his bunk one night in Da Nang by the concussion of a nearby rocket explosion. He wanted out and was disoriented, emotional, unstable and needed supervision. I was on my way to Hong Kong anyway and flew with him that far. We were then met by another IBMer, who escorted him home to the States. A few others were probably frightened during most of their assignment but were too macho to say anything that might shorten their two-year opportunity to save some hard earned money and see the world. Most others really enjoyed and thrived on the work, the foreign experience and yes, the danger. These latter types were the kind we were looking for and were the men that really contributed to the mission, to each other, and to the stories in this book. These were the IBMers who went home healthy, stronger in spirit and more self-assured because of their experiences in Southeast Asia.

During those years, and probably ever since, we were both the most endangered group of IBMers in corporate history and the most privileged. We were professional mercenaries and while in Vietnam enjoyed the best of what the military and the local Vietnamese economy could offer. In the line of duty, we traveled free on military aircraft - C130s, C124s, helicopters, and an occasional jet or a prop driven reconnaissance aircraft. We met and socialized with many fine enlisted men and military officers. One Air Force Colonel at TSN became my regular chess protagonist whenever he could leave the base. We could either shop for our food in the local Vietnamese outdoor markets, ask our housemaids to do the same, or use our contractor privileges at the military PXs and commissaries. We could either dine at home, or in the many fine French, Chinese or Vietnamese restaurants in and around Saigon or Cholon or eat with the military when we wanted a good old American style steak, hamburger or home-style meal. I remember one small but popular military mess near Tan Son Nhut that served huge juicy cheeseburgers and chocolate malts that reminded me of home.

In Saigon, we lived in fairly comfortable homes, called villas, to the envy of the more imbedded IBMers living in cramped portakamps or military barracks upcountry. We had an IBM housing allowance with which to pay rent and furnish these homes in a semi-comfortable and fashionable manner. Bamboo and rattan furniture was popular and most of the houses were furnished in cheap, sparse Asian eclectic and whatever else we could scrounge. Whenever an IBMer rotated home, his furniture was quickly picked over or re-assigned to a new arrival. However, this semi-crude furniture was supplemented by the very latest and best stereophonic equipment that Uncle Sam's PX musical departments could provide. As an example, John, one of our sales reps, took a weekend trip to Hong Kong to do some personal shopping, and he made the mistake before he went of offering to buy stereo equipment for the rest of us in Saigon. He really did some big time shopping at the 'Navy Store' PX. A few weeks later 62 medium sized crates arrived via APO mail from Hong Kong containing the latest Sony tape decks, Pioneer tuners, Sansui speakers and Garrard record changers. There were probably a few good super-8 movie cameras and 35 mm cameras in that shipment also. John had spent almost two full days at the PX buying, addressing and mailing and did a whale of a job.

Money for such things wasn't a problem because we were being paid from 160% to 175% of our Stateside salary while in country, much of which we could afford to send home directly into savings. We also qualified for USA tax exempt status if we remained outside of the U.S.A. for 510 days out of 18 month periods. Any actual tax obligations could be deferred legally until our return home because we were living in a war zone. IBM also provided a 7-day all expenses paid R&R for every six months on assignment plus one trip home during the assignment. Some men were allowed to defer or to save and accrue their R&R time until the end of their assignment if their particular expertise could not be spared, but, in general, we were all encouraged to take a good vacation every six months to relieve stress and maintain high morale. After all, it only took one day to travel to a beach in Hawaii or Australia or a bridge in Paris or Amsterdam and another day back into the war zone! We took advantage of the opportunities and may have been the best traveled, best vacationed group in the whole world!

While in Vietnam, if our work duties were completed and customer responsibilities well covered, we were free to do and go anywhere we wanted within reason - with the following provisos: always inform someone and/or call in to the base radio station as to where you were or were going (we all carried Motorola handy-talkies). The rules specified that we play it safe with respect to known danger areas, obey the strictly enforced curfew hours and always return to the work location on time. We carried the "non-combatant" card, mentioned earlier, in our wallets and were therefore, by definition, peace loving and innocent civilians. The theory was, that should anyone of us be captured by the enemy, we would show the card and automatically be released. Yeah, right! What a joke!

Many of us also carried a wide assortment of hidden personal (unauthorized) weapons. We were given GS equivalent level government ratings by our military sponsors, which provided certain privileges of rank if and when mixing with the military. We were asked by IBM to buy our own cars. In addition there were several IBM owned vehicles for visitors or company business; these were white Ford station wagons in Saigon and a number of Toyota 4-wheel drive jeeps upcountry in hardship places like Qui Nhon, Da Nang and Cam Rahn Bay. Vietnam mud in the rainy season required the 4-wheel option to enable CEs and SEs to meet their service obligations.

This freedom of movement, a good communications system and good transportation let us drive to the restaurants, date the French and Vietnamese women, belong to a few social clubs, shop for food and recreation, drive through the war torn countryside and to the beaches as well as the required back and forth to the IBM office compound and our customer data processing locations. A few IBMers belonged to the elite Circle Sportif Club for swimming, tennis and luncheons (Arthur Ashe played a demonstration match there in late 1968 after winning the U.S. Open). Others used the Club Nautique on the Saigon River for water skiing and socializing at the club's remote private island. We could also play golf, tennis and use the huge swimming pool at MACV, managed for and by the military. A few of us became active with competitive volleyball and were members on a team at MACV. We played weekly matches during lunch hour against other Marine, Air Force and Vietnamese Ranger teams. I was in the best physical condition of my life, and as I said, we worked hard and played hard. There was no lack for things to do in or around Saigon!

Saigon, and the other Vietnamese locations where we worked and lived, was dangerous. There was always a huge feeling of relief whenever one climbed aboard an Air Vietnam or Thai Airways flight for a business or vacation trip out of Vietnam. In country, we learned to stay alert - stay away from crowds, watch for anyone suspicious who might be a VC planting plastique in a car or building, keep the car doors locked and house gates closed and locked, not to do stupid things which might draw undue attention in public, stay out of certain city areas and certain nightclubs, obey the curfew laws, keep our weapons hidden but available. I actually carried a huge razor sharp Bowie knife under the seat of my VW and had even learned to "stick it" in a practice tree from ten or fifteen paces. I hoped I would never have to use it to defend myself. We learned to play it smart. We were living in the equivalent of the old American Wild West - Dodge City in its heyday - and the only thing missing were quick-draw gunfights at *High Noon* on the main street of town. Almost everyone else was carrying a weapon too!

Saigon's reputation was so bad that more than just a few military men, who were assigned to the Tan Son Nhut Air Base area, never left the base during their twelve-month assignment. They never even drove the three or four miles into downtown Saigon. As an example, we were eating a fine dinner at BOQ-1 and an Air Force Major came over and sat with us. He wanted to know about civilian life on the economy and although he had been in country for eleven months he had never been off base, thinking it too dangerous. There was safety behind the guarded gates, gun emplacements and the concertina wire at the bases. We boastfully said that Saigon probably wasn't as dangerous as Tan Son Nhut since all the VC rockets were aimed at TSN and MACV, but added that the difference in town was the fear of the unknown. In actual fact, VC rocket accuracy was notoriously poor, and many of those aimed at the bases arbitrarily strayed into Saigon residential areas. We quickly learned the term 'Incoming' and occasionally, one of us would experience the following scenario: boom! Four blocks away. Boom! Three blocks away. BOom! Two blocks away. BOOOM! One block away. BOOm! One block away on the other side. BOom! Two blocks away and finally, Boom, boom, boom as they passed out of ear shot. We didn't dwell on this aspect with the Major and I hope he went into town before he left for home. The downtown Saigon adventure was worth the effort.

*Saigon Du Notte Light Show*

We were successful in having our MACV sponsor issue fifty M-2 rifles to our IBM office along with a couple of clips of ammo for each gun, and we were invited to use the local gunnery range for firing practice. I had never shot a gun in my life, didn't know how to and didn't want to unless needed, but I kept my M-2 and ammo in my villa near where I slept and definitely handy. We re-issued all the M-2s to almost every IBMer, to be considered as a defensive weapon and used only if under attack. Fortunately, the need did not arise, but we all certainly felt psychologically safer. Some of our M-2s were inappropriately used each New Years and each 4th of July for shooting at stars, just to make sure the guns were in fine working order. At such times, the spent ammo would fall back to earth and sound like heavy hailstones as it clattered off all the surrounding tin roofed houses.

Periodically, we had to account to MACV on the status of these weapons and we kept them for a couple of years before they were re-claimed and given to the Vietnamese Army during a later period of 'Vietnamization'. IBMers also had other weapons - things like .38 and .45 revolvers, AK-47s, various other carbines, grease guns and even hand grenades. It was known that one IBMer had an M-16 with a generous

111

supply of banana clips and the CEs in Da Nang had several parts lockers in their villa filled with a veritable arsenal of weapons with hundreds if not thousands of rounds of ammunition. This was probably justified in Da Nang. Some of the IBMers were probably better armed than the military (buying a gun was fairly easy), but our management team told the guys that we did not want to see or know about all this extra hardware. One time I was helping clean up an IBMer's vacated room after he had returned to the States. When we moved his bed we discovered a whole box full of hand grenades. I don't know what happened to the grenades because when I turned my back to help out somewhere else, they suddenly disappeared. The military provided several locations where one could dispose of illegal weapons and there were no questions asked of those doing so.

The IBMers who volunteered to work up-country (e.g. Da Nang, Nha Trang, Qui Nhon, Cam Ranh Bay, etc.) had to be a special breed and may have been, by design or by self-preservation, the wildest of our group (See Chapter 11). They sometimes got into trouble and the following story about a guy, whom I will call Steve, illustrates the point. Steve drove a big Yamaha motorcycle that had a characteristic deep-throated rumble. This gave it (and him) a unique trademark wherever he went when compared to the small puttering, sputtering motorbikes driven by the locals. One evening he and his girl friend were driving down the main street of an up-country city when a Vietnamese woman pushing a soup wagon turned immediately in front of Steve's motorcycle and across his lane of traffic. It was probably done on purpose since that was a good way to extract money from the rich Americans. Steve had no opportunity to stop or to turn and avoid her. The impact of the collision caused her wagon to tumble on its side spilling all her soup, which, of course, represented her entire day's income. The motorcycle ended up on its side, but fortunately no one was physically harmed, at least not then. The woman accused Steve of causing the accident and demanded that he pay for the soup as well as for the banged up wagon. Steve tried to explain that she was at fault for having failed to yield right-of-way. A large crowd gathered and became hostile toward Steve whose Vietnamese girl friend had apparently abandoned him. Things began to get out of control and Steve attempted to leave without paying, but each time he bent down to pick up his motorcycle, the crowd closed in on him. It was a sticky situation, but just then the girl friend returned with friendly, armed guards who worked at Steve's villa. Their presence changed the balance of power and enabled Steve's group to make a hasty but uncomfortable escape. Steve felt that he had done no wrong and that the incident would soon be forgotten; not so! The following day his maid returned from the market with news that Steve was now a marked man and would die for not paying the woman. Steve was too comfortable in his setting and discounted the rumors. About a week later while Steve was in Saigon another contracting company's American employee borrowed the throaty motorcycle and was driving through the city after curfew. He was shot and killed by a 'National Guard' type Vietnamese who recognized the sound of Steve's motorcycle. Curfews up-country were sometimes ignored, so despite the theoretical justification for shooting a curfew violator, the act was clearly an act of retribution and murder. The Vietnamese was not prosecuted. When Steve was seen the next day by a few local citizens, who knew of the shooting, they believed that they were seeing a ghost and reacted accordingly. He was still a marked man. Steve needed no further warning and within twenty-four hours was packed and gone. He spent the remainder of his four-year tour in Saigon and married the woman who had retrieved his compound guards.

The R&R (rest and recreation) policy was one of the best benefits we could possibly have and they were anxiously planned by each man and judiciously used. R&Rs to various exotic places in the world almost became a "can you top this" competition. Information about interesting places, good hotels, modes of transportation, availability of women, beautiful beaches, good bars and restaurants was enthusiastically exchanged before and after each man's trip. Mere side trips to nearby Thailand (even though it was a vacationer's paradise), Singapore or Hong Kong were far too commonplace and our bachelors began traveling to places like Katmandu, Rangoon, Nairobi, Bali, Sydney, Copenhagen, Paris, Rome and stops along the way. IBM picked up the airfare for all but the most lengthy trips, paid for the hotels and meals up to a per diem limit and we paid for the fun and the souvenirs we sent home. My homes, ever since, have been well furnished with items like Hong Kong rosewood and Taiwan teak furniture, Korean bronze lamps, Japanese silk screens and Thai silk and dinnerware. In addition to these countries, I was also able to visit New

Zealand, Australia, Tahiti, Fiji, Malaysia, Mexico, Jamaica, Greece, Italy, France, Spain, and Denmark as well as a couple trips home to Honolulu. I once went from Saigon to Miami on a business trip via Singapore, Sydney, Auckland, Papeete, Acapulco, Montego Bay and finally after eight days arrived at my IBM meeting - on time! I was probably typical of our well traveled group. The only R&R rules were that we had to be back in Vietnam within ten days of departure and keep track of our expenses. What wonderful stories came out of these R&R trips!

The IBM Corporation tried to downplay its involvement in the Vietnam War, and because of this our Marketing Reps and System Engineers did not qualify for the coveted 100% Club or SE Symposium, back in the states. I guess the Corporation did not want it known that we were on sales 'quota' and that we were actually selling IBM products in the war zone - even though we were. They said it was a paper quota only. I therefore, missed three 100% Clubs for those three years in which I exceeded the paper quota (this limited my 100% Club attainment to 16 Clubs and 2 SE Symposiums during my 25 years with IBM, prior to my retirement in 1987. Looking back, this seems a very small thing, but at that time the number of Clubs achieved was a huge measure of IBM success) and I always felt that these 3 misses should have and could have been re-instated after Vietnam.

However, in lieu of these public recognition events, IBM did do something that was perhaps even better than the traditional recognition events. They gave us the "Hong Kong Education Conference", which became an annual three-day bash at the Hong Kong Hilton Hotel. The Federal IBM team from Branch Office 560 based at Camp Zama, Japan also attended. High-level management was brought in from DP Headquarters in New York or Washington, D.C. and the IBM Regional Office in San Mateo, California. They talked with us about new IBM products and successes, and they tried to better understand our Vietnam responsibilities and environment (It was somewhat of a boondoggle for them too). They also needed to discuss, within their own management ranks, whether IBM was doing the right thing by supporting the war effort on such a large scale, but by that time there was no way that top management could have unilaterally slowed our involvement, the military was too dependent on us. Outside speakers were scheduled for the

Conference and one year the Charge d' Affairs Officer or Vice-Consul at the Hong Kong U.S. Consulate gave us a complete report on the Golden Triangle poppy fields and how opium moved to markets all over the world. He had names, maps, routes, volumes and dollar value statistics. It was interesting but left an impression with me that if all that was known then the U.S.A. wasn't really trying to stop that source of drug trafficking.

Recognition awards were handed out to well deserving SEs and Marketing Representatives, skits were presented by our members, personnel performance evaluation interviews were done by managers and a good time was had by all in peaceful and beautiful surroundings. I especially enjoyed the Conference one year because I was nurturing a Chinese girlfriend who lived in Hong Kong. I volunteered to go to Hong Kong a few days early to make arrangements with the Hilton for food, rooms, banquet hall, and entertainment. My new friend 'Ling' was an actual professional singer on the Kowloon side and she and I, after some private extra practice (no sex involved – really!), ended up singing a duet one evening at the Conference's main banquet. The Hong Kong Conference was small and personal, in our special honor only, and a welcomed respite from the war and very much appreciated by us 'wild ducks'. The Conference also provided an opportunity to become acquainted with what Hong Kong had to offer, including all the best restaurants, nightspots, shopping, and a few bargirls.

While writing this book, I learned that one of the Hong Kong Conference's visiting IBM Headquarters executives somewhat insulted one of our Saigon based administrative employees and asked him to do one extra thing too many. The executive had checked a number of library books out of a Washington, D.C. public library to read on his trip and after the Conference asked that our man package and air ship the books back to his home (I guess, so he would have space for all his other Hong Kong purchases?). Our 'wild duck' thought that this was a bit much so he wrapped them up, properly addressed the package and promptly boat shipped the overdue books on a container ship bound for the West Coast. We don't know when they arrived in D.C. or how large the overdue fine was, but justice was served.

IBM made a major investment in supporting the U.S. Government's effort in Vietnam. Approximately 250 professionals were sent to Southeast

Asia and we were supported by a dedicated Federal team in Honolulu; by Western Region management in California; by GEM Headquarters personnel and Branch Offices in Bethesda, Maryland who marketed to and serviced the Pentagon and Military Headquarters in and around Washington D.C.; by IBM's Federal Systems Division in Gaithersburg, Maryland; and indirectly by various IBM headquarters staffs in New York. This was a corporate commitment, which has been all but forgotten today except by those of us who were there. Without this book, that commitment will be completely forgotten.

The IBM Corporation also made some money during the war, and at one time I figured that just our Saigon based Branch Office alone could account for roughly $70,000,000 to $80,000,000 in purchase, rental and maintenance service revenue during my three year assignment just in Vietnam (I don't know how to come any closer to these dollar figures and they are based solely on my memory). Our mission may not have been particularly profitable because of all the added expenses, but I strongly doubt that IBM lost any money in Vietnam; although, I did hear that IBM was once asked by our Government to return a certain portion of those revenues. IBM paid for housing, transportation, office and upcountry vehicles, meals, inflated salaries, vacations and R&Rs, the single side band radio equipment, and many long distance management trips in addition to the normal cost of the equipment, spare parts and overhead business expenses. I can guess that IBM was somewhat exposed to political criticism from stockholders and that portion of the general public who embraced isolationist and anti-war philosophies which began to tear our nation apart as the war progressed.

While in Vietnam, I was pretty much unaware of the anti-war feelings becoming progressively stronger in the States, especially because I had come from Hawaii, which was and still is so closely tied to the military. I am glad that I didn't understand what was happening. However, I did have a subliminal sense that there was a decreasing sense of urgency by our east coast IBM plant locations. It was a slight feeling, but quite real. Early on, in the mid to late '60's there was an enthusiastic sense of purpose in the processing of new orders and shipments of machines by those involved in meeting our Vietnam requirements. All crates were clearly marked with bold red letters, which said "IN SUPPORT OF SEA", and the schedules and shipments took priority preference over everything else that IBM produced in the States. As time went by, things became less urgent from the plant scheduling point of view, more follow-up was needed to insure that we received the correct order and ever so slight delays began to occur. Again, I cannot site any specifics about this; it was simply a gut feel, but symptomatic of the attitudes about the war by those not involved or by those protesting our presence in Vietnam.

As volunteers, each one of us made a significant individual commitment. Yes, we wanted the adventure, excitement and pay increase; but, we were putting our lives on the line and doing something out of the ordinary. We were also putting our careers on the line (without necessarily knowing it at the time). Prior to accepting the Vietnam assignment, there was an implied promise that if we did go to SEA for the two-year, or more, assignment then our careers, upon return to stateside work, would be "taken care of and rewarded" with good follow-on opportunity within the company. It may be that the very personality traits which caused us to volunteer in the first place were in fact strengthened while in Vietnam and that the resultant independent and the "we did something great, the world owes us" attitude caused IBM management to disregard their implied promise of help and to avoid sponsoring any of our careers. Whatever; I do believe that those of us who returned to the U.S.A. went into career declines or at least holding patterns during the following years with IBM and unfortunately were employed in more normalized and comparatively boring or lesser jobs.

Many others sought and accepted follow-on IBM foreign assignments to countries like Australia, Korea, Germany, Okinawa, Thailand, Brazil and even Saudi Arabia. I believe that along with our pride, we carried a stigma of having been associated with the Vietnam War or for having been a foreign assignment mercenary. The unwritten sponsorship and opportunity did not materialize and our exploits and the history contained in this book were swept under the corporate rug, just like so many other creative accomplishments that took place in Vietnam. This is not sour grapes (I don't think?) but rather an objective post-Vietnam evaluation of many careers. On the positive side, the independence nurtured by the Vietnam experience eventually enabled many of the men to excel in other countries or in non-IBM endeavors and they are probably better off today than if they had remained "true Blue".

Life in Vietnam brought us into contact with various other aspects of living in the tropics. The country contained sixty known species of snakes, including poisonous cobras, kraits and vipers. There were a wide variety of undesirable insects such as mosquitos, lice, fleas, ticks, mites, spiders, scorpions, ants, termites, bedbugs and large flying cockroaches. Some of these critters were new to our assignees and required some attitude adjustment. There was also the added danger of dysentery from either bad water or unclean food eaten at any number of restaurants. The only afternoon of work that I missed while in Vietnam was due to a sandwich mistakenly eaten at a handy but unsanitary restaurant near our office. One of our Da Nang based CEs did contract dysentery and almost bled to death and another IBMer contracted hepatitis. Finally, for those men who were not careful, there was always the possibility of contracting several types of venereal diseases from the readily available prostitutes – be they biker girls, massage parlor hostesses or bar tea girls. All these things helped justify, in our minds, the extra pay we received while in Southeast Asia.

The very best thing that did happen was that no IBMer was permanently injured or killed in Vietnam. Other contractors did lose personnel. I believe it was Control Data Corporation who lost a manager who was shot and killed in his Saigon home. Vinnell Corporation lost four American employees when a popular Saigon River restaurant was blown up. One IBM/FSD employee was involved in a serious motorcycle accident and spent weeks recuperating at the Army's 3rd Field Hospital near TSN. (I remember visiting him several times and seeing, smelling and hearing the many seriously wounded as I walked down the hospital corridors). Another IBM CE received five bayonet wounds during a robbery attack at NKP, Thailand, and another was the man we sent home shell-shocked. Our FE Manager had the tires blown off his Mazda by a pipe bomb, and there were numerous other scrapes and bruises from living in such a chaotic environment. There was always constant tension and less frequent but genuine periods of fear on the part of many of the young IBMers who were placed in dangerous circumstances. But, thank goodness, none of us were killed!

Bruce Tomson and I shared the DPD management and marketing duties during my first year in Vietnam in 1969 and I learned a great deal from Bruce and from my own hard work. The plan was for me to assume full management responsibilities of Location Manager at the end of Bruce's assignment, so in January, 1970, after 2 and 1/2 years, Bruce returned to California and I took my turn at being responsible for the operation and safety of our IBM support mission. Five years later, Bruce Tomson again became a key player in IBM's Vietnam history as told in Chapter 17, *The Last Phone Call*.

Sometime in 1970, two of our administrative employees traveled to Da Nang to help locate some machines, to update our IBM furniture & fixtures inventory and to re-submit some overdue machine invoices. That night an ammunitions barge blew up in the nearby harbor and one of our two travelers woke up on the floor. Not knowing what had really happened, he decided to crawl along the floor in the darkness, .38 revolver already in hand, and he slowly pushed open a door leading to the villa's next room. He crawled through and bumped into his partner who was crawling toward his room dragging an M-2. They frightened each other and then started laughing.

To say that we were a collection of independent personalities would be a gross understatement. Independence, courage and self-sufficiency were requirements of the job. Vietnam was no place for the meek. It took courage to drive the nighttime streets of Saigon or Da Nang in order to respond to a late night machine outage and repair call. It took courage to drive leisurely through the war zone in a civilian car and photograph gun-ships and helicopters as they strafed enemy positions. It was stupid too! It took initiative to rewire a computer core plane with a flashlight and tweezers in lieu of a replacement part. It took independence to be the only IBM advisor within 5000 miles on a particular technical subject and then stand behind and prove the wisdom of the advice given. And, it took self-assurance to tell IBM top management or the Vietnamese police or a MACV military officer "NO"! Certain persons, offices or organizations are not accustomed to hearing "NO", but it was sometimes wise or necessary to do so.

Once during 1971, I was nominated as the IBM Marketing Manager for the month of January of the entire GEM Region, a true honor in normal times. I was invited to fly to White Plains, New York and accept the coveted honor. I told them "No, I couldn't make it. I had more important things to do." Another time a Senior Master Sergeant at MACV HQ called me and TOLD me to return the fifty M-2 carbines that had been loaned to us the previous year, because MACV wanted to give the rifles to the Vietnamese Army as part of the new Vietnamization policy. "Would I please have them cleaned up and returned ASAP"! I said, "NO!" We managed to prolong that return for another six months. We wanted those M-2s; they gave us warm fuzzy safe feelings. I don't think anyone had said "NO" to that sergeant for many years. It is just not done. On several occasions, we were asked by stateside IBM management to turn in any side arms that we just might be carrying around. They did not want any 'incidents'. We said "NO" and continued to carry them.

IBM management often asked whether any of us were seriously involved with local females or whether any IBMer actually had a 'live-in' girl friend. Again, they were concerned about any unforeseen incidents with a possible VC sympathizer, did not want to be subsidizing our housing for unauthorized female guests, and did not want any compromise of our security clearances because of a girl friend. Also, they probably did not want to have to relocate any future married personnel from strictly a bachelor-only assignment. It was a sensitive issue and sort of no ones business what we did off hours, so we always said "NO", there was nothing serious going on and there were no live-in girl friends. In actuality we almost all had either long term or temporary live-ins, or at least wished we did. Frankly, we were all healthy horny men in our twenties and thirties. We thought the Vietnamese women were the most beautiful women we had ever seen and many opportunities did exist for brief liaisons and/or genuine love.

Once, when the new Honolulu Branch Manager came to Saigon on his first recon trip, he arrived after dark and was taken to John and Cary's villa for a home cooked dinner. Several IBMers were there along with a couple of their live-in girlfriends. Not knowing how the new manager would react to the girlfriend policy, the IBMers introduced the ladies as "maids". The manager played along with the sham, but when he and I departed for the evening, he told me that he personally didn't have any objection to girlfriends, but that he wanted me to know that he was not naive enough to swallow the story about the "maids".

Speaking of maids, the real ones, there are quite a few funny stories about these little Vietnamese ladies whom we employed to clean our villas, wash our clothes, shop and generally do things around the house that bachelors normally don't do. They were paid $40.00 or $50.00 a month, plus a room, and were invaluable. The maids were known to do such things as wash wool suit coats and ties and one maid, in Da Nang, was cleaning a guest bedroom and came across the guest's removable partial-upper bridge which he had carefully placed on a night stand. Not knowing what it was, but being very efficient, she threw the bridge into the trash. The owner spent several hours without his teeth until he solved the mystery.

Saigon's main office maid was a clever older wench – maybe in her 50s - whom we called Ba Bai. She was enterprising, kind, understanding and somewhat of a mother or sister figure for most of the guys.

*We all remember Ba Bai*

She watched us like a mother hen. She spoke little English but somehow could anticipate most of what had to be done around the office.

121

She had one uncorrectable failing that went on for several years. The office had a small kitchen in which Ba Bai cooked her lunch and every day around noon we would be repulsed by the stench of her frying her lunch in nouc mam (stinking fish sauce). We pleaded with her to change her diet or cook somewhere else, but we eventually had to solve the problem by simply going out to lunch whenever the smell became intolerable. I think every IBMer who ever worked in Saigon probably said goodbye to that special maid with a tear in his eye and fondness in his heart. "Chao Ba Bai." I can still see her going about her self-assigned duties. Some 'unimportant' people are remembered for eternity.

We did play hard, but we also worked hard and we tried to insure that IBM's investment and trust were justified. Saturday was usually a full workday for everyone and at least several IBMers were in the office and others at customer accounts for a portion of Sunday. (The Customer Engineers were always on call, 24 hours every day). I recall one six-month period when I did not take a single day off, at the end of which I really had a bad case of burn out. A good R&R trip fixed me up fine! As I look back on my 25 year IBM career, I can remember three specific personal burn out periods - the Vietnam assignment was the first, another was in Saudi Arabia in the late 1970s where our office was working at 40% below authorized head count, and the last was when I was nearing retirement in 1987, and trying to make an impossible sales quota while also trying to evaluate retirement options and make the right decision about leaving a company that I truly loved.

During the Vietnam years, we made every effort to maintain IBM's

In Vietnam, we were at the end of a very long logistical and professional string that gave us wonderful autonomy. Several of us in first or second line management made daily decisions that affected customer service and the care of our personnel. The authority to make locally important decisions - independent of slow upper IBM management committee decisions - was refreshing and fulfilling. Occasionally a personnel or IBM policy issue would arise for which we had no experience, and we would consult with the American Country manager at either nearby World Trade Vietnam or World Trade Thailand. These older experienced managers were not involved with our military operation, but they were very helpful when we needed the counseling of a friend and we appreciated their extensive experience and sound advice. We returned their help when asked in the form of emergency spare parts, maintenance advice and technical education for their Vietnamese or Thai personnel.

*Dan, John, Bob, Bill, and Stu in uniform*

During the Vietnam years, we made every effort to maintain IBM's three major standards of: respect for the individual, excellence in customer service and to provide the best data processing products and support services possible. I believe we succeeded and through it all - monsoons, under threat of attack, during machine upgrades, while in transit to an account upcountry via C-130 or helicopter, in front of the military customer, and in our own office environment - we always wore our **white shirts and ties!**

# Chapter 7
## Recreation

WHEN YOU ARE WORKING 10, 12 or sometimes 14 hours a day, six days a week, then any leisure time or recreation becomes of paramount importance. There were a wide variety of activities in Saigon if one was willing to take a little risk while searching for fun. The risk to one's personal well being varied from simply driving the crazy, traffic-choked, accident-filled streets, to being in the wrong place at the wrong time, to water skiing on the toxic Saigon River and being shot at, or to venturing into the countryside to watch the war unfold in real time. The fun included parties, ample abundance and consumption of booze acquired at the base post exchanges (PXs), a wide variety of sports, discovering new restaurants, pursuing female relationships, photography trips around town, sitting in bars where one could shoot the breeze with friends, play pool, throw darts, play cards, drink the local 33 beer and talk to the bar girls, and all the other things that young bachelors do after work since there is no family waiting at home. There was, of course, the more personal time in our villas used for writing letters home, reading, studying IBM technical manuals, watching the local Vietnamese or U.S. produced television programs, music (I enjoyed playing the guitar in the evenings), evening bull sessions with the guys before curfew, planning R&R trips and sometimes entertaining certain young ladies of commercial virtue.

As I have stated earlier, the streets of all the Vietnamese cities were dangerous, not only because of the amazing volume of erratic traffic but also because the Viet Cong (VC) and VC sympathizers were busy with acts of terrorism and because of the street hoodlums (commonly referred to as 'cowboys') who were always on the prowl, robbing and stealing whatever they could lay their hands on. America had brought materialism to this Asian society and the cowboys could trade and sell our stolen imported goods on the black market at inflated prices. The cowboys were active even during daylight hours ripping fancy watches from pedestrian arms as they rode by on the backs of Hondas, breaking and entering homes to steal TVs, stereos or money, stealing cars if not locked properly, and generally doing anything illegal for their own gain, sometimes at gun point in the confines of someone's private home. There were too many of them for the local police to control.

The VC threat came via some of the same types of activities and perhaps involved some of the same people, but in addition, there were also the premeditated murders and seemingly random plastique explosions in restaurants, bars, markets and other public locations which contributed to the pervasive feeling of personal insecurity and general political disruption. On any given afternoon, one could be sitting in a small neighborhood bar sipping on a Ba Moui Ba beer, talking with friends or a bar girl, and have the front door or a portion of a side wall blown in by plastique. Mis-aimed rocket attacks could have a similar result. This random destruction always seemed to increase under the cover of darkness. Our official IBM management advice was for the men to remain home in the evenings, but for heaven's sake, if someone had to go out then drive the main streets, drive slowly within the speed limits, keep a low and pacified profile in public places and be home well before curfew. It was dangerous, but somehow, when not working, we had fun in spite of these ever-present threats. Some of the fun was natural and some was invented.

Along with the chaos in Saigon, there was still a well defined social elite which hosted afternoon garden parties, lunches at the exclusive Circle Sportif Club (a holdover from French colonial days) and a few evening parties and dances in private homes. Invitations were either formal or by word of mouth, but you made certain you were really invited or went with a friend who was. The hosts and hostesses were a few of the remaining wealthy Vietnamese, French-Vietnamese or French families who were probably trying to continue with their normal social and business functions in spite of the war's disruption. IBMers would occasionally attend these functions. We were invited because we posed no threat to anyone and we were relatively wealthy and well educated. We attended out of curiosity and with hopes of meeting the few available young French or American women (round eyes). There would be dancing to a live band, drinks and champagne provided indirectly through the PX, and most of the talk would, of course, be about the current status of the surrounding war. One or two of our IBMers did meet their future wives at these events and have lived happily ever after.

The live-in girl friends were another story and for the most part were not a problem. They were exceptionally beautiful women, at least in the eyes of the lonely IBM bachelors far from home. The women of Vietnam had a softness, but also a toughness and a resilience that was difficult for Westerners to understand, and most had already had a tough life by the time the North Vietnamese sponsored war in South Vietnam began. Many had lost their parents and had been raised and cared for by extended families. These women had a special attraction for most of our young men. Language was only a minor problem and generally treated as something to laugh about. Language has never been a problem when it comes to taking care of a household, cooking a meal, dining, watching TV on a couch, listening to music together, going for a drive or to the beach, holding hands, sleeping together or making love. These things can be done in any language and the Vietnamese women did them very well.

Some men who did not crave variety and the risks of venereal disease that went with it, wanted more serious companionship, steady loving or they simply did not care for the nightly carousing and randomly visited tea-bars and available bar girls found there. There was a poster on the MACV dispensary wall which read: "Venereal Disease - if you broke your arm five times, you wouldn't expect it to work as well as normal, would you?" There had to be a better way. Perhaps the words of an IBMer, whom we will call Craig and who tried to live a normal home life, will help to explain the circumstances of his live-in girl friend: "She wasn't poor, she simply never had any money. At the age of ten her parents were killed and her aunt took her from Da Nang to Saigon and from then on she was on her own. At the age of fifteen, she became the number three wife of a Vietnamese Army Captain. When I met her I was twenty-four and she was nineteen. She had been working in bars for about two years. My roommate's girl friend introduced me to her as her sister. We had one date watching TV and trying to communicate in Pidgin English. I really liked her but had no plans of forming a permanent arrangement. We spent the next night together and she asked me if she could move in with me. I told her "No thanks." The next day, when I returned home from work, all of her clothes were in my closet. We spent the next three years together."

Craig's story goes on: "When I first met her, she was skinny and broke, but she gained weight and saved some money while we were together, and we had a hell of a lot of fun. She knew very little about the world outside of Vietnam, but she was game. We used to sit on the floor for hours discussing life and death, politics and philosophy, with neither one of us fully understanding the other. Our quiet times were good, and when she didn't feel threatened, she could be very sweet and gentle, but I would rather face a frightened tiger than that lady when her back was to the wall. Yes, she was kind, loving and gentle, but had a heart of steel. If you can understand that, you can begin to understand Vietnamese women. Survival was the name of the game, but if a certain amount of love could be part of it, so much the better. One of my hang-ups while she was with me was that she tended to wear 'see-thru' blouses. Maybe that was the reason that I was so popular with the rest of the guys - hardly an evening went by that someone didn't come by to say hello. She didn't dress the way she did to be provocative with my friends; it was just more comfortable in the hot humid climate. It was also very sexy and the problem was that it was sexy not only to me but also to my friends. But jealousy works two ways, and were the Vietnamese women ever jealous! All of us who had steady girl friends had this problem, and in the end it was this jealousy that ended our relationship." And, in this case, caused Craig to reluctantly leave Vietnam without his girl.

Eventually we all had to return home, and when Craig finally packed and left, what he had established as a loving home relationship, another IBMer, Jim, witnessed as a tender scene from his adjoining upstairs window and which was told to me as follows: "Her American gone, she stood outside the villa gate, a few belongings in her arms and gazed up at the window that had served her bedroom for three special years. She stood a long time, tears streaming down her beautiful high cheekbones." Finally Jim thought he heard her say good-bye to the house - "goobuy how" - before walking slowly down the dusty busy street to an uncertain future.

Craig also had this to say about live-ins: "Let me try and explain about the women that we knew in Vietnam at that time. The girls were plentiful, accessible and lots of fun; but the bar scene soon became tiresome and more trouble than it was worth. A fulltime girl friend seemed to be the best way to obtain the companionship we wanted without the night after night game playing. I know it sounds callous to say that many of us were willing to pay these women money to spend all of their time with us, but it wasn't just a one sided proposition. We needed a relationship and they needed food, shelter and security (and, who knows, maybe they needed a little love also). Those Americans who left children behind to face an uncertain life of hell because of the stigma of their mixed parentage have much guilt to face up to (and many of the fathers did return for their offspring and many were adopted); but if proper precautions were taken, then it was a matter of mutual advantage. I can't speak for all of us, but in my own way I really loved my Vietnamese live-in."

By using the words *proper precautions* above, Craig made certain that his live-in girl friend used birth control pills. Thank goodness they were available! Whenever one of us was about to go on R&R or weekend holiday to Hong Kong, there were always several requests from the guys with permanent girl friends to bring back several months worth of birth control pills for each couple. I was always embarrassed to buy the pills - even in Hong Kong - but I took my turn on several occasions - and was glad that I had done so. We also brought back many colorful bolts of silk from Hong Kong or brocade from Bangkok for which the girls were most appreciative and from which they made the beautiful *ao dias* flowing glowing dresses. By keeping them happy, they kept us happy.

I myself could not allow myself the luxury of a live-in. My goodness, I was an IBM manager and had to set a good example of propriety and morals as well as establish IBM policy for the others, even though my example seemed to be uniformly ignored. There were many times that I wished my sacrifice were not so. I too had the need for companionship and the same physical desires of the others, but sometimes had to go out on the economy for my evening recreation or pursue more clandestine and impromptu female relationships. In times of serious need or boredom, my male house-mate and I could simply go stand near our front driveway gate in the early evening and in a matter of five or ten minutes there would be several Hondas, with male driver negotiating and a beautiful Vietnamese lady waiting to be selected. They would bid for our evening's physical pleasures. We did this a couple of times, but it was really playing sexual Russian roulette.

There was a better way than the quickie one-night stand (brief evening stands really; the girls usually had to be home before curfew). I developed two fairly long termed but intermittent part-time girl friends, and I kept these two special relationships as private as possible (and especially one from the other). However, one night I became pretty nervous when quite by surprise, one of the girls happened to be upstairs in my bedroom and the other *femme fetale* came to call downstairs. To my credit, neither one discovered or even suspected the other was there. Fortunately it was a large house. That event reminds me of a scene in a Woody Allen film I once saw. I managed to talk one of the girls out of the house and drove her to a nearby friend's place and then returned before the girl upstairs knew I was gone.

I would occasionally take one of the two girls to an IBM party or out to the yacht club annex for a Sunday afternoon picnic or boat ride. I made it quite clear to both that I was not a candidate for a permanent affair or marriage and that I planned to return to the U.S.A. unencumbered by a Vietnamese bride. This put a definite damper on the two girls' relationship with me, but we still had great fun. It would have been so very easy to have fallen deeply in love with either one. Both girls were strikingly beautiful, in their early 20s and I truly enjoyed their company.

One, whom I will call "Ling", had money of her own, drove a new Japanese-made car, was strong willed coupled with a dynamite personality and was sultry, sexy and enjoyed being so. She liked having fun. I believe, but never really knew the details, that Ling lived with and was sponsored by an older American Embassy attaché who kept her in style but gave her enough free reign to roam. She would drop by my villa unannounced, as above, and ask for a favor or show off a new dress or she would ask me to take her to a party or hint around that she was available the following Sunday for a picnic. She would dispense her sexual favors whenever the whim hit her, but it was often enough to keep me interested. She was independent and smart and reportedly made it to the U.S.A. prior to South Vietnam's 1975 defeat.

The other girl, whom I will call "Mai" was quite a bit different from

Ling and was perhaps more typical of a young, down-and-out Vietnamese trying to make it in the tough war-torn world. I met Mai in the hotel bar across the street from our Saigon office. I bought her a 'Saigon-tea' that first evening, but she wouldn't dance or go home with me. I was intrigued. She seemed withdrawn and shy and had a sad but hauntingly beautiful expression on her perfectly formed oriental face. She spoke only a few words of English. I wondered what she was doing working in the nightclub portion of that combination restaurant bar and brothel. Over time, I found out that Mai was not a coquette or tease or whore; she did not go home with other men. She was just a young woman caught up in the sadness of war trying to make a living by her instincts, wits and good looks. She wasn't completely innocent when I first met her, but she seemed innocent and remained my refreshingly sweet secret girl friend for the next year. Through her broken English, I found out that she had a day job at nearby Tan Son Nhut with the military that was somehow secretarial in nature. She lived fairly near my villa down a narrow alley off Cach Mang Street with her fairly strict relatives (I assumed that she was their only financial support). She never did show me exactly where she lived and she never mentioned a mother or father. She was Catholic and even though she and I would happily sin from time to time, she did know right from wrong and had high moral standards. She never did stay with me overnight and the few times that I took her to an IBM function, I was proud to show her off. We had a few mutual friends experiencing the same careful relationship, and we would share meals and good times at their homes.

I believe that Mai was true to me in her mind during our relationship, if not with her body (is that possible?), and I also knew that she wanted marriage and a means to escape Vietnam – like so many others. Again, I did not let myself fall in love with Mai - I don't think - but I still have photographs of a beautiful person and think about her from time to time, when I let myself. Like the story that Craig told above, when it came time to leave Vietnam in the fall of 1971, I left Mai standing on the steps of my villa, holding our miniature Dachshund "Peanuts" in one arm and tearfully waving good-bye with the other. Mai did escape Vietnam prior to the 1975 defeat and since then has been happily married to an U.S.

diplomat, seen foreign service in other countries and has raised three children who are fine U.S. citizens.

More than only a few IBMers married their Vietnamese or Thai sweethearts and most have remained happily married with beautiful and intelligent children ever since. These women of Southeast Asia knew how to please their men, and they knew how to control them. My opinion is that they have made excellent wives and mothers and that those marriages were matches made in Vietnamese heaven and were then, forever after, protected and nurtured in American freedom. Recent correspondence with several such families, now many years since their marriages, is proving to me that the children are the beneficiaries of both cultures and are smart, talented, loved and well cared for, have done well through their respective schools and have entered adulthood as hard working professional contributors to American society. Some of these families have visited Vietnam in recent years and certainly their ties to that far away land and that horrible war are very strong, because even my memories are strong, though I didn't bring anyone home with me. Those Vietnamese ladies were very special and enriched our overseas experiences.

One fine week it was announced that a group of six CEs were planning a weekend in Bangkok. It always worried me when too many of our maintenance personnel were away from our accounts at the same time, but this particular weekend was special. One of their fellow CEs, Bob Dillon, was to marry a beautiful Thai girl and the wedding promised to be quite the social event. Tom had completed his tour in Vietnam, fallen in love somewhere along the way and planned to remain in Southeast Asia as a business and family man. The six CEs had to attend their friend's celebration and they left Saigon on a Friday afternoon, promising to return first thing Monday morning. Bob had been popular and had participated in more than his share of pranks and adventures in Vietnam. The CEs had thought long and hard about what would be an appropriate wedding gift--something just a little different. A new TV set or dinnerware or a gift certificate wouldn't do. Perhaps these particular CEs did their best thinking while drinking, because a few weeks earlier while sharing ideas in a bar, they arrived at the perfect gift. It was going to cost around $500, but nothing was too good for ol' Bob. Contacts were made in Bangkok and a few local strings were pulled. The six CEs bought a young but somewhat large Thai elephant and made arrangements to have it presented the day of the wedding.

Bob and Dang Lek's (her nickname) reception was held at her family's Bangkok estate. The Thai family was wealthy and influential and had invited 400 or 500 friends to their large, classic, four story home, which was surrounded by beautifully manicured gardens and in the best part of town. During Thai weddings it is customary for the bride and groom to give thank you speeches, and the groom is advised to speak first in order to show his authority. Bob spoke to the guests in English from the house's front porch, gave his acknowledging thanks and said all the right things. The guests were listening from the gardens and enjoying a catered feast. Next, Dang Lek spoke and other speeches followed. Suddenly, there was a commotion at the far gate, and the guests began to murmur and step aside. A wide path was cleared through the gardens. In came the six CEs driving their baby elephant. The elephant had a red bow tied around its neck and it began bellowing loudly and trampling some of the groomed flowerbeds. It was hungry. The Thai speech maker began to tell the elephant to be quiet and the guests began to laugh. Bob and Dang Lek suddenly realized they were to be instantly blessed proud parents and the CEs realized they had selected the perfect gift.

Elephants are good luck charms, but this one caused one big interruption and also caused a 24-hour delay in the honeymoon trip to Hong Kong. The elephant was brought under control and temporarily placed in a dog kennel area behind the house. After the reception broke up, Bob and his friends herded the elephant down the middle of a few Bangkok streets to another family compound stockade and they quickly trained a maid to care and hand feed the new baby. After the honeymoon, Bob checked with local authorities and found there were no restrictions about owning an elephant, so he and his bride kept their baby for many months but finally had to donate it to Bangkok's Timland amusement park. A baby elephant drinks huge quantities of milk and Bob told me that fresh milk in Thailand was terribly expensive. The CEs returned to Saigon on time knowing they had contributed to a fun and unforgettable weekend. I recently had breakfast with Bob and we enjoyed the re-telling of this story.

There were a few single American women in Saigon in the late '60's, but not nearly enough to go around. They had their pick of the single men and the chase for their fickle attentions was not worth the effort, especially since they had not learned the oriental ways of pleasing a man, and some of our number had become quite spoiled. However, cultural ties are hard to break and most of us yearned for the personalities, background commonality, good looks and western conversation of the American women.

A couple of the guys ended up cheating the IBM 'bachelor only' requirement and either remarried a former wife, married an American sweetheart or married a Vietnamese sweetheart before completing their tour of duty. As a result there would occasionally be a lady from back home around the office as well as attending our social gatherings for brief periods. One of these women was a stewardess with American Airlines and she would bid her flight schedule for the Saigon run whenever possible. When she was in town, we put her to work in the office doing secretarial duties and she also became quite proficient at cleaning our MACV M-2 rifles prior to their final return. After awhile she could break a rifle down, clean it, oil it and re-assemble it in a remarkably short time. She also served a few good home-style meals for her husband's dinner guests. In general, Vietnam was not a good place for American women and we tried to enforce the bachelors-only policy. The liberal R&R benefit allowed the rest of us to spend time with westernized women at more peaceful locations, such as Tahiti, Fiji, New Zealand, Australia and Hawaii in my case. Those are fond memories!

Bruce Tomson and I had shared a house in Honolulu prior to our overseas assignments and during those party days had met and dated a few United Airlines stewardesses. They were good looking, young and fun loving. One of them stayed in touch with Bruce and somehow let him know that she would be landing at Tan Son Nhut airport on a specific day and hour and that he should visit her onboard their plane for a few minutes between flights. Bruce asked me to go out to meet her DC-10 with him, since there might be an extra American gal or two to talk to. We had a yearning to see a 'round eye' and hadn't talked with any American women in many months. We were allowed to board the plane and suddenly five beautiful ladies rushed both of us with hugs and modest kisses and began singing *"Happy Birthday"* to Bruce, who indeed had a birthday that very day. The girls brought out a huge birthday cake that they had baked during the long Pacific flight into Saigon and we all sat around talking about home and the war. The stews had to prepare for the departing flight all too soon, so we said our good-byes and deplaned feeling especially warm inside about some wonderful ladies, and we realized that we had been treated in a special way by a group of women who gave help and kindness for a living.

On another occasion, I received a letter from a friend in Honolulu saying that a mutual friend, whom I will call Tom, had a birthday coming soon and that she wanted to give him something special that he would remember and appreciate. Could I please help? She said that she knew Tom was somewhat shy and conservative but that he really appreciated quality. She asked that I find Tom a beautiful, sexy and loving Vietnamese girl to be enjoyed for the entire night of his birthday. Enclosed with the letter was a check for $75.00 - enough, she thought, to cover the necessary expenses. Well, this was quite a responsibility, and an interesting challenge. I asked another close IBM friend who knew Tom's tastes and together we set off for downtown Saigon to find the perfect gift. After five or six different tea bars along Tu Doc Street where we had a few drinks and the girls started to look better and better, we finally met a beautiful, tall and well endowed bar girl who spoke fairly good English and who agreed to spend the night with Tom for $25. (When converted to piasters, 25 was a generous fee for a prostitute who would usually receive only $5.00 to $10.00 in equivalent piasters for her services).

The date and surprise arrangements were set, an upfront retainer of $10.00 was given to the girl and we all waited anxiously for the evening of the birthday gift's presentation. The only problem was that the two of us had spent the entire $75.00 in the tea bars and in persuading the girl we had selected to go ahead with the deal. The next day, I wrote back to my friend in Honolulu saying that we had used the $75.00 on serious research and that she needed to send more money to reimburse us for the actual gift. For some reason, no more money arrived. On the evening of Tom's birthday, our gift showed up as promised and presented herself as a birthday surprise. As feared by all in the know, our lucky birthday boy refused to accept the gift and sent her home. Strike a mark for celibacy and prudence, something unique in that time and place. We gave it a proper try, had a great laugh and had fun with the $75.00 in Saigon conducting the talent search.

Playing golf at the Saigon Golf Club was another interesting diversion. The course was near Tan Son Nhut and in the early 1970's some of our personnel played fairly regularly on weekends. It was unusually flat and was the only course I had ever heard of that had intersecting fairways (numbers 10 and 18 crossed and one had better look before playing through). During the rainy season, there was some distance challenge to the soggy course, but when the dry season had been in affect for several months, a well hit straight ball would bound down a fairway like it was bouncing on a frozen lake. Having short-iron second shots to the par five holes was not uncommon and I remember bragging to the guys about the one time I accidentally hit one solidly and had actually overdriven the 500 yards to the green. I have been told that another IBMer scored a hole-in-one on the par four number 2 hole. The course's biggest shortcoming was its greens; they were watered and cut regularly but had the same wide blade grass as the fairways so that putting seemed like you were putting on a gravel driveway. Putting results depended purely on luck, not skill. The golf course had been the scene of bloody fighting during the '68 TET offensive, so the manned bunkers alongside several fairways were real bunkers where you could run for safety rather than the normal sand trap bunkers found on most golf courses. There were also several nearby graveyards and mined areas so that 'out-of bounds' really meant out-of-bounds!

There was a yacht club on the Saigon River near the middle of town. It was called Le Club Nautique (pronounced Cloob Nawteek) and had a great rooftop restaurant from which we could watch the war across the river. The club had an active and friendly French, Vietnamese and American membership roster that owned many small outboard motor boats used for water skiing. Bruce, John and Bill all bought small wooden ski boats, about 16 feet in length, which had been designed and built in Saigon many years earlier. A 35-horse power outboard would almost sink the boat, but it would also manage to pull a skier at speeds of 30 to 35 mph. What a place to ski! The water was green and tepid and seemed to have the consistency of watered-down pea soup. It was filled with tropical flotsam and jetsam including the dead bloated pig I once skied across. It was not a place where a water skier wanted to fall. The river serpentined past tankers, freighters and barges crowded with the equipment and supplies of war, under bridges lined with concertina wire, past armed guards and tanks and through rice paddy canals.

The yacht club owned an annex area at Tynye, an island paradise about five miles by water north of Saigon. Once, while skiing through this labyrinth of uncommon venue, I was sure that I heard "ping, ping, ping" bullet sounds whizzing just over my head all too near for comfort. My immediate reaction was to crouch on the skis as low as possible and yell at the ski boat driver, "faster, faster!" I felt awfully naked standing on two pieces of wood in my swimming trunks in the middle of a narrow river with ten-foot bushes on either side. Target practice with me as the target was not my idea of a water sport. I think we set a speed record to Tynye that day.

In order to join the Club Nautique, an interview with the club commodore was necessary. The commodore was a respected Vietnamese doctor with a medical practice in town. I dropped by his office one afternoon with my completed application form in hand. The doctor dropped whatever he was doing and began to ask me a series of questions about my boating experience and ability to pay the yacht club dues. Halfway through the lengthy interview, I began to hear a low moaning sound coming from the back room of the doctor's office. The doctor got up from where we were sitting and parted an old lace curtain covering a doorway. He beckoned me to look. There, lying on a wooden bench, was a this old man covered with large, belly-filling, blood-sucking leeches and attached to other oriental suction devices and herbal placebos. I could see many large mason-type jars on the surrounding shelves which were filled with leeches and who knows what other ancient remedies. The patient's eyes were filled with pain and fear. He was being purged of his disease the old fashioned way, but the commodore doctor seemed to be more interested in my yacht club application than with his moaning patient. I apparently passed the stringent application test, was welcomed into the club, and I politely left that office as soon as I could, hoping that I hadn't caught anything while there that would need a similar disgusting cure. That was one unique interview and yacht club!

The yacht club annex at Tynye was a world away from the war - or so we wanted it to seem. During the dry season (winter months) a few IBMers would either drive their cars there or motorboat there almost every Sunday afternoon – after spending Sunday morning in the office or at an account. During the monsoon season, the club would sometimes be open, but subject to the pass-ability of the muddy and rutted access road. The annex was a flat piece of privately owned yacht club land. It was situated on a wide and quiet tributary of the Saigon River, surrounded by rice paddies, a few farm houses, and large trees and jungle along the river banks. There was a long low wooden boat dock, an open-air restaurant, a good sand volleyball court and a large grassy area with palm trees and shrubs that was perfect for picnics, throwing the football and Frisbee or just socializing. Many of the members were the remainder of the French or French-Vietnamese aristocracy or diplomatic corps and the club language of the day was French. Americans were tolerated but were somewhat shunned by most of the French, even though it was recognized that our club dues were needed and that we could play a pretty good brand of volleyball. We kept score in French during the volleyball games, so most of us learned how to count up to 15 in French.

One hot day we were playing six man touch football on the grassy area, and after about an hour of hard play a military friend sat down in the shade, rolled over and began to complain of dizziness and sharp chest pains. He said he had no history of heart problems but we decided to treat the situation as a worst-case scenario anyway. We had to act quickly since we were about fifteen miles from the nearest hospital and the roads were barely passable, even with our four-wheel drive vehicles. We did have good communications with our office via our Motorola handy-talkies, so we called home and urgently asked our base radio operator to call and convince the Army to send a helicopter - immediately! The friend with what appeared to be a serious heart attack was a 38-year-old Army Captain.

One of our IBMers had a winning way with children and he organized the kids at the club so that a large "X" was formed with beach towels in an open area to mark a landing spot for the helicopter. The chopper arrived soon afterward and hovered over the landing area as we waved and shouted, "This is the place." The children all ran for cover. The captain was quickly lifted away to the nearest Army hospital. However, the Frenchmen at the club, who had their Sunday disturbed by the incident, seemed to feel that we had intruded on their domain and they were brash enough to say so. On the way home that afternoon, some of the IBMers stopped at the hospital to see how our Captain friend was doing. He was sitting up and thanked us profusely and gave much credit to our Motorola network. His doctor said that the Captain had experienced a massive heart attack, and that if it had taken any longer to get help he most likely would not have survived. We were pleased to have played a small part in saving his life.

The yacht club property was surrounded by barbed wire and had a gate and guard that limited access to "Members Only" and was located at the end of a long rough dirt road through farms and river lowlands. I do not recall ever seeing the peaceful and isolated atmosphere being broken by any effects of the war - other than the frequent over-flights of helicopters and jet aircraft on their way in and out of Tan Son Nhut. However, during the above episode with the captain, the elderly Vietnamese guard, who was employed to protect the club civilians, tried to attract the attention of one of the passing helicopters. He fired a flare gun near the low flying machine without success, but he did set fire to a nearby farmer's rice paddy. On most Sundays, a few helicopters would temporarily hover close overhead in order to ogle the shapely bikini-clad girls, but there was never any trouble. Bathing suits were the accepted dress, with shirts required in the restaurant. The French and Vietnamese girls kept our attention focused on the latest style and tiniest bikinis. Keep in mind that the French were the inventors of the bikini and the Tynye girls had to carry on their great tradition. Our volleyball, water skiing and observation skills became vastly improved on those Sundays, in that little bit of paradise. I would not mind a membership in that club even today.

Jim Strandine and I played as much volleyball as time permitted. Bump, pass, hit, slam and serve - we actually became pretty good for Saigon standards and played well together. We had a kind of unspoken communication on the court and always seemed to sense where the other guy was without looking. I could just feel when Jim was ready to dig out a tough serve or be running for the next pass that he would blindly set over his head to the left hand corner for my slams. We were invited to play on the MACV team in the all military league. There were about six cement courts at MACV and highly competitive games were played among the Air Force, Army, Marines and our MACV team during noon lunch breaks. Jim and I played in lightweight sneakers and were especially careful not to be stepped on or kicked by errant combat boots.

My most memorable set of games took place in a nearby Vietnamese Ranger compound, between our MACV team and the best Vietnamese players in South Vietnam. The compound reminded me of an old 'wild west' fort, kind of a stockade with high wooden walls and patrol ledges on the inside from where other Rangers could either shoot their machine guns toward the outside or cheer their team on the inside. We were much taller than the Vietnamese, but those smaller players could really jump; a couple of the five foot six inch Rangers could easily clear the eight-foot net with a good hard slam. It was somewhat un-nerving to me to be surrounded by a hundred or so well-trained, battle-ready, armed and cheering Rangers, but the competition sparked good friendships and at the end of a close match we all wanted to play another time. Jim and I also played two-man ball against French-Vietnamese teams at the Circle Sportif Club, and when I left Vietnam, I donated ten new volleyballs to the club to say thank you and promote continued enthusiasm for the sport. I hope they are still playing there.

There were many other things to do in Saigon. One of the most popular hobbies for many of us was photography, either with 35mm still cameras or with the then new Super-8 movie cameras. We shutterbug enthusiasts would generally take our equipment with us whenever we would drive anywhere. There was always another great scene waiting for us just around the next corner. In addition to a new Sony Super 8 movie camera that I sometimes used, I carried a little Rolie 35 that took excellent photos and was small enough to fit in the palm of my hand or be hidden away in a pocket. That way I didn't have to worry about some cowboy ripping it away or having it stolen out of my car. There was a sunroof in my VW and while a friend would drive, I would stand on the front seat, stick my head and movie camera out the top and record the action as we cruised through town. The streets of downtown Saigon were laid out in a general grid-like pattern interrupted by several large traffic circles. These circles made particularly good photo hunting grounds.

We filmed a long list of scenes: of amazing traffic clashes; school girls in their uniformed white ao-dais walking by concertina wire; ladies with their conical hats or more fashionable parasols; sandbags, guns, and tanks around town; refugee shanty towns; the U.S. Embassy (now removed), National Assembly Building and President's Palace; black market wares being displayed for sale on the city sidewalks; the open food and flower markets full of interesting shoppers; cheap oil paintings of Asian scenes displayed on downtown walls; bicycle racks with up to 500 neatly placed bikes per rack; whole families of 5 or 6 riding on one motor scooter; downtown public buildings so often then seen in the TV news; colorful pagodas; peaceful country home sites which turned into battlegrounds at night; huge piles of trash for which there was a totally inadequate collection system; military convoys; the ever present street kids who never tired of having their pictures taken; and finally photos of each other taking these photographs and movies. You never knew when you could take a photo of something like a Honda and driver covered with white geese headed to market, the geese hanging by cords tied to their feet which would cover the Honda so completely that it resembled a Pasadena Rose Parade float. These photos have reinforced my memory of Saigon and Southeast Asia.

There were other leisure time activities. During New Years, TET or 4th of July evenings, it was common practice to shoot one's firearm into the sky. However, it was dangerous to be out of doors without a helmet, to watch or listen, because the spent ammunition could be injurious or even deadly and would sound like large hailstones falling on all the tin roofs in the neighborhood. We invented a unique form of entertainment for evening yard parties. Someone would fill rubber balloons with propane gas from the gas nozzle of a kitchen stove, tie the balloon off and then tie a long streamer of toilet paper to the balloon. Then, we would light the bottom portion of the toilet paper as we let the balloon go. The burning TP and balloon would rise rapidly and when the flame reached the balloon at about 100 feet, there would be a loud bright explosion and screams of delight from the neighborhood kids. We were fortunate not to have set any homes on fire.

There were many fine restaurants in Saigon and perhaps some of you will recall: La Casita behind the National Bank which served an excellent bouillabaisse on Fridays (any other time there was a good chance for Ho

Chi's revenge); The Alley with its selections of fried sea bass, wild boar, rabbit in wine sauce, and strawberries in red wine; La Cave, which had a genuine French menu and was quiet, secluded and intimate (we were there one night when Brigadier General Jimmy Stewart, of Hollywood fame, sat down at a nearby table for dinner); the Red Door in Cholon which served Chinese food; the My Le Hoa, also in Cholon, which served spicy fried crab, dove, roast suckling pig, Peking duck and other succulent Chinese dishes like chicken feet; the Mayfair with its quiet atmosphere and great French onion soup; the William Tell south of the Saigon River with the best vichyssoise in the world; Ramoutcho's in the Eden building; La Dolce Vita for cream of chicken soap and many more dining places now lost to memory. Every few weeks, a small group of us would try to eat out at a new restaurant where none of us had yet eaten. It became a game of what to eat at the most unique restaurant without becoming sick. I learned how to read and order from a French menu, practiced often with chop sticks and enjoyed some of the few remaining French wines still served by the finer restaurants. However, I never did summon up the courage to dine out at one of the many street side mobile soup carts, which sold a popular Vietnamese snack called "Pho", and which were fondly referred to as 'Howard Johnson' lunch wagons. Some of our men swore by them, or was it at them?

One of the delights of working overseas as a well-paid contractor was that money never seemed to be a problem. I had experienced this same delightful phenomena during three years in North Africa in the early '60's. It is only when one returns stateside that money and bills once again become a major concern. There are no monthly bills if housing, meals and travel are all paid for by the corporation. We always had more than enough cash to do or to buy what we wanted. However, money in Vietnam was not taken lightly; it was one of the reasons we were there and it was a complex subject. We carried at least three types of money - U.S. currency that was seldom used and not legal exchange, Vietnamese currency that constantly changed in value with inflation, and the U.S. military script (or MPC) which was required for all purchases at the base PXs, BOQ restaurants and military commissaries. I remember the script as being artistically interesting money that could not be easily counterfeited. It was printed in various bright colors and had pictures of war inspired aircraft, tanks, soldiers, guns and ships within the borders of each bill.

There was an official exchange rate between Vietnamese piasters and the U.S. dollar and the script, and in addition, there was the black market exchange rate. Vietnamese citizens were not supposed to possess or use script, but some of them were especially adept at exchanging it. When the difference between the official rate and the street rate became too extreme or too much script had bled into unauthorized hands, the military would call in all of the old script and issue new. This would happen every six to ten months and the idea, for those who wished to break the law, was to exchange old script for piasters at the inflated rate just before they thought an exchange was scheduled. I believe that a few IBMers and I know that many military men made handsome profits dealing in this money exchange scam. We tried to discourage the IBMers from any illegal activities by stating that anyone caught dealing in the black market would be sent straight home. Our people would also witness and/or be aware of large money exchanges made by U.S. military officers. Shame on them, but the temptations were many!

The exact day that the script was to be withdrawn and re-issued was not supposed to be known in advance. It was simply announced at the bases that old script could be exchanged - one for one - that day, and there would be a wild scramble to make the exchange from the old to the new so that things could be purchased at the military stores and so that the black market and street exchange rate could be re-valued at fair levels. There was a story going around that a GI took good advantage of one of the MPC changes. On the day of the exchange, he immediately hit the downtown bars with a pocketful of money from his Monopoly set and tried to hire half the girls in town for his sexual pleasures, before they found out what the new script looked like. Military script represented a massive amount of money and had a major influence on the economy. One time, it was announced that an issue of old script would be exchanged the next day, but when the next day came the exchange locations were mysteriously closed. It was then announced by the military that the new script was not yet needed. What really happened was - a huge portion of the new script (a large truck load) had been stolen on the way to the military banking system. Everything in Saigon could be stolen, and was!

The SEAWA gong at the IBM office was used at least once a day and "Southeast Asia Wins Again" became a constant explanation for the idiosyncrasies of life unique to only Vietnam. Bill tells the following story: "Vung Tau is a popular beach town about 30 kilometers due southeast of Saigon on the coast. However, it was almost 80 kilometers by road and not an easy drive. The road was also subject to intermittent VC terrorism. Once there, it seemed like a true haven - white beaches, warm water, peace and quiet, and really no thoughts about the conflict throughout Vietnam left behind - until one day when John, Bob and I went down to the part of the beach that was protected by the U.S. military. We had our ladies with us and were having a grand old time, swimming in the surf, building sand castles and eating our picnic lunch. Then three Vietnamese soldiers showed up and demanded that we all go to the local police station because the women were in a 'restricted zone'. When we argued that the American MPs had allowed them to come with us to the beach, they said it was not American territory. We said, 'OK, then these Vietnamese ladies have a perfect right to be on this beach.' At that point they said, 'No they don't because this part of the beach is controlled by the U.S.' Huh? So we, and about ten other couples, went down to the local police station, where a young Corporal seemed to be in charge. When we asked him what was going to happen to us, he said it was up to the Major. 'Fine', we said, 'Where's the Major?' 'He's not here', we were told. 'Then what should we do?' 'That is up to the Major', he replied. And so it went, for about two hours, until all the parties seemed to be tired of the game and everyone was released. Southeast Asia Wins Again!" And time to go hit the SEAWA gong.

I had my own share of minor frustrations and surprises. The Saigon public water system was highly suspect and sanitary drinking water was a serious concern for anyone who did not want to risk occasional bouts with dysentery (called Ho Chi Minh's revenge). The city's pipes were old, rusted and contaminated. You either boiled all water used for drinking or obtained it at known potable sources. I had instructed my maid to fill a five-gallon jug regularly with potable water from a known dependable location, which was about a city block or two from the house. She had agreed that that was a good idea. This 'good' drinking water was then kept in pitchers in the frig and used for ice tea and ice cubes. The maid faithfully kept my household in pure water for as long as I lived in the big house on Cach Mang - or so I thought. One day I returned home early and watched in horror as she filled the pitcher and ice cube trays from the kitchen sink tap. I said, "Hey, how long have you been doing that?" She said, "Oh, many months now. I no like walk, and you no sick, so no problem." Southeast Asia Wins Again and go hit the SEAWA gong.

This is probably an appropriate place to tell a few Saigon traffic stories, and as I have said, the traffic was a major hazard and probably came right behind rockets, terrorism, robbery and VC attacks on the risk scale. The problem may have stemmed from the fact that the Vietnamese had never learned how to queue up as in the age-old custom of America and England. Lane integrity simply did not exist. The Vietnamese, and the rest of us trapped within, endured a level of traffic chaos that can never be adequately described to anyone who has not experienced it. One of the busiest streets in town was Cach Mang Street that carried the bulk of the traffic between downtown Saigon and all the military facilities on and around Tan Son Nhut. Cach Mang ran right by my house and there were times during rush hour when I literally could not exit from my own driveway. About halfway into town (or halfway out to Tan Son Nhut) there were railroad tracks crossing Cach Mang and a freight train passed by a couple times a day. One IBMer remembers stopping with the traffic heading into town behind the lowered track barriers. A longer than normal train went by and cars, trucks, taxis, cyclos, pedicabs, Hondas, carts, bicycles and people continued to pile up in all lanes and expand to the opposite normally empty left hand side of the street until there was a mass of waiting traffic stretching from sidewalk to sidewalk all going into town. Finally, the train passed and guess what? The other side of the tracks was also filled sidewalk to sidewalk so that two massive crowds faced each other and neither could move ahead. It took the Vietnamese 'white mice' (police) a good hour to sort that one out.

A nearby street where two of our IBMers lived was a curiosity: it was actually a narrow <u>one-way</u> alley, but not only did it have two way traffic, but the traffic in the forbidden direction always seemed to be the heavier of the two. This ridiculous situation became even more baffling when you observed that a Vietnamese policeman would stand in the middle of the exit end of the street and watch an endless flow of traffic pass by him and enter in the wrong direction. In that same busy area, an IBMer in his car pulled up to a traffic light. A Vietnamese on a Honda pulled up to his left and another Honda pulled up to his right. When the traffic light turned green, the Vietnamese on the left turned right and the Vietnamese on the right turned left and collided with each other in front of the IBMer's car. He said that he suspected what was going to happen and had fortunately waited a few seconds and did not run over either of them.

Another IBMer tells the following three stories: "One of the few times that I was able to stand back and really laugh at mayhem was when I was visiting an account in Cholon. The office was off an alley, where I was standing; I had already parked a few blocks away. A bus was trying to park, and as it jockeyed back and forth to maneuver into its space, cars on either side of it began to fill the narrow street. When the bus finally pulled into its parking slot, there were four lanes of cars facing each other. Horns blared, people shouted, tempers flared, and I walked to my car, laughing."

"Another day I was driving on a six-lane road (on the way to Long Binh), and I noticed that there were four lanes of traffic headed toward me rather than the anticipated three, so I moved over farther to my right. Then a jeep with full armament was passing the four lanes coming toward me and I moved over farther to the right. Next an ambulance with all sirens blaring tried to pass the jeep and was heading straight at me. I was forced off the road and sat for a while in the stifling heat trying to catch my breath and regain my nerves for the remaining road ahead. One morning, as I left my home for work, I turned onto the two-lane Yen Do Street off of Cach Mang and fell in behind a slow moving, open-ended truck. There was a dead body inside wrapped in a shroud and suspended from the roof in a makeshift hammock. The family and friends were walking alongside. There was no way to pass on the narrow road. I had to follow at their pace and arrived at work late that day feeling sick to my stomach." Unfortunately, that scene was fairly commonplace along the streets of Saigon.

It is probably more appropriate to end this chapter on a lighter note, and in doing so, I will pass along an important piece of information. From time to time, we would talk our girl friends or housemaids into cooking and serving "Cha Gio". If that didn't work, we would go to a Vietnamese restaurant, lunch or dinner, and order this special oriental treat. It is difficult to describe, but was enjoyed by all. Follow this recipe and try it yourself!

## Recipe For Cha Gio
1 pork chop
A small amount of crab meat or chicken - optional
5 small onions
1/4 potato
Some thin noodles
1/2 teaspoon sugar
1/8 teaspoon seasoning
1/4 teaspoon salt
A pinch of pepper
1 teaspoon nouc mam * See below.
1 egg
Rice paper

Chop pork into very small pieces. Add chopped onions. Chop up potato (or use bean sprouts) and add to the mix. Soak noodles 10 to 15 minutes with spice leaves. Chop up noodles and spice leaves and add to the mix. Add sugar, seasoning, salt, pepper, nouc mam (or, in lieu of nouc mam, use A-1 sauce), and one egg. Mix all together. Cut the rice paper into 1/4 sections. Rub a little sugared water on the rice paper to make it soft. Fold one end of a paper over a small amount of the mixture. Fold in the sides. Roll it up tight. Repeat this with the rice paper until all the mixture is used. Deep fry in cooking oil - oil should cover the Cha Gio.

*Note: The ingredients are fairly arbitrary. All Vietnamese make Cha Gio differently, so feel free to improvise. To eat the Cha Gio, the Vietnamese dip each roll into a sauce made of nouc mam, sugar, garlic, lime and red pepper. However, it is excellent in itself or wrapped in thin lettuce leaves. Nuoc mam is a fish sauce that is as popular in Vietnam as catsup or salsa is in America. It has to be smelled to be believed, and savored to be appreciated. It can be made by burying a fish in the sand for a sufficient time to make it liquefy and then processed God only knows how. Alternately, on a more commercial basis, the fish are highly salted and placed in vats where it is compressed for four to twelve months. As it ages, bacteria causes fermentation. The smelly juice is then drained off and bottled as nuoc-mam. In Saigon, after our initial revulsion - which lasted for up to a year - most of us learned to love it (in small doses) almost as much as the Vietnamese, but our liking depended on the age, smell and quality of the sauce. Its presence can easily be detected and at some point, one should open all windows and/or doors. Some Chinese fish sauces can be found in America, which approximates its unique aroma and flavor. Good luck!

# Chapter 8
## Angkor Wat, Cambodia

OVER THE PAST MANY YEARS, I was fortunate enough to visit a few of the world's more famous ancient ruins: Leptis Magnus in Libya, Balabak in Lebanon, Persepolis in Iran, the Pyramids of Egypt, many ruins in and around Rome and Athens, the Pyramids of Teotihuacan near Mexico City and a few others. I have not yet traveled to the Inca ruins in Peru, or up the Nile to Luxor or to Yucatan or even to the ruins of Nan Madol on Ponape Island (even though I worked in the Marshall Islands for awhile), but I would like to see these latter sites in order to compare their scope and mysteries to those hidden away in the jungles of northern Cambodia. In my opinion, the ruins of Angkor Wat and Angkor Thom are, without a doubt, the most spectacular, most artistic, most mysterious and most grand of anything I have ever seen. For anyone who loves to visit and photograph ancient ruins, Angkor is a must, the visit of a lifetime! That is if you can travel there safely, which in the '70s was problamatical.

I had heard about Angkor from a few IBMers who had visited there on vacation the previous year and I decided to do the same as soon as an opportunity presented itself. In 1969 Cambodia declared itself a neutralist country and thus it was supposedly safe for casual tourism. I wondered whether this was really so. One of the neighboring families to our Saigon office compound was French Vietnamese and the daughter, who was quite lovely, had become a business friend and our IBM travel agent. Her name was Leontine and we would turn our travel plans over to her with the confidence that hotel reservations and airline tickets to anywhere in the world would soon be delivered to the door. Our IBMers were constantly on the move so we made an excellent client base for her. In return she produced the tickets efficiently and correctly - not always an easy task in that chaotic environment. Four of us wanted to go: John, Jim, Cary and myself and we scheduled a departure for September 15, 1969. In retrospect, I believe that all four will agree even to this day that the trip to Angkor was probably one of the best short vacations of our lives. I would eagerly return.

In spite of being lesser known than some of its famous rivals and in spite of its location - at the center of civil strife and recent massive genocidal atrocities - the Angkor complex had not been forgotten. Photographs, articles in magazines and, as I write this in1996, limited travel tours are again popularizing trips into Cambodia. Daily flights from Phnom Penh to Siem Reap may be currently available, although somewhat regulated, and the Grand Hotel where John, Jim, Cary and I stayed is operating again with overnight accommodations for those visiting the ruins. Much earlier the temples had been forgotten by the outside world for literally hundreds of years and the jungle had almost completely reclaimed the area, which at one time served as the center of the Khmer civilization. In 1860 a French naturalist by the name of Henry Mouhot stumbled upon the ruins by accident while paddling up the Tonle Sap; his comment on what he had found was, "Angkor is grander than anything left to the world by Greece or Rome." A more recent author, Virginia Brownback, put it this way: Angkor is "The ultimate unveiled art treasure of the world", and Somerset Maugham wrote, "I have never seen anything in the world more beautiful than the Temples of Angkor." Glowing descriptions, but not exaggerated.

The Mekong River is the eleventh longest river in the world and flows approximately 2,600 miles (by contrast, the mighty Mississippi River is 2,348 miles in length) with its headwaters starting as far away as Burma and China. He river is one of the predominate physical features of Southeast Asia and governs much of the lifestyles and economies of the peoples of Laos, Thailand, Cambodia and Vietnam. It is navigable for shipping as far upstream as Phnom Penh. The river floods to massive proportions during the summer monsoons (June through November) and then reduces to just a very large river on the scale of the Mississippi during the winter dry season. A strange phenomenon occurs along the Mekong every year. Cambodia's largest lake, the Tonle Sap, flows southeast for half the year via the Sap River and into the Mekong at Phnom Penh. Then, during the late summer flood months when the flow of the Mekong River, swollen by the monsoon rains, increases to a level where its outlets in the delta cannot handle the enormous volume of water, the Sap River reverses itself and flows back into the Tonle Sap. The reversal makes this large lake a natural reservoir and a valuable resource for the rice farmers of the area. The Tonle Sap rises by as much as eight meters and triples in surface area each wet season. There is a yearly Water Festival celebrated in Phnom Penh in late October or early November, after the Mekong crests, which corresponds to when the Sap River again begins to reverse its southerly flow back into the Mekong.

Before departing on our weekend adventure into Cambodia, I did some reading about the history of the temples we were about to visit. A brief synopsis follows: the Khmer Empire, which occupied present day Cambodia and parts of Laos, Thailand and Vietnam, existed between the 6th and 15th centuries. The Khmers, whose descendants are what remains of today's Cambodians, are first known to have lived along the lower and middle Mekong River in northern Cambodia and southern Laos. Their capital was near the present city of Kompong Thom in central Cambodia but was moved around the year 900 to the Angkor area, which soon became the location for a magnificent city. The splendor of Angkor Wat and the surrounding monuments has never been equaled since by any of the other mainland Southeast Asian cultures. Khmer art, architecture and culture were strongly influenced by a religious heritage from India (Hinduism) and represented in the extreme by the stone images, statues, and carvings which now lay in partial ruin due to time, neglect, war and the ever strangling jungle. The Khmers were constantly at war with the neighboring Mon, Cham, Annamese and Thai peoples. The Thais were finally victorious in the 14th and 15th centuries. After constant raids, Angkor was abandoned suddenly around the year 1434, and the capital was moved to the more central present day location of Phnom Penh. Angkor was then lost to the world for over four centuries.

The immense temple complexes of Angkor are larger in scale than the Egyptian pyramids and are ranked among the masterpieces of world architecture. The greatest temple is the huge Angkor Wat of the early 12th century. It covers an area of 1,500 by 1,300 meters and is surrounded by a vast dry moat, 180 meters wide, this making it the largest religious building in the world. Along the causeway leading to the enormous entrance gate are balustrades shaped as giant serpents. The temple proper consists of towering complexes of terraces and cloisters surmounted by five towers in which were contained the principal icons. Rows of shrines line the galleries with walls covered with elaborately carved reliefs that illustrate Hindu mythology. The Khmers believed in an intimate relationship between their mythical universe and earth. By reproducing the ideal on earth, they opened a gate for their Gods, thus assuring harmony between the two worlds. The sculptures reveal the stories. Angkor Wat eventually became a Buddhist religious center, and during our visit we saw clusters of saffron clothed monks strolling by the statues, carvings and friezes or in quiet meditation. They gave a sense of reality to the otherwise surreal surroundings. Over the years these monks have helped protect the temple, worked hard to restore it and temporarily halted the ever encroaching jungle vegetation.

A few kilometers away is the second most spectacular temple, Angkor Thom, a walled city of about ten square kilometers (four square miles). Angkor Thom was built by King Jayavarman after defeating the Chams from Vietnam, who had destroyed much of Angkor Wat in the 12th century. It was built to re-establish Khmer glory and again the results were spectacular. The city is enclosed by a wall twelve kilometers long and eight meters high, and at the exact center is the most outstanding feature, the Bayon, a temple of fifty colossal towers up to 45 meters high with more than 170 gigantic faces all with different expressions. The Bayon bas-reliefs stretch for twelve hundred meters and incorporate over eleven thousand figures, most of which depict scenes from everyday life in their 12th century kingdom. There are many other lesser temples in the immediate areas, in various stages of decay, but none so breathtaking as the two described above. At least several days are required to gain a fair appreciation of the entire ruin complex.

Both Air Vietnam and Royal Air Cambodia flew to Phnom Penh and Siem Reap in 1969. We chose Air Vietnam's 727 because of an earlier trip that Bob Dillon and a couple of other IBM CEs had taken on Cambodia's airline. They had flown with Royal Air Cambodia in an old DC-6 from Phnom Penh to Siem Reap, and one of its starboard engines had spewed oil throughout the 45 minute flight. After safely deplaning, they noticed that the right side of the plane was blackened with engine oil and that an oil tanker was pulling up to the plane for a refill. The name of the plane was "Angkor Thom". They spent four fascinating days exploring the ruins, and when it was time to return to Saigon, there was old "Angkor Thom" waiting for them and again being scrubbed down and being re-filled with oil. They asked a few questions and found out that Royal Air Cambodia did not have any spare DC-6 engines or any money to buy one. The airline's plan was to just keep flying with the leaky engine until it quit and as long as the oil held out. Sure enough, it spewed oil all the way back to Phnom Penh. They arrived safely but that was warning enough for me.

In spite of the chaos at Tan Son Nhut, Air Vietnam departed on time and again we experienced the now familiar sense of relief in departing Vietnam. The short flight took us over the pock marked B-52 bombed areas to the east of Saigon and then over the Mekong River on the approach to Cambodia's capital. John, Jim, Cary and I all took notice of the tight spiraling descent of the 727's landing pattern, and it was explained later that it was far safer that way as an added precaution against being shot at from unfriendly forces in the Cambodian countryside. Immigration, bags and the taxi ride to the Raffles Hotel Le Royale all went smoothly, but the ride into town provided us with many scenes of infrastructural decay of a city that during the colonial era had once been considered the loveliest French city in Indochina. There were many hints of the economic troubles, which lay ahead for all of Cambodia. Tourism was still a viable source of income and we were treated well during our three-day vacation - in exchange for the American dollar.

We arrived at mid-day, which gave us an opportunity to tour Phnom Penh prior to our departure for Angkor Wat the next morning. Soon, four drivers with cyclos were rounded up and we were off at a good trot bound for the Royal Palace, which we had identified from the air due to the glittering golden roofs. The palace was unoccupied by any royalty at the time, so tourists had almost full visiting privileges. The main gates were open and we spent almost two hours wandering the beautiful grounds and photographing the ornate palace buildings. We were especially lucky, because there just happened to be a dress rehearsal for a welcoming ceremony being prepared for visiting heads-of-state. There was a huge dance pavilion, crowned in the golden Khymer fashion, which was open on three sides when fine weather permitted. Inside were perhaps fifty young dancing girls (we guessed 15 or 16 years of age) all adorned in bright and multi- colored native costumes.

They were swaying and circling to the "cling, clang, clong" that served as the classical dance music of Cambodia (quite similar to the music of Thailand), and each ballet movement and gesture of their pointed fingers and toes was done in perfect unison. We were held spellbound by the beauty of the girls and the rhythm of the dancing. All around the dancing area were even younger girls who followed with their eyes the instructions of the dance mama-sans and hoped that they too would be chosen some day to represent Cambodia. (I wonder how many of those beautiful little girls escaped the terrors of the Khmer Rouge and might be alive today?).

The day was passing too swiftly and we had much to see of the city, so we pulled away from the fascinating, once-in-a-lifetime scenes around the palace and headed back to our waiting cyclos. Cary suggested that we should do the peddling and let the cyclo drivers ride. That sounded like fun and soon the four of us were racing down one of the main streets toward the central marketplace. (This was kind of a stupid high profile thing to do, but what the hey!) We finally stopped at the market and caught our breath. The cyclo drivers enjoyed their rare rides and seemed to join in on our fun.

*Professional Cyclo Driver*

I remember that big John turned out to be the best peddler and we kidded him about always having a profession to fall back on should things not go well with IBM. It was warm and humid, especially after our race through the streets, and the marketplace was crowded and stifling, so the next stop was for some Cambodian beer and then back to the hotel. This was 1969 and the vivid memories I have of Phnom Penh will always bring a smile. It is hard to imagine the systematic killings, torture and atrocities that took place in and around such a fascinating city, only a few years after our visit. Just two miles south of our hotel is the present day Tuol Sleng Museum, which served Pol Pot's forces as a prison and extermination center for the aristocracy and where, at one time around 1975, up to one hundred victims a day were tortured and killed. Fifteen miles to the southeast of our hotel are the remains of the "Killing Fields of Choeng Ek" where an estimated 20,000 people were murdered. We had absolutely no hint in 1969 of the terrors that lay in the not too distant future.

We dined at the hotel, went for a swim, had poolside cocktails and turned in early in anticipation of a long drive across central Cambodia the next day. Vietnam was just 60 miles away, and we slept peacefully in neutralist Cambodia.

The next morning our rented white Peugeot sedan was ready and waiting for us in front of the hotel. We left Phnom Penh heading north on a bright sunny day. It was 30 kilometers along the west bank of the Sap River to the ferry that would take us across a broad expanse of the swollen river to Highway 6 that led to Siem Reap and Angkor. There wasn't much traffic and we were the second of three cars which rolled onto the old rickety ferry boat, and I wondered where we would end up down river if the noisy one lung diesel, which powered the ferry along at about four knots, should ever fail. Approaching the other side of the river, we passed several picturesque bamboo houses built on stilts but were still some distance from shore - probably good fishing but pretty isolated if one wanted to go somewhere. After the Prek Kdam Ferry, we had about 250 kilometers to go before reaching our destination, and most of the drive was past rice paddies and rice paddies - as far as the eye could see - rice paddies. It was beautifully emerald green and looked to me from a distance like a huge golf course, broken only by a few trees, stick and bamboo huts along the irrigation canals and the people working knee deep in the mud or walking the higher dry paths of the levees shaded by their traditional broad conical straw hats. (Author's Note: The topography of the area also looked to me like a huge basin in which to explore for natural gas or oil. Could central Cambodia be a gigantic synclinal basin? Time will tell whether the riches of such a natural resource will reward their ancient heritage and present day impoverishment.) We stopped to take photos of some water buffalo and of children who were fishing in the irrigation ditches. The children were especially friendly, as all children naturally are. We did not realize that we were at the geographic center of a massive Khmer Rouge buildup that was preparing for an all out bloody war with the U.S. backed Cambodian Government.

After an hour or so, we stopped in a small town (there were no large cities in Cambodia other than Phnom Penh) by the name of Kampong Thom to buy gasoline, cold drinks and look around. We encountered what seemed to be a cautious but contemptuous attitude from the people in regard to our presence there - call it animosity or just plain distrust. What were four American tourists doing wandering around the central shopping area of their quiet rural village? We moved through the open air market slowly, quietly and cautiously, bought our drinks and decided that we were not welcome and that it would be wise to move on. It was a strange feeling received in that town, not imagined, and probably justified. The road to Siem Reap was a good one, well paved with only a few chuckholes, and we made good time. By noon we were at the Grand Hotel.

During the 1970's and 1980's, the Siem Reap and Angkor area was the scene of heavy fighting and the drive we took across the rice bowl of Cambodia would not have been possible even six months later. In 1994 the only way a tourist could visit Angkor was to travel by air with the schedules and itineraries heavily controlled by the Angkor Tourism organization. On January 22, 1995 I ran across the following newspaper article, which was titled *"Khmer Rouge Threatens Tourists"*. It read, "A Texas woman and her Cambodian interpreter were killed and her husband was seriously wounded last week when Khmer Rouge guerrillas fired on their vehicle at the Angkor Wat temple complex. The Americans were part of a four-van convoy of more than a dozen tourists on an excursion to the famed archeological site 150 miles northwest of Phnom Penh. Citing a weakened but still active Khmer Rouge insurgency, the (US) State Department has warned Americans of high levels of crime and banditry in Cambodia. Several foreigners have been killed and the guerrillas have threatened to harm others. Cambodia's own monarch recently urged tourists to stay away because of terrorism." End of article.

We were lucky we timed our own trip when we did, because by June of 1970, the Angkor complex was controlled by a combination North Vietnamese and Khmer Rouge fighting force and by the following January, the French archeologist overseeing the restoration of the temples was expelled and his team of Cambodian workers executed.

Soon after, heavy fighting for control of Angkor erupted accompanied by air strikes and continuing warfare. We four saw the temples just before they were scarred by Cambodia's civil war.

The temples of Angkor are the remains of a succession of cities built over nearly five centuries by the rulers of the Khmer Empire, which at its height governed an area of almost all of what we know as Southeast Asia. It is thought that its capitol of Angkor Thom may have had a population of a million people. We wanted to see as much as possible that same afternoon and the next morning, before having to return to Saigon. Angkor Wat was just five kilometers north of the Grand Hotel, so we were soon walking into the grandeur of centuries past and at the right time of day - Angkor Wat faces west and is best seen in the afternoon. The ruins cover an area approximately 1.5 kilometers by 1.3 kilometers and as I mentioned earlier is one of the largest temple complexes in the world. We parked the Peugeot some distance away and crossed the 180-meter wide moat on foot across a wide stone causeway. That led to the main temple entrance, past a large sandstone statue of Vishnu and other carvings and friezes and strolled in awe down the 475 meter long paved avenue to the central temple. We took photographs as we walked and spoke in hushed tones. Few other people were present except for an occasional Buddhist monk with their shaved heads and saffron robes. The central structure is grandiose and is capped by a huge tower that ties all the other features together and forms an architectural crown.

We continued to whisper out of respect for what had been accomplished and gradually climbed to the top up a wide and steep stone stairway. Sitting down to rest and take in the view westward of where we had just walked and climbed, Jim turned to his right and gazed in amazement at a bearded, hippie-clad American. Jim said, "Pablo, is that you, my old San Marino neighbor?" He replied nonchalantly, "Yeah, hi Jim, what are you doing here?" Sure enough, it is a small world. Jim had run into an old friend from San Marino, California, half a world away, at the top of a hidden temple. What a coincidence! I have a favorite photograph from that same spot which looks out over the temple grounds well below where we were standing and at the sun setting behind a thick green ageless jungle.

*Three Monkeys (Look Close)*

Cary, Jim, John and I probably desecrated the sanctity of the religious carvings that afternoon by posing in front of the ancient and beautiful bas-relief carvings that encircle the lower portions of the temple, climbing up on the statues of horses and Hindu gods and pretending to dive into what had probably once been a king's swimming pool carved from sandstone. No one was there to object except the ghosts of past civilizations. The most famous of the bas-relief scenes at Angkor Wat is called the 'Churning of the Ocean of Milk' which is a carved scene of devils and gods churning up the ocean with a huge serpent in order to extract the milk-like elixir of immortality while other Hindu deities participate or look on the carved event. Angkor Wat represents the ultimate Khmer architectural achievement and ever since our visit I have wondered what the torture of twenty years of war and thievery has contributed to the further deterioration of the temple. Hopefully, a recently begun restoration effort will help remove bullet holes and bomb damage so that others will again be able to enjoy Angkor as much as we did.

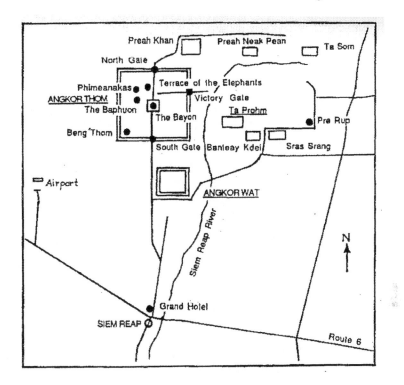

## Siem Reap, Angkor Wat and Ankor Thom

A good dinner and sound sleep at the Grand Hotel that night prepared us for another spectacle the next day - a morning visit to Angkor Thom and the Bayon. The Bayon temple is built in the exact center of a walled city and connected to four city gates by broad roads that were used by people and by elephants. The carvings at the Bayon were fascinating and depicted everything from scenes of women selling fish in a market, to cock fights, to battle scenes of past wars and even a wounded king. We were in a hurry and could not do justice to what was there to see; our Air Vietnam flight was scheduled for 2 p.m. We did see one more ruin on the way out which for me was perhaps less grand but even more memorable than those mentioned above. We left Angkor Thom by walking down the Terrace of Elephants and out the Victory Gate and walked through a heavy forest to a different site called Ta Prohm (The Jungle Temple). This last ruin was built as a Buddhist temple in the 12th century and has been left undisturbed since it was discovered in 1860. The paths and massive stone carved building blocks have been overgrown by great tall fig trees, their root structures encircling many of the partially decayed and destroyed buildings and looking like the tentacles of a giant octopus strangling an ancient prey. The trees were so large that the entire ruin was engulfed in permanent shade - even on the brightest of days - and moss and lichens added to the mysterious feelings we experienced about the place. In the heightened humidity of the jungle forest there was an almost stifling smell of things growing and things dying and of continuing decay. More photos were taken to prove that such a place did actually exist. Children led us through the maze and seemed happy to walk along with us without begging or being obnoxious or overly aggressive in order to sell some cheap artifact. However, we did buy a few small cowbells made from bamboo and a small cleverly constructed replica of a Cambodian cart, also made of bamboo pieces, which presently resides on my bookshelf at home. These children were also fascinated by Cary's bright red hair, as if they had never seen anyone in Cambodia with such bright hair color.

*Ta Prohm, Anchor Wat, Cambodia*

All too soon it was time to depart. We found our car, unmolested, and drove the few minutes to the local airport. Air Vietnam was on time; we processed through immigration, climbed aboard and were soon on our way back to the war and our more serious responsibilities. The three-day trip and especially the two days at Angkor was then, and remains, a true anachronism and something I will never forget.

If I had an opportunity to revisit some of the places I have traveled in this world, Angkor would certainly be at or near the top of that list. However, I suspect it will be many years before Cambodia regains any real national pride or economic success? Almost half of Cambodia's population of 7,000,000 died during the '70's and '80's and the country was left with the highest number of amputees per capita of any country in the world due to the hundreds of thousands of remaining land mines. (One estimate states 4,000,000 land mines and 20,000 amputees, but these numbers are probably conservative). Cambodia initiated a slow systematic mine detection and removal process using American help, but meanwhile each month hundreds of innocent citizens continue to be injured by stepping on the mines. What a tragic commentary about modern Cambodia when compared to the grandeur of its earlier centuries or the carefree weekend that we spent there in 1969.

# Chapter 9
## Fears And Tears

EVERY AMERICAN WHO SPENT ANY real time in Vietnam has a special story to tell; the experiences there were that different. This chapter tells two of those stories: they are about George, an IBM Customer Engineer assigned to the Long Binh computing accounts and about Gloria, the wife of an American contractor, living on the economy in Saigon.

**GEORGE'S STORY** - An IBM Customer Engineer On the World's Largest Army Base. A September 1993 letter:

"Dear Dan:

I was in Viet Nam with IBM from August 1967 to April 1969, and was at Long Binh the entire time. I will put together a set of stories on my time there and forward them to you for use in the book. Some of the adventures will include: the time I was shot down in a helicopter during the 1968 TET, getting blown up during a rocket attach on Long Binh, flying door gunner on a Huey helicopter (yes, as a civilian!), adventures in my red '66 Mustang fastback, getting a broken back in a jeep/motorcycle accident, the weapons we carried as civilians, and other tidbits as I think of them.

Yours truly, George League"

George was true to his word and sent the following:

### "A Short History of my Time in Viet Nam"

"It all started when my boss called me into his office in the spring of 1967 and asked, 'How would you like to go to Viet Nam?' I had spent three years in Japan and Korea with the Air Force from 1962 to 1965 and was still single, so the idea of returning to the Far East intrigued me. I wasn't all that excited about going to a war zone, but hearing that I would receive a 75% increase in pay, a better income tax deduction and full expenses for two years, tipped the balance in favor of going. In other words, greed won out over common sense.

I went off to New York City for three months to train on the IBM 1410 processor, then on to Philadelphia for an additional three weeks on the 2301 disk file. Back in those days, they taught you every circuit in the machine; it was your job to trace the trouble down to the individual card or component. Diagnostic software was very primitive at that time, so it was mostly scope and voltmeter work plus an occasional sniff test for burned circuitry.

Two other men, Bob and John, left the mainland with me in August of 1967 and traveled to Hawaii, where we were to receive a briefing before going on to our destination. It was really a free week's vacation; sort of a 'last meal before being thrown to the lions'. They only held the briefing on Tuesdays. IBM scheduled us to arrive on Wednesday, giving us a whole week with nothing to do but sightsee and have fun. It was highly appreciated.

From Hawaii we traveled to Camp Zama, Japan, just south of Tokyo, where we met our new FE Branch Manager. After a few days there, we received our travel orders and boarded a C-130 for a flight to Saigon. That flight was the worst 12 hours I have ever spent in a plane. We sat on webbed seats that ran along both sides of the plane, with huge pallets of cargo stashed down the center. For those of you unfamiliar with the climate control in a C-130, it has two temperatures - 95 degrees or 32 degrees Fahrenheit. We had to stuff these big chunks of pink wax in our ears to keep from going deaf. For 12 hours we were on a roller coaster, going up and down, up and down, all the time either roasting or freezing. About half of those on board got air sick, and I knew that the big Texan sitting next to me would never wear THAT hat again!

When I arrived in country, Bob and I were assigned to work at Long Binh, at that time the largest army base in the world. Bob worked at the 14th Inventory Control Center on the main part of the base while I was assigned to work at the 506th Field Depot, which was in a newly cleared part of the jungle about a mile outside of the current base boundary. The Army had just finished building this million-dollar climate controlled computer center in the middle of nowhere. Later on, warehouses and support buildings would be built near by, but at that time we were the only things out there. There was a high embankment built all around the computer center, with manned machine gun nests in each corner.

A few weeks later, the computer equipment arrived, and we started uncrating the various machines and moving them into the computer room. Of course, the government, being what it is, purchased the raised floor from the lowest bidder. After we had the 7010 mainframe and all the tape drives positioned, it was time to roll the big monster 2302 disk drive onto the floor. It was by far the heaviest piece of equipment IBM made. As we pushed it up the ramp and onto the floor, the wheels started sinking into the raised floor and the huge 2302 came to rest on its bottom frame rails. We had to procure some huge sheets of 3/8 inch steel plating, jack the 2302 out of the floor, and keep it installed on the steel plates from then on, so it wouldn't go through the flooring again.

During that first year in Vietnam, I actually lived in the CE parts room next to the computer room. It was quite large and was air conditioned, whereas the quarters that the Army provided at that time were open bay barracks. The customer liked it (me in the CE room) because I was right there to fix anything on a moment's notice, and I liked having private and comfortable quarters.

Another IBMer, by the name of Tom, arrived in country shortly after I did, and he brought with him a beautiful bright red 1966 Mustang 2+2 fastback. After a couple of weeks in Saigon, he decided he did not need a car, so I bought it from him for $2500. Needless to say, that car turned a few heads wherever I drove it. I went into Saigon to try to transfer the title and license plates, only to find that it would take about 3 months and several hundred dollars in bribe money to get it accomplished. So, I said to hell with it and left it in Tom's name and with his license plates.

The only gas station near Long Binh was an old Shell station halfway to Bien Hoa. I think they cut their gasoline 50-50 with water 'cause that Mustang sure wouldn't run on it. So, the problem was, where could I get some good gas...hmmm. Let's see, I work at the field depot, the computer prints out all kinds of requisitions, and what do you know, here comes a bunch of gasoline requisition forms off the printer. Take the forms over to the POL dump, fill up the Mustang and give the form to an amazed private at the gate. It worked for almost two years, no problem.

Mustang maintenance was no problem either. A couple cases of beer to the guys at the motor pool, and whatever I needed, I got. I even landed a set of new tires on chrome rims from those guys. Great deal.

That car served me well, and I wish that I still had it. Two years later, I sold it to a renegade Army sergeant for 413,000 black-market Vietnamese piasters. He was buying piasters from Hong Kong for about 300 P to the dollar, so his price for the car was only about $1377. I took the piasters and turned them into IBM at the official rate of 118 P to the dollar. IBM used the piasters to pay the rent on the villas in Saigon, and I got $3500 for the car. Everybody made out on that one. As far as I know, the car is still in Tom's name.

Living at Long Binh was strange to say the least. At the center of the base were five beautiful homes where the Generals lived. I mean, the lap of luxury - Italian marble and all that stuff. As you moved outward, next came the quarters for Colonels and Majors, which were individual air-conditioned rooms. Then the lower officers in open bay barracks, etc. until you arrived at the perimeter where there were guys living in bunkers. Rank definitely had its privileges.....

There were 7 or 8 parking spaces just outside the post exchange, and of course, these had signs on them 'RESERVED for 0-6 and above'; that's Lt. Colonel and above. Like when was the last time you saw a colonel or general in the PX? Everyone else had to park a block away and walk. Well, our civilian orders gave us a rank of GS-13, which was the equivalent to a 0-6 in the military. Here I am, a 24 year old Lt. Colonel, so I come wheeling into the PX parking lot and zip right into one of the privileged spots. Before I can even get the door open, there's two MPs standing there, giving me a ration of crap about how I can't park there. Talk about a change of attitude... I showed them my I.D. and it went from, 'You can't park there, you asshole; can't you read the #$#@*& sign?' to 'Excuse me sir, go right in.' I left a couple of bewildered looking MPs standing there, but wisely I didn't push my luck too often.

Good old Bob damned near got himself fired about two weeks into the job at the 14th ICC. We had preventive maintenance (PM) scheduled from 7 to 9 in the morning. I was going to help him that day because we had some engineering changes (ECs) to put on the tape drives. Well, 7 a.m. rolled around and the massive inventory update job, which the customer had been running all night, hadn't completed yet. So, instead of waiting, Bob says, 'you agreed to give us the machines at 7 a.m. and it is now 7 a.m.'. He then walked over to the computer and hit machine Reset on the console. I thought they were going to kill him on the spot, but he ended up with a serious discussion in the data processing CO's office about who was in charge there. At least he never did that again.

I was technically a civilian, but wore fatigues, flak jacket and a helmet just like the military (Author's note: almost all the other IBMers wore white shirts and sometimes ties in the traditional IBM manner, but in George's case there was some justification as you will soon find out). The VC didn't care if you were a civilian or not, they just liked to shoot at Americans. We were definitely not 'unarmed'; some of the IBM guys were better armed than most of the soldiers. I had an M-3 .45 caliber 'grease gun' that I bought from a soldier for $30.00; also, an AK-47 which I bought from a Captain for $85.00, as well as a Chi-com SKS carbine and a pistol. One of our CEs had a mortar and I believe somebody even had a bazooka.

I remember one night when we were still the only building in the depot, there was supposedly some VC activity in the field approaching the computer center. We set an M-60 up on a table in the CE room and were shooting out the open window. There were some Huey choppers hovering above the building shooting out into the same field, and the machine gun nests on the surrounding embankment were also firing. I don't think we hit anything, because there were no bodies in the field the next day.

One sight I will never forget is the first time I saw a 'Puff' C-47 gunship operating at night. They were circling a target out near Bear Cat, and it looked like there were huge red laser beams coming out of the side of the plane, just a solid red line from ship to ground. Every fifth round is a tracer, so I was seeing only 1/5th of the actual firepower. It was incredible. I can't imagine what it must have been like to be underneath that thing. However, for shear terror, nothing could compare to the B-52 raids. They were bombing 20 miles away one night, and yet the ground where I was standing shook like an earthquake. To be under one of those raids must truly have been hell.

Another sight I won't forget is the first time I saw them bring in a dead GI. I was at the heli-pad waiting for a hop to Saigon when a med-evac came in. They unloaded a stretcher with a body on it, and it was covered by an olive drab blanket. The only part visible was his boots. It struck me like a hammer that he had put those boots on that morning, had laced them up - and never thought that he would not live to take them off again. I never saw his face, but I will never forget those boots.

In early February 1968 the VC made coordinated attacks all over South Vietnam to try and win the war; they almost made it. It was called the 'TET Offensive' after the Tet holiday (Lunar New Year) when it took place. I was unable to leave Long Binh for two weeks, until almost all of the fighting was over. The folks in Saigon had it much worse with many civilians trapped without food or supplies for a long period of time. Near the end of the second week I was given the OK to travel from the Commander, and decided to catch a chopper into Saigon. We were flying near Highway 1, which runs between Long Binh and Saigon, when we were hit by ground fire. It was really strange, in that you didn't have time to get scared. Bullets came through the floor of the Huey, but didn't hit anyone. However, some bullets did hit the engine and we started to go down. The Green Beret Captain sitting next to me whipped out his .45 and hollered, "they're not taking us alive!" I told him to speak for himself and grabbed the M-79 grenade launcher off the rack over the doorway. The pilot was very good and was able to auto-rotate. We dropped rapidly and the rotor blades continued to spin because of the air passing over them as we descended. Just before we hit, the pilot cranked in full pitch to the rotors, which slowed us dramatically. We crashed into a rice paddy and sank in thigh deep mud, but no one was really hurt. No enemy were in sight, so we slogged through the mud and shit until we made it to the highway where we were picked up by a deuce-and-a-half and rode on into Tan Son Nhut air base. I tried to sneak off with the M-79, but one of the crew made me give it back.

After the TET offensive, our IBM office in Saigon issued everybody M-2 .30 caliber automatic carbines, a supply of ammunition and a case of C rations. That's right, IBM issued us all weapons!

167

I worked at Long Binh my whole tour, but other CEs rotated in and out of Long Binh. Guess I was just lucky? I had arranged my work schedule so I would have ten days on and then four days off, and alternated weekends with the other CE. It was great because during the four days off I could fly to Bangkok or Hong Kong or Japan. Bangkok had the most beautiful women in the world (to my taste) and things were amazingly cheap. Japan was much more expensive, but I spoke the language and felt more comfortable there. But, my favorite place was Hong Kong! I had a 21-foot cabin cruiser built out at Saikung Harbor in the New Territories and had a girl friend there named Jenny Lee. When I went to Hong Kong, we would take the boat and go out to one of the many uninhabited offshore islands, with their white beaches. It was great; plus, Hong Kong had the best food I have eaten anywhere in the world. You could also take the high-speed hydrofoil from Hong Kong to Macao in about 45 minutes (which the author, Dan also did). Macao was a strange place; it was physically part of communist China, but administered by the Portuguese. They had gambling casinos, but every hour on the hour you would hear messages from Chairman Mao being broadcast from speakers that were hung on poles all over the small picturesque city.

Sometimes I would just go to Saigon for my 4 days off and stay at one of the IBM villas. I remember sitting on the roof of Ron Vess' villa, watching the F-105s and Skyraiders dive bombing near the racetrack in Cholon - the Chinese section of Saigon. We just sat in our chairs on the roof and watched the war. Ron and I and a guy named Jerry were sitting on that roof one warm night when we heard a whizzing sound, then a thud. A stray bullet had passed between us and lodged in the wall behind where we were sitting. We decided to call it a night. Another night, same roof top, I was sitting alone watching the airdropped flares in the distance, when an ARVN C-47 transport flew right over me with its right engines completely engulfed in flames; he was trying to get to Tan Son Nhut, but didn't quite make it; he crashed and exploded on base.

At the end of the week when they were bombing Cholon, I needed to catch a hop back to Long Binh. I went to the heli-pad at Tan Son Nhut, but there were no flights out. An Army Sergeant was also waiting to go to Long Binh. After awhile a Lieutenant came running in and said, 'I'm going to Long Binh, but I don't have a crew. Anybody wanna go?' The Sergeant and I raised our hands; the pilot told the sergeant to fly in the co-pilot's seat and asked me if I knew how to use an M-60. I told him I did and he assigned me as door gunner. We took off and circled low over Cholon, which was in flames from the bombing and then headed for Long Binh. I was just waiting for something to shoot at, but the trip was uneventful.

Things gradually became more civilized around the 506th as the complex grew. The army brought in civilian contractors to do the computer programming and run the tape library, and the new commander decided that it would be best if I moved out of the CE room and into quarters on the main base to avoid jealousy on the part of the other civilians. At the 506th we had a supply sergeant, who could get ANYTHING. The guy was incredible. We cut 55-gallon drums in half and made charcoal broilers out of them, and on Saturdays we would have grilled steaks and imported champagne. I don't know where he got the stuff, but no one was complaining. We also had a mascot, a mutt dog appropriately named 'RERUN', in honor of all the computer work that had to be re-run.

One day when I drove to the center, I noticed that there was nobody around the computer room. After searching around, I saw a bunch of guys standing in line over at one of the warehouses. Turns out that somebody had snuck a prostitute into the base, and she was hard at work in one of the storage rooms. At the end of the day, she wobbled out of the warehouse, sore but well paid.

Besides my car, I also had a little Honda 50 motor scooter that I rode around on base. On January 18th, 1969, I was riding along MacArthur Blvd. at Long Binh, when a sergeant driving a jeep pulled out from a side street right in front of me. He saw me after he was fully across my lane, so he stopped dead right there. I laid the bike down trying to stop, but there was loose gravel on the road. I was up on the foot pegs trying to kick the bike away from me when it hit the side of the jeep. The bike stopped and I slammed back into the seat, then onto the side of the jeep and finally ended up in a ditch. The impact had crushed two vertebras in my spine (L1 and L2). I think I was unconscious for awhile, but I'm not really sure. Luckily, the impact was completely parallel with my spine and there was no lateral motion, hence no spinal cord damage. The Army ambulance came and took me to the 23rd Med Evac Hospital, where I stayed for a week. I couldn't wait to get out of that place; they brought in battle wounded every day and guys died in my ward every night. They would scream, or cry, or just moan, but in the morning they would be gone. After six days in the Med Evac, I was transferred to the 5th Army Field Hospital in Bangkok, where I stayed for a month. That was a whole different world. I received physical therapy for an hour every day from the most beautiful six foot Swedish blonde you ever saw. While I was there, Gypsy Rose Lee came to visit us; I have a picture of her in bed with me. She was in her 50s by then, but still looked good to us. I recovered from my accident and returned to Long Binh to complete my assignment.

It was about 2 o'clock in the morning on a Tuesday in April 1969, and I was lying in my bunk reading a book. I was waiting for the computer operator at the 506th to call me like he did almost every night, with some problem either real or imagined. Usually they would get an error saying they were unable to write to a tape drive. I would ask if they had a write enabling ring in the tape reel and I would get assurance that there was; 'after all, we're not stupid, you know.' And, of course, when I arrived, there would be no ring in the tape and they would blame each other.

My room was the last room on the first floor of the officers' quarters. Next to my room at the end of the barracks was a bunker, then a tennis court (yes, you got it, a tennis court; this was a weird war!). The bunkers were made by taking a road culvert about 12 feet in diameter, cutting it in half to make kind of an above the ground tunnel, then building a wooden frame around it and filling the frame with asphalt. Barriers were placed at both ends to keep the shrapnel out. These were effective for near misses, but a direct hit would take one out. Anyway, that night there was a battery of six 155mm self-propelled guns up on the ridge, and they had been firing out towards Bear Cat for several hours. Boom-boom-boom-boom-boom. After a while you didn't even hear them. Boom-boom-boom-boom-boom. Then, boom-boom-boom-boom-boom---KA-Whump! Ka-whump? Ka-whump??? That's not out-going! That's IN-COMING!

I rolled out of my bed and shot out the door clad only in my jockey shorts and ran like hell for the bunker. I was about half way there, when a 122mm rocket landed in the tennis court, not more than 20 feet from me. It was so close that I never heard it explode; I remember seeing the explosion and fire, but no sound. It blew me backward about 30 feet into the mud, but the bunker was between it and me and the bunker took the brunt of the shrapnel. I crawled to the bunker as fast as I could and scrambled inside. Eighty-seven more rockets came in that night and I think I counted every one of them. Each time one landed, I was sure the next was going to kill me.

The Chaplain lived in the room above me and he was asleep when the first rocket hit in the tennis court. He awoke, dressed and went to his duty post, wherever that was. He came back about dawn after the attack was over and we talked for awhile. He then went upstairs to his room, whereupon I heard him exclaim, 'Jesus Christ!' I ran upstairs to see what the problem was. The wall of his room that faced the tennis court looked like Swiss cheese. There was shrapnel in his ceiling, his mattress, his pillow and even in his refrigerator, yet none touched him while he slept. I guess he worked for the right guy.....

After that attack, I decided that I had pushed my luck far enough and that the time had come for me to take the money I had saved and run. The rocket attack had really shaken me. I had not seriously been afraid before, but those hours in that bunker with death raining down from the sky really got to me. I had almost completed my two year assignment and I left Long Binh the next day; and, I left Vietnam for good the following Saturday. I'll never forget it."

George League retired from the IBM Corporation in July of 1992 after 27 years of service and lives happily with his family in a southeast city in the U.S.A.

**GLORIA'S STORY** - The Adventures of a Contractor's Wife in War Torn Saigon

"I was raised on a farm in Holbrook, Arizona and had little experience with foreign countries, war or poverty until November 1969. At age 23, I joined my husband Stan in Saigon, South Vietnam. Stan was a computer programmer in Los Angeles and had volunteered to go to Vietnam on a two year assignment with a civilian contractor (not IBM in this case). It was a good job and was an opportunity to save money and see the world. Stan went to Saigon alone, but after six months of sizing up the situation he decided it would be safe for me, and our fourteen-month-old baby boy, to join him. Stan met us in Hong Kong and we spent a week in that marvelous city prior to traveling on to new experiences.

My first night in Saigon was terrifying to the degree that I almost told Stan I was going to return home on the first plane out the next day. Missiles were exploding, an apartment building down the street was blown up and several people were killed. Gunfire continued throughout the night and the next morning there was an abandoned dead man lying in the street. What a beginning! This was safe? Stan made me stay indoors with the baby for most of the next two weeks in order to make a slower adjustment to this foreign life. We hired a Vietnamese nanny by the name of "Gee Nam" for the baby and a maid by the name of "Thu Nuygen", who served us as housekeeper, washed my clothes and helped with the meals. Thu Nuygen had several good references from previous American employers and she eventually became our son's Godmother. We supplemented the strange local dishes with known food types from the military commissary out at Tan Son Nhut. Much of what the maid prepared was a variety of soups consisting of vegetables, noodles, and mystery meat. (Would I have eaten that in the States? I don't think so). There was also the delicious Cha Gio wrapped in rice paper and dipped in nouc mam fish sauce as well as various spicy seaweed dishes with wonderful fruits such as mango, papaya and leeche nuts. It was quite a change from Arizona but I could cope.

I finally wanted to see the city and since Stan's company provided him with a company car, we began a series of tours of Saigon. My only field of reference for those first trips was the vacations my family used to take me on in Mexico. I wasn't used to seeing people living in cardboard boxes or begging for food and money. I naively wondered why the Vietnam government couldn't take care of all the children and old people who were living in the streets. I learned there was only the very poor or the very rich, but no middle class. Only the strong would survive. Ghettos extended for many city blocks and the people looked haggard and undernourished. Few good jobs were available and the younger women were forced into prostitution to help feed their families. Stan wanted me to see everything, so he took me to a Saigon bar and introduced me to the mama san and a few of the bargirls. I became a novelty there and the girls started asking about life in the United States. Most of them wanted to marry an American, move to the U.S. and then transfer their extended families as soon as they got settled. Many of them did just that. On the way home that same day, we fell in behind what I thought was a parade; rather, it was a group of Buddhist monks in their saffron robes walking behind and carrying an elaborately decorated casket. I felt I had learned enough for one day.

Stan's company also provided us with a nice house on a quiet side street. We were across the street from the home of a Chinese Embassy diplomat and his family. The home was heavily guarded and even had armed guards walking the roof during the night. The diplomat would be picked up and delivered home in a chauffeur driven limousine each day. He would sometimes stop to talk to our son as he played outside with Vietnamese children. One day, when I returned from work, I was greeted by one of the Chinese guards at my own front gate. I was told that the diplomat's wife was asleep in my maid's room, that she had gone shopping and had locked herself out of her home earlier and that she needed to rest since she was pregnant. She remained in my home with a guard at her door until her husband returned late that afternoon. He came in to fetch his wife and was preceded by four guards who entered my compound with guns drawn. He quickly realized the situation, shook my hand and humbly professed his gratitude. He was also very embarrassed about the armed guards. Three days later his two maids brought us an especially prepared and delicious Chinese dinner. After that our two-year old son was often invited into the diplomat's home since the Chinese believe that if a woman who is pregnant holds and has another boy child around her, she too will have a boy child. Another benefit resulted from this chance meeting. The Chinese security guards watched and cared for our son while he played and even gave him a tiny puppy as his own pet.

Our young son grew up speaking a combination English, Vietnamese and French. His father, Stan, and his Vietnamese nanny both spoke French around the house and he would mix all three languages. A few years later, after we returned to the U.S., his nursery school teacher told me that he was having a hard time adjusting. He had been used to playing war games with the Vietnamese children in Saigon and she said he was very aggressive with the American children

Soon after arriving in country, I began volunteer work at a local orphanage, which housed somewhere between 100 and 150 children in horrible conditions. The orphanage was run by a wealthy woman who told me that her brother was an influential and powerful person in the Vietnamese Government. I later found out that he was indeed very high up. My first day at the orphanage was perhaps even more of an eye opener than my first day in town. At first, the children were frightened of me because I was a foreigner and I had to work hard to patiently gain their confidence. There was a younger boy there who could speak some English and who acted as interpreter for me. The orphans were approximately ten to twelve years old and all wore old clothes, had no shoes and were undernourished. They had lice and fleas in their hair, worms in their stools and bug bites on their arms and legs. The smell of the barn-like building was repulsive, garbage was everywhere and a few small babies were sick with pneumonia. Some of the babies had limbs missing from grenade explosions and the only medicine available was some iodine and gauze. One crib at the end of the house contained a baby who they said was being left there to die. They wouldn't let me see her and I never knew why. We set up a separate area for a simple clinic and talked a medic from the nearby American base into giving us some additional medicines. We began cooking better meals in big cauldrons outside in the orphanage yard, and served the children some soup and fish dishes, but there was only enough for one bowl of soup per child. The children began to accept me.

After a few weeks at the orphanage the children led me into the main dining room and we sat on mats on the floor. A few children played with my hair and were fascinated by my light makeup. They would try and mimic my every gesture. One of the women brought me a bowl of soup and all the children stopped what they were doing to watch and see if I would eat the horrible smelling fish broth. I hadn't eaten much fish in Arizona but I had to save face. I drank it down with pretended relish and the children returned to their own soups re-assured. There were many local customs that had to be learned and one day a Vietnamese women asked me to please stop patting the children on their heads. I had been innocently putting evil spirits into each child's head. It was believed that they would go crazy and a form of exorcism had to be performed on each child to release the spirits.

One day, the wealthy benefactor said we would soon be visited by some important people and that we should begin cleaning up. We hauled trash for two days and Stan even brought some of his contractor friends to help. The visitor's day finally arrived and a room was opened up which was nicely decorated and contained new clothes and toys for the children. Each child was given one toy and some clothes to wear. We had occupied most of that morning bathing the children and everything appeared clean and nice. When the visitors left, the toys and new clothes were taken away from the children and returned to safekeeping. I learned that the wealthy madame financed the orphanage through donations from foreigners and she wanted everything to appear clean and successful. It was the wife of Vietnam's Vice President who visited the orphanage, with her entourage, newsmen and cameras. The local TV news would show her bestowing gifts all around and then after she departed the gifts would be collected and again locked up so they would be fresh for her next visit. It was so artificial and shameful. We were once visited by three English ladies, whose husbands were in the local diplomatic corps. They planned to give money to the orphanage, so all the children were put in rags for that particular visit. They asked me about the orphanage and I told them the truth. I really didn't have the stomach for what went on at that orphanage and it was best that I soon find another job. Stan knew some of the IBMers through his computer programming job. I got lucky and spent the next two years as a part time radio dispatcher working at 115 Ming Mang Alley with the IBM-GEM organization helping out with their Single Sideband network.

I had a compulsion to try and help wherever I could, so for several months I also worked at a hospital for a Dr, Long near Tan Son Nhut Air Base on my days off. I was a volunteer helper in a ward for the recently wounded. Ambulances would go out to a nearby field to meet helicopters filled with wounded. Screaming men would be placed on sort of a conveyor belt to be hosed down with water and disinfectant because they were so muddy and so bloody. We would take large scissors and cut the clothes and boots off bloodied limbs and try to clean them up as much as possible to get them ready for surgery. My uniform would be splattered with blood and some of the wounds were truly repulsive. After surgery they would be taken to a ward and I would clean myself up and then just sit and talk with the men who couldn't or wouldn't have to fight again. There were several hundred beds in the ward and they were nearly always filled. We talked about home and I would help them write letters to their families in the U.S. They were scared but happy to see an American women and the simple act of holding their hand or listening to their stories seemed to help calm them and get them through that rough period. I soon got to where I didn't want to see any more carnage, but I did go by the recovery wards off and on for the next year and a half to help when and where I could.

Life could be scary in Saigon too. One morning Stan and I were awakened around 2 a.m. by a huge nearby blast that shook the house and knocked dishware off some shelves. We didn't move for quite some time, fearing any follow-on explosions. Stan became curious and went to our compound gate and saw a car ablaze only about a hundred yards down our supposedly quiet street. Car bombs were one of several forms of Saigon terrorism. Another morning, as I prepared to go to work at IBM, I found a straw doll just outside our front door. I didn't know what it was or why it was there. I took it to IBM with me and asked one of their Vietnamese employees about it (Nam Phoung or Ming Chi). She told me that it was a voodoo doll and was intended to bring me bad luck. I found out that some of the IBM bachelors, who had Vietnamese girl friends, had also found similar omens under their pillows and mattresses or at their doors-- strange herbs or dolls of local superstition. There was a lot we Westerners didn't understand.

I became a close friend to an older Vietnamese woman, a Madame Anh. She was wealthy and influential within the Vietnamese social elite. Why she and I were attracted I will never know, but for almost two years she and I were close confidants. She would send her chauffeur to my villa and we would spend the day talking of her 65 years in Vietnam and abroad; she was widely traveled. She introduced me to local Vietnamese cooking (such things as sea-weed jello, cha gio and other delicacies). She had a large home, many servants and her pride and joy was an atrium, built by her husband, which was filled with exotic birds from all over the world. My favorites were the nightingales with eyes like Cleopatra's. She had several *ao dais* made for me by her servants, and I would dress like a Vietnamese and we would go shopping in Saigon's fashionable women's shops or to the open marketplace, I in my ao dai and conical straw hat. Many months after developing our friendship, I went to her house and she seemed very frightened. She told me that she had received a visit and a warning from a government official about the fact that she was entertaining an American woman in her house and that she should be more circumspect. A neighbor had turned her in. From that day on, we met outside her home and in the homes of several of her wealthy friends where I posed as an English language tutor.

Madam Anh had a wealthy niece who lived in Bangkok, and we were introduced when I was there to renew my Vietnam visitor's visa. We too became good friends. We would visit the silk factories in Bangkok and the gold markets and I often stayed overnight at her Thai-style villa. I once bought tea in a Bangkok market and when I returned to Saigon, I was temporarily detained at customs because they thought it was "hash". Through these two gracious ladies, my foreign experiences were greatly enriched, learning and trying to understand the Asian customs.

Finally the day came we were to leave Vietnam. Several of the IBMers came to see us off and wish us fond farewell. However, it wasn't that easy. One of the customs agents asked to speak to our little son and learned he was fluent in Vietnamese. Stan and I were told that we were free to leave the country but that our son would have to remain. Immigrations was convinced that he was Vietnamese in spite of his blond hair, green eyes and relatively light complexion. Or did they simply want a payoff? We had to return to town. Since we had given up our apartment we were invited to stay at another contractor's home until things could be cleared up. I had packed my son's birth certificate, not anticipating any immigration problems, and we spent the next two days trying to convince the American and Vietnamese Embassies that he really was our son.

The U.S. Embassy finally agreed to write a letter to the Vietnamese Embassy stating that they would take responsibility for the situation. I took the letter to the Vietnamese Embassy where I was made to wait several hot hours. Finally, after noticing that one particular office seemed to be the busiest with employees going back and forth, I told my son to go into that office. Soon after, following along on my charade, I went to rescue him. My little three-year-old was talking in Vietnamese to a much older Vietnamese dignitary who sat behind a huge desk. The man asked me if he could help and I had my opportunity to explain the situation. Soon after, I left his office with the necessary paperwork. An honest official and my son's innocence and friendliness had won our release. Our little family traveled much of Asia and Europe for the next four months and the memories of our Vietnam hardships were soon dimmed by the fantastic sights of India's Taj Majal, the ancient ruins of Greece, the Swiss Alps, Madrid bull fights, Rome's Vatican City, the Eiffel Tower in Paris, Salzburg and Bavaria and finally our own Statue of Liberty from the deck of a homeward bound luxury liner. It was quite an experience for a little girl from Holbrook, Arizona.

# Chapter 10
## The Sail Of The "Demasiado"

WHEN I THINK OF ALL the crazy things that any of the IBMers did while on assignment in Southeast Asia, the one adventure that immediately comes to mind is the one about the four Customer Engineers who bought a 40 foot sailboat in Hong Kong, sailed it to Vietnam by way of enemy territory and then at the end of their Southeast Asia assignments started out for California across the wide Pacific. From time to time the IBM Corporation would grant time off for what was called "an opportunity of a lifetime" and our Vietnam CEs were definitely going to do something different with that opportunity. Certain adventurous men have always dreamt of buying a boat and sailing away to paradise, but few have actually sailed out of a war zone and few have attempted to cross a major ocean without any previous experience at sea. What follows is the story of the "Demasiado".

When I first arrived in Vietnam, I moved into a two story villa, near the IBM office compound, which was being occupied by a couple of CEs who had already been in country for almost two years and were planning their trip home. I learned a great deal from these men in a short time about operating on a day-to-day basis in and around Saigon. I also learned that in addition to being quite talented and well educated in the disciplines of repairing IBM computers, they were also ruggedly adventurous. They were planning a unique way to return to California. "Let's buy a boat and sail home", someone had suggested months earlier. "We'll take a few months off prior to being re-assigned in the states and see all the exotic islands between Asia and America." The idea jelled and trips were made to Hong Kong and the Choey Lee Shipyard there. An order was placed for one of the newer designed Choey Lee 40s. About my second night in Vietnam, I was talking with my new roommates, Robert McGrath and Ron Vess, and said I was kinda wondering what was going on with the full size boat plan layout that was marked off on the living room tile floor. I mentioned that I had done some sailing during past years. Out came the boat plans that were immediately spread across the living room floor, and the two friends outlined their ideas for sailing home. They wanted to know what I thought. The Choey Lee 40 looked adequate and sea worthy enough for the adventure and I knew that the Choey Lee line of yachts were the finest built, at that time, in the western Pacific. The yachts were relatively slow because of the extra weight of all the teak wood used in the fiberglass overlay, joinery, decks and bright work. She would weigh in at 22,400 pounds, had a beam of 10 feet 9 inches, a draft of 6 feet even and a water line length of only 28 feet (way short by today's designs). She was a yawl and carried 4 tons of cast iron and concrete ballast inside her keel and used a Perkins 36-horse power diesel engine (too small for that boat weight). The sail inventory included working jib, genoa jib, spinnaker, main, mizzen and mizzen staysail. The boat carried 100 gallons of diesel fuel in two tanks and 100 gallons of water in one tank. Masts were aluminum and winches were Australian Barlow 30s. They were going to name her "Demasiado", which means either "proud" or "too much" in Spanish. They were to find that both meanings would apply in the months ahead. I asked Robert and Ron how much sailing they had done and whether they had any celestial navigation experience. The answer to both questions was, "no practical experience at sea, but Robert has taken two correspondence courses from the Coastal Navigation School in Santa Barbara" (Footnote *). "Whoa, this was going to be interesting", I thought to myself.

During the next few months, the two CEs visited Hong Kong on their weekends off to spend time at the Choey Lee yard, to monitor the boat's construction progress and to plan provisioning and their departure dates. They also employed a professional ship surveyor based in Hong Kong who was supposed to certify and approve various construction stages and provide written progress reports until final completion. Soon, the boat was scheduled to be ready, but when Robert arrived at the Choey Lee yard to take delivery, the boat was nowhere near finished. It stood neglected under a shed near many other unfinished hulls. Robert went ahead and completed the paperwork anyway and when he returned to the yard the next day, Demasiado was literally covered with Chinese workers. The following week, the boat was completed, launched, outfitted with compass properly swung and prepared for sea. A short final sea trial, with the yard's surveyor aboard, was done and the adventure was underway. The plan was to sail "Demasiado" the 625 miles to Saigon and moor her in the Saigon River near the Club Nautique until IBM work assignments were finally completed. There were no other sailing yachts of that magnitude in the river or even in the war zone (to my knowledge) and we were all anxious to see the first leg of the adventure completed successfully. The trip was almost a disaster, but allow me to use excerpts from the actual ship's log to describe what happened on the initial shakedown voyage south.

Footnote * - Robert had completed both "Offshore Navigation" and "Celestial Navigation" while in Vietnam. He later told me, "the forms provided by these two courses were great. The celestial work was soon reduced to a noon sun shot. The North Star was also used until we got near and south of the equator where the star was too low on the horizon. Many parts of the offshore navigation course were used - light lists, charts, sailing directions, British Sailing Directions, The Pilot, radio beacons, aero beacons and later we even navigated off Malaysia by using bottom soundings from the depth sounder." I had once sailed down the west coast of Central America in a forty footer and knew that the Southern Cross cluster of stars made an excellent reference as one neared the equator.

## Hong Kong to Da Nang

Crew List:
+ Robert McGrath, 32, Californian
+ Ron Vess, 35, Virginian
+ Harry Hetrick, 28, Pennsylvanian
+ John Stewart, 38, Canadian
+ Duane MacInnis, 23, Canadian
+ Ship's Log:

26 Jan. 1970
6:15 AM    Up anchor and away on time. Departure from Royal

Hong Kong Yacht Club. Motoring through Victoria Harbor at 120 degrees.

12 Noon   Heading of 220 degrees Southeast, bound for RVN.

2:00 PM   Fresh water line broke and all fresh water (100 gal) dumped in bilges. Pumped it overboard (see explanation below).

6:00 PM   Set night watches. Some sea sickness aboard.

27 Jan.

8:00 AM   Heading 190 degrees.

12 Noon   Sun sight places Demasiado at 112 44.3' E Long., 20 1.6 N. Latitude. Heading changed to 210 degrees.

28 Jan.

1:00 AM   Polaris sight position 112 18' E, 19 30' N.

12 Noon   Sun sight position 112 6.1' E, 18 42.5' N.

29 Jan.

7:50 AM   Heading of 210 . Calm and clear. Freighter "Susanne out of Bergen, Norway passed astern, waved and tooted.

12 Noon   Sun sight position 110 38.9' E, 17 16.5' N.

1:00 PM   STEERING LOST, RUDDER POST SHEARED? We try jury rig with rudder and continuing under power.

6:00 PM   Heading of 140 no good. LOST ALL STEERING, RUDDER LOST OR MISSING. Storm squall hits, rigged sea anchor & secure.

30 Jan.

8:00 AM   Still stormy. Heading 140 Put up storm jib and tacked to 320 degrees. No rudder control.

12 Noon   Stormy, cloudy rainy... No noon sun shot.

4:00 PM   Tacked back to 180 degrees.

31 Jan.

8:00 AM   Course variable by 10 or 20 degrees. Sailing about 340 and about 200 on other tack. Jib and mizzen only. Cloudy. Tried several sail combinations to control direction.

12 Noon    Sun sight location 109 36.4' E, 16 57' N.

3:00 PM    Ship to shore communications tried but received only Vietnamese. No response.

1 Feb.

8:00 AM    Various tacks, wind shifty. RDF picks up Hue, Qui Nhon and Da Nang. Got good fix on Qui Nhon only.

12 Noon    Sun sight loc. 108 51.1' E, 16 32.1' N.

8:00 PM    Course 360 degrees North. Flares to west sighted.

12:00 PM    Tack to 180/190 degrees, as best we can.

2 Feb.

3:00 AM    Da Nang night glow sighted. Hooray!

4:00 AM    Ships sighted. Vary pistol fired & strobe lit. "Assistance needed!". U.S. flag raised. No response.

7:00 AM    Cu Lao Cham Island sighted

9:30 AM    John & Harry over the side to check rudder... No rudder!

Mizzen mast boom made into jury rigged rudder by strapping oars on boom to give some steering. Without rudder, boat circles under power. Engine started.

6:00 PM    Da Nang Harbor

7:30 PM    U.S. Navy Harbor Security pick us up & escort to safe anchorage. Secured for night & contacted IBM.

Two events were separately explained by McGrath and follow: "Near evening the first day, Duane entered the main cabin and discovered the bilges full and the floorboards awash. Duane thought we were sinking and wanted to return to Hong Kong immediately. We started the bilge pump and began to look for the leak; we discovered the culprit to be a broken hot water line. The boat's hot water is created by running the water through a heat exchanger on the exhaust manifold of the main engine; our water valves were set wrong, so the water eventually became steam and blew out the line; the demand pump took over and neatly pumped our fresh water tank dry. Our bilges were filled with fresh water, not salt." McGrath didn't say what they drank or cooked with after that, but I hope they had plenty of beer on board.

The second event was described as: "After we lost the rudder, we found that we could only sail across the wind. The prevailing wind for February was southwest so we would sail generally northwest for a number of hours and then southeast for an equal amount of time. Our noon sun shots, therefore, put us on a sailing track directly for our South Vietnam destination (Huh?). We began trying various sail combinations and on a yawl there are quite a few choices. Once, when the crew was setting the spinnaker, the heavy wooden spinnaker pole sky'd (Author's note: they didn't have the knowledge at that time to use a restraining downhaul line prior to setting the chute) and trapped John's arm between the pole and mast. John began yelling for help and thought his arm would break if relief didn't come soon. McGrath was at the helm, but couldn't turn the boat to relieve the pressure without the rudder and the crew finally released a spinnaker sheet and freed John's arm." McGrath said that it seemed like every time they put the spinnaker up, they got into trouble. (Author's note: even experienced racing crews get into trouble with spinnakers; they are big, powerful and unruly in unskilled hands. These men had no previous experience with a spinnaker. On the later leg from Da Nang to Cam Ranh Bay, they tried the spinnaker again in light winds; however when they doused it, the sail went into the sea and filled with water stopping the boat and jamming the spinnaker pole against the mast. The wooden pole exploded and left them only the pole end fittings as reminders of what not to do with a spinnaker).

This account seems pretty matter of fact and the navigation is not much better than good "dead reckoning", but it was good enough! This shakedown cruise indicates the type of things that can go wrong with inexperienced sailors and if a boat is not properly checked out and fully tested prior to a major departure, but our heroes did not have the luxury of sailing around in Hong Kong waters prior to returning to work. Quality control in oriental boatyards was not what it should have been in 1970 and, even so, Choey Lee was probably the best of them. I think what comes out of this brief description is that McGrath and crew were technically skilled enough to overcome difficulties by being innovative, patient and perhaps somewhat lucky. They made the trip in 178 hours for an average speed of 3.5 mph. Soon thereafter, an article appeared in a Vallejo, California, newspaper which describes this initial voyage even better; I quote:

"They wished us well when we sailed out of Hong Kong but said we were crazy for going", said Robert McGrath, skipper of the 40-foot yawl "Demasiado". McGrath is skipper of a 40-foot yawl that limped into DaNang harbor after drifting six days without a rudder. McGrath had taken a correspondence course in navigation, but none of the five (crew) had ever been to sea. They set sail Jan. 25 and made good time for the first 3 days, though all admitted to being seasick. On the third night they realized the boat was steering in a tight circle and would not respond to the wheel. They discovered the steel rudderpost connecting the rudder and wheel was split in two places. The craft drifted all the next day and weathered a storm with 15-foot waves breaking over the deck that night. 'We felt like dice in a crap game', Stewart wrote in his diary. When the sea calmed, the crew dived under the hull to repair the rudder. It was gone. McGrath's charts showed they were between Communist Chinese Hainan Island and the treacherous Paracel Reefs about 150 miles east of the South Vietnamese coast. They hoisted sail to take advantage of the westerly wind but discovered that without the rudder the boat tended to head into the wind rather than run before it. McGrath set a zigzag course, first north, then south, and drifted west with the prevailing breeze. 'I'll have to admit there were times when I didn't think we were going to make it', McGrath said. 'Our radios wouldn't work and we were afraid to signal other ships until we knew we were out of communist shipping lanes'. When they did spot some ships offshore, he added, the yacht's flares didn't attract any attention. 'I was concerned', Hetrick said, 'It was the first time I'd ever been on a sailboat in my life and we hadn't seen land since we left Hong Kong. I had worked in Danang before and I knew that if we drifted too far north we'd come up on unfriendly beaches.' McGrath's navigation proved accurate and the Demasiado sailed into DaNang harbor Monday night. 'The US Navy harbor security patrol met us in the river.' Vess said. 'They wanted to know who we were and what the hell we were doing. I guess they hadn't seen many pleasure yachts come in before. One of them asked if we knew there was a war on.' The boat was tied up at the harbor security pier and a damage control man, L.C. Stanley Fain, of Kentucky, began designing a new rudder for the craft. McGrath and his crew will sail south for Saigon next week. The three Americans say they plan to take 18 months leave of absence next January and cruise across the Pacific to San Francisco." End of news article.

The adventurers made it to Saigon a few weeks later, but not without another incident. They lost the second rudder and had to limp into Cam Ranh Bay under similar conditions and results, but, at least it was in friendlier waters and they had more sailing experience under their belts. The boat was soon tied to a mooring in front of Saigon's yacht club and the pretty yawl lent a bit of class to the barges and war ships which were its neighbors. Talk about an anachronism! Through the summer months which followed and when the monsoon rains were not too severe, the IBM sailors used their big beautiful toy on weekends and days off for parties and short river sails. They developed some sail handling capability on the narrow twisting river as well as some confidence needed for the next part of their adventure. They also found out that one can sail and drink beer at the same time (a well known capability among seasoned sailors). I did hear about one afternoon on the Saigon River that may have been a first in the entire history of sail - they were sailing downwind with spinnaker up and seriously ripped the light weight sail by running into a large jungle tree! IBM work assignments neared completion and the boys began their departure plans for their next sail to Bangkok, Thailand. Again, I will borrow from excerpts of Demasiado's log book.

## Saigon to Bangkok

Crew List:
+ Robert McGrath
+ Hank Wholihan
+ Ron Vess
+ Lee Goff
+ Bud Bjorge
+ Kieth Murphy
+ Mike Dwyer

(Author's Note: This group of Customer Engineers was key to our maintenance responsibilities in Saigon, so a great deal of anxiety accompanied this particular sail of the Demasiado. McGrath took a well balanced highly technical support group with him, and almost left our branch office high and dry.)

Ship's Log

21 Nov. 1970

| | |
|---|---|
| 0830 | Customs Dock for Checkout |
| 1300 | Slipped mooring & departed down river. |
| 1800 | Vung Tao Harbor. |
| 2130 | Offshore, heading 205 degrees |

22 Nov.

| | |
|---|---|
| 0400 | Main & jib set. |
| 0700 | Light winds, jib down, genoa up. |
| 0900 | RDF fix on Vung Tao aft and Phau Thiet ahead. |
| 1200 | Heading of 238 degrees and got good noon sun shot. |
| 1400 | Heading change to 320 degrees. |
| 1800 | Heading 205. Circled by Vietnamese patrol boat #701. No wind & under power rest of night. |

23 Nov. 1970  Birthday at sea, McGrath turns 33. No cake.

| | |
|---|---|
| 0500 | Got polaris shot. Heading 180 degrees. Circled and hailed by U.S. Navy patrol boat; asked to display our ensign and if we needed any assistance. |
| 0800 | Both batteries dead. Wrong switch left on; engine won't start. More @&*#@*. Charged batteries with Honda generator. |
| 1030 | Out of gasoline for Honda, but was able to start engine with both batteries. Hooray, motoring and charging. |
| 1200 | Noon sun shot. Position is 105 6.5' E, 8 14.3' N. |
| 1300 | U.S. Navy patrol alongside. Did we need anything? 26 hours of motoring; where's the wind? |

| 24 Nov. | Into the Gulf of Siam |
| 0100 | Heading 320 & passing many fishing trawlers |
| 0700 | Hon Panjang Island sighted |
| 1200 | Noon sun shot. Pos. is 103 32.9' S, 9 48.8' N. |
| 1300 | School of playful porpoises all about - for about ten miles |
| 1500 | Sea now full of sea snakes. Crew took turns on bow with my .30 cal. Ruger Blackhawk killing snakes. |
| 1630 | Fixes on islands. Kas Tang and Poulo Wai. |
| 2200 | Change course to 350 to avoid islands ahead. |
| 2300 | Tropical deluge, squall. All sails down and heading 290 to get around island |
| 2400 | Back to heading of 318 degrees. |
| | |
| 25 Nov. | Uneventful day on heading of 318 degrees |
| 1200 | Noon sun shot. Position is 101 57.6'E, 11 21' N. |
| | |
| 26 Nov. | |
| 0200 | Group flashing red lights ahead. Change heading to 290 degrees. |
| 0400 | Back to heading of 320. |
| 0700 | Engine off, sails up. Heading 295 degrees. |
| 0900 | Entered Sattahip Harbor. Anchor down. |
| 1000 | Got some help from Navy School and Thai Navy to find customs and immigrations. Waited for officials. |
| 1500 | Anchor up. Sattahip to Pattaya. Heading 300 degrees. |
| 1800 | Several beacons. Orange light used for bearing. |
| 1900 | Correct Pattaya beacon identified. The orange light was the burn off from the oil refinery above Pattaya. |
| 2000 | Anchor down and secure for the night. |
| | |
| 27 Nov. | |
| 0930 | Drove to Bangkok to clear immigrations. Took all day. |
| 1630 | Cleared, except for Wholihan who didn't show up from Pattaya. |

| | |
|---|---|
| 2230 | Vess and McGrath return to Pattaya to bring boat up river to Bangkok. Rest of the crew scatter for good times and return to Saigon. |

**28 Nov.**

| | |
|---|---|
| 0630 | Depart Pattaya. Motor sailing in high wind from N.W. |
| 1500 | Spotted lightship and pilots off Bangkok Bar. |
| 1600 | Stopped by customs boat and went ashore for declarations. One Thai official put aboard for rest of trip. |
| 2130 | Moored alongside customs because drawbridge was down. Searched for contraband by several customs officials. |

**29 Nov.**

| | |
|---|---|
| 0630 | False start up river as bridge did not open as scheduled at 0600. Walked to bridge, phone wouldn't work. Finally logged a 10 AM passage. |
| 0940 | On station waiting for bridge. Opened exactly at 1000 and we powered through to our shipyard. |
| 1030 | All secured. McGrath departs for Saigon. R. Vess in charge of re-provisioning and maintenance for next leg of trip home. |

This was the end of the log entries for a while. Demasiado was hauled out at the Bangkok shipyard for cleaning, hull inspection and new bottom paint. The trip described above took a little over 8 days to go approximately 750 miles and again demonstrates a certain innate skill and patience on the part of McGrath and his crew. It also indicates a lack of wind and a relatively slow boat by today's standards. The boat needed maintenance after spending the monsoon season in the slimy Saigon River and there was work to do to prepare for the long Pacific journey ahead.

After refurbishing and laying on stores, McGrath and his three sailing friends - Bob Brubaker, Jerry Evans and Ron Vess - departed Bangkok and headed southeast across the Pacific bound for California. They had visions of tropical beaches, warm nights and warm maidens plus an enthusiasm born from a few tough years in Vietnam, hoping for more peaceful adventures on the many islands that lay ahead, 18 months to pursue an opportunity of a lifetime. Their first destination was Singapore and in route they watched British Commandos in training on the small island of Palau Tioman. From Singapore they headed east through the Java Sea to exotic Bali (which at that time was still relatively unspoiled by tourism) where they encountered mine fields, an aggressive tanker, whales and pirates. Next came the small island of Palau Komodo, but they didn't see any of the famed Komodo dragons; rather, they made some friends by helping some children who had been seriously burned. Next came Timor and eastward across the Arafura Sea to Australia's Thursday Island in the Torres Strait. Demasiado and crew were doing fine, but the high humidity and heat of sailing along 10 degrees South latitude are poor shipmates and when they arrived made the island's Australian Grand Hotel extra special. They relaxed and saw a few movies at this northern most extremity of Australia. Soon after the next departure they experienced some extreme currents, tides and reefs in the Torres Straits area. Sea sickness remained a problem. A schedule of weekly radio contacts with friends in California was established about this time and our adventurers were able to talk with relatives and girl friends via phone patch procedures. Mail was received at various points along the way via general delivery "Post Restante". Another 600 miles easting past the Warrior Reefs and Murray Islands finally brought them to Port Moresby, Papua New Guinea where the Port Moresby Yacht Club, a side trip to the central highlands town of Mount Hagen and a yacht race provided some needed diversion. They had safely cruised the thousand Islands of Indonesia and the northern extent of the Great Barrier Reef. Robert even took a few days personal break from the sailing and flew back to Vietnam to visit a Vietnamese girl friend and rejoined his crew again in Port Moresby. Many of us, like Robert, had warm ties and tough goodbyes in Vietnam.

Moving *"Ever Onward"* (ancient IBM song sung at Sales School), our sailors cleared the east end of New Guinea and next visited Trobriand Island, famous for being the home of the original bungi jumpers, and then across the Solomon Sea to Honiara on Guadalcanal Island. There they had some adventures at the local yacht club, had to employ a local mechanic and somehow temporarily lost Demasiado. A self-steering device was finally installed on the stern for the long trip ahead. Demasiado experienced a spreader dip knock down (boat actually lays over 180 degrees on her side with mast spreaders touching the water) the first evening out of Honiara, but had no damage from the sudden squall other than to the crew's mental condition and a mess in the main cabin. Next came an attempt by Demasiado and crew to plow a trench through the coral heads of Parkington Reef (little damage except to navigator's ego) on their way southeast to the New Hebrides. When asked about his navigation, Bob said that Parkington was such a little dot on such a huge ocean, he didn't think they could possibly hit it. They stopped at Efate to enjoy a local pub and see more movies before sailing on to Suva, the capital of the Fiji Islands (Author's note: I spent two wonderful months in the late 70s cruising the waters around Fiji and can easily identify with the Demasiado and her crew at this destination. The beauty and cruising grounds of Fiji are still a well kept secret).

Unfortunately, skipper McGrath became seriously ill with appendicitis and spent more time in Suva than planned--ten days in their hospital. Demasiado sailed east northeast and McGrath rejoined the crew in Western Samoa, minus his appendix. There are more stories about good times at famed Aggie Grey's Hotel, friends and girlfriends, but by now the boys are tired of the constant sailing and pressures to reach California. More boat troubles lay just ahead. On the way to Pago Pago, American Samoa, the "#$%%#@&" rudder shaft broke again, and with the 3,000 miles of Pacific between them and Hawaii, the broken rudder gave good reason to change plans. They limped back into Apia, Western Samoa whereupon Jerry, Bob and McGrath flew home to the good ol' USA and Ron stayed to make arrangements to deck-ship Demasiado to San Pedro, California in a cradle.

Demasiado finally reached its San Francisco destination on a truck bed amid talks between the sailing friends about another cruise to Hawaii that coming summer. Work and money requirements reared their ugly heads, social aspects of life here on solid land became complex and a future Pacific sail for the Demasiado soon became a dream in history. Demasiado was eventually sold to a cruising type, who planned to cross the Pacific in the right direction - east to west. I do not believe that any of the four have done much sailing since, but with so many peoples and islands seen, it truly was an opportunity of a lifetime for these IBMers. What an adventurous way to come home from a war!

# Chapter 11
## War Zone Memoirs By Ed Baker

THE FOLLOWING PAGES ARE FROM the memory of IBM Customer Engineer, Ed Baker, written for this book many years after his four-year assignment in South Vietnam. Ed had an adventurous spirit, was a valuable asset to both IBM and the military and is a good storyteller, as you will read.

"I joined the IBM Corporation in October 1963 as a Customer Engineer trainee. By February of 1966 I was working in Reno, Nevada fixing machines, but was dissatisfied with my position and personal life. I notified my IBM manager that, in a few months, I wanted to quit and return to school. I had no idea what I wanted to major in; I really just wanted to change my life and "returning to school" was socially acceptable. Some weeks after that conversation with my manager a notice was posted that there was to be a branch CE meeting for a major corporate announcement. IBM was looking for single CE's to work in support of the US Military in South Vietnam. My immediate response was, "I will go". I did not pay any attention to the mention that there would be pay incentives. I was just interested in the overseas adventure aspect. Since my manager was already looking for a replacement for me there was no objections on his side. But, weeks went by with no further action by IBM. I was in the mood to go, but disappointed that IBM was not doing anything to tell me where or when. Finally I took a day off, drove to San Francisco, looked up the Control Data Corp ("CDC") office address and presented myself to the office manager as an IBM computer technician who wanted to go to Vietnam as a CDC computer technician. After signing a paper that CDC had not recruited me, and being told to expect a phone call in a few days I returned to Reno. In a few days I did receive a phone call offering me a position in South Vietnam where I would work for two years and then be transferred to a European assignment for an additional two years; my start date would be in four weeks, I would attend a one month training class in the USA and then relocate to Saigon. (Author's note: Ed was fortunate that he did not accept the CDC offer, because, to my knowledge, CDC had very few machines for him to maintain in Vietnam) Ah, this is the way a company should function. The next day I told my boss I was giving four weeks notice, and why.

The very next morning, I received a phone call from someone identifying himself as an IBM Vice President in Armonk, New York (IBM HQ). He apologized for the delay in communicating with me, but if I would reconsider my employment termination IBM was prepared to have me fly to Hawaii in three weeks as the first step toward the Vietnam assignment. I told him I would think it over. The next day I told my manager I would not accept CDC's offer and would happily remain an IBMer. I then had to make a very embarrassing phone call to the CDC manager.

Within a few weeks I got my passport in the mail - since this was my first one I did not recognize the perks of having a red passport saying that the bearer was traveling for the benefit of the US Government - this passport was later stolen in Saigon and the replacement, alas, was the normal non-diplomat blue. Finally, in July of 1966, I was on my way. When I landed in Honolulu, I was met by the Branch Manager, Bob Tanner. On the same incoming flight was Carl Williams, a CE from Philadelphia, also going to Vietnam. The three of us waited for another flight bringing CE Ron Hawn. Bob then took all three of us to the Outrigger Hotel. There were no reservations but after some haggling, we ended up in a three-bedroom suite with about 30 feet of glass walls overlooking Waikiki beach. Nice to travel first class! We received some briefings at the Honolulu Branch office, enjoyed a few fine days in Honolulu and then left for more orientation at Camp Zama, Japan, IBM Branch Office 560. Ron had a serious case of sunburn.

We were met at the Tokyo airport by Milt somebody driving his own car in Tokyo, and getting lost trying to find Camp Zama (about 25 miles southwest of central Tokyo). We had two or three weeks at Zama doing not much of anything except being tourists in Tokyo. Karl, Ron and I rode the bullet train and spent a couple of days in Kyoto - that was certainly interesting as we stayed in a Ryokan hotel where no one spoke English. Karl, being large and very black really stood out and gathered a lot of attention wherever we went. After a trip to Yokohama I vowed to never ask a Japanese for help. I wanted to take the train to Yokohama. The train station was confusing and so when I saw a Japanese businessman I crossed my fingers that he spoke English and asked him where I could get a ticket. He did speak English, asked me a few questions about where in Yokohama I wanted to go and then got in line with me. When our turn at the window came he talked to the clerk and then told me how much to pay. I thanked him and he said he would show me which train to take. When he said to get on this one I thanked him very much, again. Then he got on the train with me and showed me my seat. I again really thanked him and then he sat down! He had bought a round-trip ticket to Yokohama also just to make sure I got off at the right station. Unbelievable.

In August 1966 we finally departed, by PanAm for Saigon, with an authorized two day layover at the Hong Kong Hilton. First class again! From Hong Kong, Carl went to Bangkok for some special training, and Ron and I went to Saigon.

The landing at Saigon was interesting in that the PanAm pilot made a very steep descent so as to provide a tougher target from any ground unfriendlies. We went through customs, got our luggage, walked out to the main terminal and did not see anyone who looked like they were waiting for us - this was a bit upsetting. But, when we walked out of the airport to the street, Larry Leskanitch walked up to us, asked if we were IBM, and when we said yes, took us over to Ron Vess and his car, parked in a red zone in front of the terminal, He handed each of us a shot glass of whisky, and said, "Welcome to Saigon". The way a company should be run! Ben Burdette( was the FE manager when I arrived. IBM had two villas across the street from each other. The original villa was where the manager and a few CEs stayed and was also the administrative office and bar. The "new" villa across the street was where the rest of the CEs stayed and it served as the parts office and storage. I think Ron Hawn and I were the 7th and 8th IBM-USA CEs in country. Burdette and CEs Larry Lesknitch, Ron Vess and Jeff Baker were there ahead of us.

Actually fixing equipment was not much different in Vietnam than anywhere else, just more difficult travel and logistics problems. Most of my memories then are not of unusual machine maintenance problems but rather of places, people, and traveling – always traveling!

Since I had IBM telecommunications experience (and in the early 1960s not many CEs could say that) I ended up with a Top Secret clearance with a Crypto endorsement. This allowed me to take service calls at secure Stratcom communication centers. There were feelers put out about submitting me for a NSA (National Security Agency) clearance - I knew about this from my own military experience and said that under no circumstances would I want one. The few IBMers that had that clearance had to initially have bodyguards with them (later relaxed) if they went out of country to Hong Kong and other such locations. Not for me, I wanted freedom, not a high level clearance.

Since my expertise was unit record and telecommunications equipment and not computer systems there was no functional requirement that I could only work in Saigon. I wanted to see the country so immediately volunteered for taking upcountry calls. These calls all involved going to Tan Son Nhut and finding a military flight going to where I needed to go and then making a reservation. After a few such trips I found an Army officer that cut me some special orders allowing me to fly on any military aircraft since I was traveling in support of the military. My orders allowing me to be in Vietnam gave me (as explained in an earlier chapter) the equivalent of a GS-13. After getting the army orders I never had problems flying on anything. I flew in USAF, USN, Army, Air America, and RMK/BRJ (one of the main American construction firms used by the military to build roads, bridges, airports, etc.) aircraft and twice in the cockpit of Air Vietnam in-country flights. These orders were re-issued every 12 months by different Army groups. I think I accumulated more air hours than any other CE, probably more land miles too. I had the army issue me a driver's license, allowing me to drive anything up to and including a 2 ½ ton truck. I used this license once to check a jeep out of the motor pool in Qui Nhon just to see if I could, and twice to check out a truck in Cam Ranh Bay when there was a lot of IBM equipment to be moved. To be on the safe side, since we drove a lot, Gene Murdock and I also got Vietnamese drivers licenses. We had to take a written test, which we passed by giving the person that was in charge of the scoring a bottle of Johnny Walker Red.

I worked with two CEs from IBM Korea, Mr. Koo and Mr Kim. They were stationed, as I recall, in Qui Nhon. They did not have any kind of security clearance and once I had to have a second CE help me on a Stratcom call. Only Mr. Koo was available which put the Stratcom commander in a bind. Finally we figured out how to drape a lot of blankets from the security entrance to where Mr. Koo needed to work so that he could not see anything secret except a portion of the 360/20 computer system that he needed to service. The Koreans were corporately interesting to us CEs. They were on loan from IBM World trade prior to the assignment of IBM Americans. There were several other Korean CEs, but I do not remember their names or where they were working. They were also able to fly in military aircraft as Mr. Koo went upcountry several times. I think Mr. Koo went on to fill a high-level management position in IBM Korea - he certainly was polite, spoke good English, knew his equipment and was an exceedingly hard worker. Gene Murdock, Carl Williams and I always addressed the Koreans as Mister "(last name)". We never called them by their first names. (Author's Note: Ed was probably not aware that South Korea had the second largest contingent of foreign troops in South Vietnam after the United States. They had the reputation of being ferocious fighters, "Take No prisoners". Approximately 320,000 South Korean soldiers served one-year tours of duty and their in-country numbers peaked to a level of 50,000 men in 1968. They were all withdrawn by 1973. Mr. Koo may have been quite comfortable near all those countrymen).

A service call that sticks in my mind was one that came in over our IBM radio network. The caller identified himself as an Army technician calling from a location in Thailand that he was not allowed to identify. "They" were setting up a new remote data processing center and had transferred some equipment there that had been previously working. His problem was that a 407 would not power up. He had been trying for the last two hours to determine what the problem was and finally had been ordered to contact us for help. It took me about 5 minutes to identify the problem. There was no power to the wall outlet that he had plugged the 407 into. It then took him only two minutes to determine that the wall outlet was not connected to anything. I didn't need much traini ng for that one.

The most interesting service call I had was in Pleiku, First Cav HQ. The army had, at some time before the Vietnam War, taken IBM 047s and put them into Conexes, along with a radio transmitter. I had worked on 047s at Sierra Ordinance Center in California. For the 98% of you IBMers that have never even heard of an 047: this was an 026 standard keypunch that was modified so that when the holes in an IBM punched card were read, the information was converted into an analog signal that would normally be transmitted over a phone line to a distant 047 that in turn would punch an identical card. Not very sophisticated, just early teleprocessing. Well, there weren't any phone lines in the Vietnam highlands! What the army had done with the equipment was convert the output signal to one that could be radio transmitted, (ie. the radio transmission took the place of phone lines). By being in a Conex (a metal box about 10' by 10' by 8') the military could put 047s on a plane, or attach them to a helicopter, and fly the Conex to a forward command area. The only other requirement would be a generator to provide power. The First Cav had four of these units. They did not work because they probably had been sitting, back in the states, unused for several years. To get them functional the Department of the Army sent two radio technicians to Pleiku and IBM sent me. I was in Pleiku, living in a tent, for several weeks. I tried to troubleshoot, but ended up placing new contacts in most of the relays in the four 047s because the existing wires were flat where they rested against the contact bar and thus any dust or accumulated grime prevented a contact. Once all the contacts had been replaced the troubleshooting was much more straight forward. Working with the radio people was interesting, and finally we did get the units to work. Whether or not the Cav actually used them I do not know, as I never saw them again. I was given an IBM Means Service award, mostly for this work in Pleiku.

The military also used 1013s to transmit data. These were a bit of a bother to work on as they were hard to test. To preserve my sanity I did design a loop-back test circuit. I never received any acknowledgement from IBM about this idea, other than the standard "thank you for your submission". I modified every 1013 I worked on in Vietnam as it really saved testing time.

The first American CE in Vietnam was, I think, Jeff Baker. He was flown in as needed from Korea and then transferred to Saigon, as was Ron Vess. When he was transferred to Saigon Jeff shipped in his car, a red Triumph Herald convertible. When he rotated back to the USA, I was living in Saigon and bought his car. Although I drove it mostly in Saigon, I also made a few trips to Bien Hoa, where it was pretty much out of place and always stared at by the American combat troops. I had no thought of maintaining a low profile, figuring if I was going to get shot at it did not make any difference what I was driving. In August of 1967 I was transferred up to Nha Trang and IBM provided me with a company owned Toyota Land Cruiser, so I sold the Triumph.

When I was living in Saigon it seemed to me that it would be a good idea to have a weapon, at least to keep in the house; break-ins were common and, being Americans, we were automatically "the enemy" to the 'cowboys' and part time VC. I subsequently checked out a revolver from the Air Force. A month or so later a missive arrived from IBM management at Camp Zama saying, in no unclear terms, that "any employee who thinks it is necessary to carry a weapon in South Vietnam can get on the next flight back to the United States". This certainly rubbed me the wrong way, since I was the only person who, at least openly, had a weapon. I seriously thought about taking the next plane back to the states. Not that I was worried about being in South Vietnam without a weapon but rather the tone of the memo, and it being sent by someone who had no idea about the living conditions in Vietnam. Ben Burdette, my CE manager, counseled me to respond when my head was cooler. I decided that I would rather be where I was than not, so I bit my lip and turned in the gun. Of course, as there got to be more IBMers in country and most had weapons, some even issued by IBM (MACV M-2s), that early memo was forgotten (Author's Note: IBM's official position remained "No personal weapons!").

I purchased another pistol in Taiwan, and later bought an AK-47 from a Special Forces guy. Getting ammo for the AK was never a problem, I would just take a couple of six-packs to the nearest Special Forces enclave and walk away with however much ammo I wanted. Fortunately I never had to fire for protection. Once in a while who ever was staying in Nha Trang at the time and I would go to a nearby abandoned coconut plantation and shoot up a few trees. The only time I fired the rifle other than to make holes in trees was when Gene Murdock and I were driving up to Qui Nhon. The road was two-lane and passing was always a difficult act due to curves, potholes and on-coming traffic. We were stuck behind a Vietnamese bus that was driving in the middle of the road, moving over only to let opposite traffic get by. After about 20 minutes of this, I told Gene, who was driving, to try and pass the bus. When Gene pulled out the bus moved over in the way. I fired off about 5 rounds and the bus immediately jumped to the right, driving on the shoulder to give us maximum room - an early example of road rage.

IBM domestic had a policy for CEs that any assignment outside the USA would be for at least two years, and a CE could only have two such assignments. I had stated that I would like to remain in Vietnam as long as possible, so at the end of my first two years I was reassigned there. My manager at the time wanted me to have some more equipment training so I was scheduled for class time in Chicago and Los Angeles before starting my second tour. I also wanted some personal time off so there was a break of almost a year between ending my first two years and starting the second. I took advantage of the return to the USA and purchased a six-foot long airline ticket: Saigon-Bangkok-New Delhi-Moscow-Leningrad-Copenhagen-Paris-London-San Francisco-Chicago-San Francisco-Los Angeles-San Francisco-Los Angeles-Tahiti-American Samoa-Western Samoa-Fuji-Singapore-Bangkok and back to Saigon! Gene Murdock and I traveled together to India, Russia, Denmark and France (to view the French Grand Prix), then Gene went somewhere and I went to England for a couple of months to check out Scientology. The time Gene and I spent traveling is a story by itself, as is my return through the South Pacific. However, they have nothing to do with IBM so are not included here.

Once when I was driving from Nha Trang to Cam Ranh Bay I was passed by red MG! It had a male driver and two female passengers, all of which looked to be in their 20s and most certainly French. There was, even then, a small French community outside Saigon. There was an empty, but well maintained, French plantation house between Nha Trang and Cam Ranh Bay. When Dan Feltham was on an upcountry inspection tour we took him there (Dan speaks of it elsewhere).

One time Gene and I drove into the Central Highlands to Ban Me

Thuot because I had read about a hunting bar/restaurant that was popular with the French. We needed an excuse so we told everyone that we were doing an inspection of IBM equipment that was supposed to be there - we knew that there was none. The building we were looking for, sadly, had been blown up. We did talk to a few local Frenchmen in a non-descript bar; they were still living in the area. They paid tribute to both side, the NVA and to the local South Vietnam officials, and were not bothered by either. They said that farming was too difficult to do anymore because of the US Army driving tanks and trucks everywhere, and that ranching was impossible because the NVA shot the cattle for food and the local officials stole their horses. They were mainly still there because it was their home and they did not want to have squatters in their houses or on their land. They had sent all the family females and children to France; their hope was that once the Americans got tired of the war and went home they could go back to running their plantations, regardless of what type of government came along, so they simply waited and drank.

Another time I decided that it should be safe to drive from Nha Trang to Saigon, going via Dalat, so Gene, who was always open to road trips, and either Karl Williams or Bob Dillon, drove with me to Dalat the first day. We were not able to drive from Dalat to Saigon in one day as we had a flat tire and, as the spare was also flat, we had to get both fixed. We ended up, to the southwest, at nightfall in Bao Loc on highway 20. We asked the tire fixer where the French hung out and were directed to a bar/restaurant. Sure enough, two tables with drinking Frenchmen. One of them lowered himself to speak English. We asked him if it was OK to drive after dark, he shrugged, in a true French-like gesture, and said that he did. We then asked him if there was a hotel in town. He identified a local whorehouse with some extra rooms usually available without having to purchase a woman. I had no association with the French in Saigon, but upcountry found them always helpful, if not overly friendly. We did go to the identified location, I slept alone and Gene didn't - the next morning he said he was quite satisfied.

As an aside, when I first arrived in Saigon I had to deal with the US Embassy on some matter and found the people there exceedingly unhelpful, unfriendly even. IBM did not have any formal emergency evacuation plans at this time, or ever did that I knew of (Author: Apparently Ed didn't know about the four water ski boats on the Saigon River). I went to the British Embassy, identified myself as an ex-colonial whose ancestors had come to the Americas in the 1600s from England, and could they, the Embassy, help me if there were problems and if the Americans would not. The response was "if you need to get out of the country in a hurry and cannot go any other way come and see us, we will get you out." I thought that was the way an embassy should be run!

In the four years I lived in Vietnam I was only sick three times. Gene and I wanted to fill in our roads traveled. We regularly drove from Nha Trang to Qui Nhon and then often into the highlands to An Khe and Pleiku. We decided that it was time to drive to Da Nang and then, with some of the CEs resident in Da Nang, went on to the DMZ, (Author: a trip up highway 1 of well over 250 miles! Crazy!) This we did, spending the night in Hue. Our Vietnamese secretary in Da Nang decided that she wanted to go with us. This was good, as sometimes it was convenient to have someone along that could speak both English and Vietnamese. When we got to Hue we found a small hotel. Later came the sleeping problem, as there were not rooms for everyone. The secretary asked if she could share a room with me as she did not sleep with Americans, and of all that were on that trip, she thought that I would leave her alone (perhaps a dubious compliment?). It was one of those good news bad news situations. So I agreed. But, there were Vietnamese soldiers sitting in the hall and when we retired for the night they started making crude, and somewhat threatening, comments about Americans and their Vietnamese whores..

We went to bed. I awoke with the horrible feeling of immanent diarrhea. The rooms, of course, did not have attached bathrooms. They were down the hall. For the sake of the modesty of Miss Hua, I was sleeping in my underpants. I made it to the bathroom, but not quite to the toilet. After washing and disposing of my now useless underpants in the trash barrel, I pranced nude back to the room and the seemingly sleeping Miss Hua. I put on another set of underpants and went back to bed. I'm glad to say, that was the only case of diarrhea I ever had in Vietnam, but a somewhat common ailment.

My second sickness was a bit different. I was at an army base in the highlands. I remember I was putting print wires into a 026 keypunch - a thankless task, with several army types watching me. My next memory was two days later of crawling, nude, like a snake, across the floor of my Saigon villa to the bathroom so that I could lie under the shower to cool off my burning up body. No in-between memories at all. Apparently, I finished the keypunch repair, packed up my stuff, got out to the landing field, caught a flight to Saigon and got a taxi from Tan San Nhut to my villa, all without thought or memory? I don't know what that was. My third sickness was social and of little interest.

I wanted to visit as much of South Vietnam as I could and I usually traveled alone. Gene and Bob Dillon and I drove to Dalat, but I made two other trips there without IBM companions - going to Dalat was for fun, there were no military bases there, no business reason to go there. One of the highlights of my life happened on the first Dalat trip. We stayed at the Dalat Palace, 'the' hotel at the time. On our first evening there we ate in the hotel dining room and ordered wine. I was the designated taster, and the wine was so bad that I told the waiter it was not acceptable - all my life I had wanted to be able to send a bottle back. He did bring a different bottle that was OK. The first one was probably from a batch of Algerian that they kept for Americans, figuring that we would accept anything.

An interesting aspect of Dalat was that there was an atomic reactor there intended to produce electricity!!! It was put in under the Eisenhower administration's "Atoms for Peace" program. There was also a major dam and a cog railroad to the coast. The dam was intact, but the cog railroad had been rendered unusable by both sides in the war. Dalat, being in the highlands, had been the second home to the moneyed French and Vietnamese elite, also a lot of nice colonial villas. A few miles outside Dalat was a waterfall that was considered the romantic place to take a date. Not really much of a waterfall, but actually the only one I ever saw in Vietnam.

One time I flew down to Saigon, borrowed a car, and with Bob Dillon drove to My Tho in the Mekong delta. This involved a few local ferryboats and a lot of local looks. We stopped in the middle of nowhere at an open-air restaurant to get something cool to drink. We assumed that not many American civilians stopped there. By the time we finished our drinks there were at least 20 persons, mostly kids, watching us and when we left we could see several more running across the fields to see the American civilians.

One of my more memorable trips, almost surrealistic, was while driving to An Khe. The road was completely deserted - not an unusual situation. In the middle of a beautiful valley was a single forested hill. There was also one jet in the sky, making continuous dives at the hill and firing one rocket on each pass. Then, on a road between An Khe and Pleiku I was driving close to a forest and an elephant came out of the woods, looked at me, and went back into the forest. There were very few wild elephants left in Vietnam and I felt privileged to have seen one. I wonder how many were killed by the war?

Immediately after the Americans invaded Cambodia and then withdrew, Gene Murdock and I decided that it was time to travel from Phnom Penh, Cambodia to Saigon by road, a trip of approximately 150 miles. We flew to Bangkok, and then to Phnom Penh. We stayed at the Hotel Le Royale, because it was where the press that had covered the invasion stayed and we figured that they would be the best source of information on how to proceed. We contacted a man who owned a Mercedes, who had been renting to various reporters and told him what we wanted to do. He said that he could not take us all the way to the Vietnam border, but that he would take us as far as possible. It helped that he still had a "PRESS" placard in the front window. He would pick us up at 9 AM the next morning, so we closed the bar with the press corps late that night - a hard-drinking group.

A white Mercedes pulled up right on time the next morning. We put our two attaché cases with our change of clothes in the trunk and took off. There were many, many roadblocks manned by Cambodian soldiers. The driver explained that we were press corps and they waved us on. We came to a very long line of cars and trucks waiting to cross a canal that had been bombed and the bridge had been replaced by a two-car barge. Our driver simply drove on the shoulder of the road past everyone and straight to the barge. We were the next car on - ah, the power of the press. At one roadblock the soldier, all of probably 16 years old, would not accept the words of our driver. He demanded our IDs. I told the driver to tell him that we just got into the country the day before, our passports and IDs were all with his Immigration Office but that we were so eager to see his country that we did not want to wait for our official papers. The soldier then demanded some proof of who we were. I gave him Bob Dillon's official looking AmThai business card (Bob had left IBM at the end of his assignment to get married and remain in Thailand) and showed him the Bangkok address and phone number. I said he could phone that number and they would verify that we were Bob Dillon and his assistant. The soldier accepted the lie and let us pass.

Finally, at a village the Mercedes driver said he could go no further, that the country was under the control of the South Vietnamese. But, he did talk to the driver of a small bus and the bus would take us as far as possible. However, we would have to sit in the middle of the bus so as not to be easily seen and at each checkpoint to crouch down. The bus was stopped several times, but only once did the soldiers seriously look at the passengers. Since they were Vietnamese we held up our American passports and they nodded and let us go. After a while the bus stopped and everybody got off. The driver looked around and then came back with a young man. The driver pointed to us, and then him and then down the road. The young man had a motor scooter. So, just like locals, all three of us hopped on the motor scooter, Gene and I each holding our attaché cases in one hand and the back of the person in front with the other. We congratulated ourselves on deciding to only take one briefcase each on this trip. The motor scooter trip lasted a very long half hour, then he stopped and we got off. He pointed to a shot up sign that identified the Cambodia Vietnam frontier. I was really sorry I had not brought a camera, but had felt, and I think rightly so, that there was too big a chance for it to be stolen or confiscated. We held out the remainder of our Cambodian money and the driver took some of it, waved and left.

The Cambodian customs post was off to the right and Vietnam's in front of us. We decided that there might be a problem on exiting Cambodia since we obviously should not have been able to get here in the first place, so entered the Vietnamese customs post. We said "Hello?" and an overweight Vietnamese appeared. We showed him our passports and said we wanted to enter Vietnam. He spoke a little English and asked, "Why". I replied "Tourist". He called out and two other Vietnamese appeared. He chatted with them, turned to us and said, "You first tourists in three years!" They brought us tea and crackers. After about a half hour we said we needed to leave as we had to get to Saigon and it was getting late. The official said, "difficult" and walked us to the door. He pointed down the road and said, "Army, one kilometer". We thanked him and now in Vietnam, walked to the Vietnamese Army post.

We stopped at a gate and a Vietnamese Major came out and asked who we were and what we wanted. We said we were businessmen working with the US Army and we needed to go to Saigon. He said that he could not take us to Saigon, but he could take us to the main highway where we might catch a bus. He came back in a fairly new French Citroen with Cambodian license plates. "Nice, no? War spoils", he said. On the way to the highway he explained his need for a US Army jeep. We said we would do what we could to help him so he gave us his name and phone number. He dropped us off at a bus stop on Highway 1 and said, "Don't forget".

The first bus that came by that said 'Saigon' we flagged down and got on. The driver spoke a little English, asked where we wanted to go. We gave him the IBM address in central Saigon. There were lots of complaints from the other passengers when we got to Saigon, since he drove straight to our villa on Cach Mang Street. When we got off the bus, it was dark. We gave the driver a little more than he asked for, waved at the other passengers and so finished a long day of unauthorized travel. Well, there was quite a bit of drinking and talking at the IBM villa that night, entertaining our interested co-IBMers about our crazy trip (Today, the trip can be made by air-conditioned bus in about 6 ½ hours for a ticket price of just $11 – not so in 1970).

During the Tet celebration of January 1968 I was living with Gene Murdock and Karl Williams in Nha Trang. Karl and I sat on our villa's rooftop veranda and, with binoculars, watched ground attacks on a hill on the all-too-close outskirts of town. Gene was not interested and spent that night in his room with his current houseguest. Every so often there would be a kind of high pitched noise passing overhead. "What's that?" Karl asked with some concern. "Bats" I said, "Ah, OK", Karl replied. And, maybe they were bats, but I think not – we did not see any bullet holes in the house the next day. But, it always seemed strange that that was the only night we heard the bats.

The Tet offensive was also offensive to the three of us. Our housekeeper-cook was visiting family in Dalat at the time and could not get back to Nha Trang because of travel restrictions on buses and trucks. We drove to the military base for meals, since the town restaurants were all closed.

This was interesting as no vehicles were supposed to be on the streets. We were never got shot at directly, but we did receive one warning shot and were stopped at several checkpoints. Once on the local army base the gate guards did not want to let us back out. This was when we had to play our "we are civilians and you have no power over us" card. After a week we were quite worried about our maid, but we had no contact information for her so could do nothing. After a week and a half she finally showed up - she had walked the 128 kilometers from Dalat to Nha Trang. Her most immediate concern was that were we OK and how had we managed to eat without her. Being informed that we were not harmed and had taken meals with the military she relaxed. She said that she didn't sleep at night worrying about us and she apologized several times that it had taken her so long to get back but she was old and just could not walk very fast any more, especially since she had to carry her own food and clothing. Her tale made us feel bad because she cared so much for our welfare. She certainly could easily have waited a few more days for the roads to reopen and return to Nha Trang by bus. Once befriended, the Vietnamese were extremely caring and faithful.

Why IBM was a great company to work for: While I was living in Nha Trang my sister phoned the IBM office in Oakland California and told the operator that her brother was working for IBM in South Vietnam and he needed to know that his mother had fallen off the roof of her house, had been in intensive care for two days and was still in the hospital with a broken back. The Oakland office passed this information on and I received a call on my company handie-talkie, relayed the information from the Saigon office to Pleiku, where I was working. As soon as I finished the service call, I caught a military flight to Nha Trang and then the next morning another to Saigon. I went to the IBM office and said that I wanted to get to San Francisco as soon as possible. Previously, when I was in Honolulu on my way to Tokyo I was given an Air Travel Card. This was an internationally recognized credit card that could only be used to purchase airline tickets. I was soon booked out of Saigon that afternoon to San Francisco with a change of planes in Hong Kong and Honolulu. I stayed in California about 10 days - my mother made a full recovery. I then went to a local travel agency and bought a return ticket. Nothing was ever said to me by anyone in IBM about my sudden departure from Vietnam, about repaying IBM for the tickets nor about the two weeks I had taken off - the time was never charged against Vacation time. Thank you IBM!

Our Nha Trang villa was broken into several times, nothing of importance taken. But, disconcerting as it always happened at night, and most nights some or all of us were sleeping. I set up a simplistic alarm system in my room. I left the door slightly ajar and put a large screwdriver on the top of the door. Sure enough, about a week after I started doing this I awoke to the sound of the screwdriver hitting the floor. We chased two young Vietnamese over the fence. Gene, who was responsible for the villa, decided that enough was enough and that it was a danger to us to have these midnight visitors. He went to the local Special Forces enclave to present our problem and came back with two Nungs (part of the Montagnards - and one of the minority groups from the Vietnam highlands) to be live-in guards. They had been trained by the Special Forces but were no longer needed. They were entirely self-supporting. The Nungs had a ruthless reputation and according to a Special Forces person, they didn't care who they killed. Gene simply paid them weekly. They showed up each afternoon and left by mid morning, we guessed to sleep and eat but we never asked where they went. Their presence stopped the uninvited from visiting and we treated each other with respect.

Toward the end of my second tour my return to IBM USA was discussed. I had been in the Reno office originally. Reno functioned as a sub-office of Sacramento, CA. Since Reno was a small office there was no position for me there, so I would return to the busier Sacramento office. After the freedom and importance of working in Vietnam to go to Sacramento and probably be responsible for a room full of keypunches and other unit record equipment, going in at 8 AM and leaving at 5 PM, was something I could not face. Way too boring! I asked about going into Systems Engineering. "No." At the same time Bob Dillon kept mentioning that his Thai in-laws had a travel agency permit that they were not using and why didn't I come to Bangkok and run it. Under the circumstances this was not a difficult choice. I gave my 30-days notice, shipped my few possessions to an APO (military mail) address in Bangkok and somewhat reluctantly departed IBM.

It was November 1970. In Bangkok I rented a wooden Thai house, hired the ex-cook and housekeeper of the Swedish Ambassador (an excellent Thai/European cook) and settled in. Since I had three bedrooms I offered their use and provided meals to several IBM CEs for a small monthly fee that helped with the rent. After being in Bangkok for a while I partnered with a Chinese-Thai and we opened a bar on Pat Pong Road, called The Jockey Club. My secretary, the bar cashier and a bar hostess all became part of the IBM family by marrying three of my fellow CEs. Several IBMers took local tours through the travel agency, called 'Liat Travel', that I ended up running and a small group took a tour with me by rail and car from Bangkok to Singapore.

Working so close with the military in Vietnam, I did not have much more contact with the Vietnamese culture than the GIs did, even though I was living on the local economy. I think if I had stayed in Saigon and worked mostly in that area I would have been more politically aware. As it was, I was only involved in Vietnam in regards to its history, physical aspects and getting my job done. The effect of the war on its people and the rightness or wrongness of the war did not concern me. Should it have, of course! But, being in my 20s, single, with no real concerns about money or the details of responsible living, just did not lend itself to deep philosophic thought. The four years I spent in Vietnam was the first of the few aspects of my life that I consider outstanding. I have always had a soft spot in my heart for IBM for providing those years."

Ed closes his story by saying that his years working in Vietnam was a bit "stressful" – perhaps an understatement. As indicated in earlier chapters, it was stressful for all of us. Ed was certainly a 'wild duck' and the type of person the Vietnam assignment definitely needed – independent, adventurous, oblivious to danger, and willing to experience everything that came his way. In Ed's case, the wild duck not only fled the IBM barnyard, but also fled the USA. Many adventures followed and today Ed is well and living happily in California, but with possible retirement plans for a move to Europe.

# Chapter 12
## My Vietnam Years, By Curtis Maxwell

(AUTHOR'S INTRODUCTORY COMMENTS: SOME OF what follows is very technical, and those portions will probably be enjoyed more and understood better by old IBM retiree techies or by true computer historians. However, Curt's description of life in the war zone represents the true depiction of an outstanding IBM Systems Engineer who proved to be a very valuable asset to our military forces while under extreme working conditions. What Curt describes in this chapter was also typical of the technical support provided to all other IBM accounts throughout Southeast Asia. Curt gives some insight into the mindset of a real problem solver. What follows here is a piece of history and a portion of Curt's own life story (somewhat edited), written for his family in the year 2011. It is a testimonial to Curt's vivid memory, still intact, after a long successful career with IBM that lasted 41 years).

### IN COUNTRY

"My memory of arriving in Viet Nam in March of 1967 is very vivid. Stepping out of the airplane onto the tarmac at Tan Son Nhut airbase, the heat and humidity hit me like a hammer! My previous five years had been spent in Alaska, the last three in Fairbanks where it was not unusual for the temperature to dip to 50 degrees below zero for weeks at a time and I am sure that it was well above 90 degrees and 90 percent relative humidity in Saigon on that day!

The civilian air terminal was hot, dirty, and chaotic. I was met by the first two IBM Systems Engineers working in Viet Nam: Larry Pulliam and John Soss. John had a American muscle car, a Mustang, into which they packed me and my baggage for the short trip to the IBM "villa" situated just off Cach Mang street. Along the way we passed a very picturesque waterway on which were lots of wood and metal scrap huts on stilts. Larry informed me the locals called the water way "stinky creek". It was aptly named.

The "villa" was not at all what I had envisioned, however I was told the little hotel/bar/brothel just down the alleyway held promise. Several other IBM folks lived there as well. A few Customer Engineers lived full time on the large Army supply base north of town servicing a variety of computers and unit record equipment. Later I was to receive the traditional plaque showing a man in black pajamas wearing a conical hat, carrying a briefcase in one hand and a rifle in the other. It was inscribed with my name and labeled "VC Dodger number 13". I was the 13th American IBMer in country.

The next few days were spent obtaining my Vietnamese ID card, my MACV non-combatant card (does the card stop bullets, I wondered?), and getting oriented to the fine French/Vietnamese restaurants downtown. Initially, I was not at all certain that I would be able to "take it" in VietNam (that heat problem, it was nearly unbearable to me). My boss, Sam Fitzpatrick, was due in from Camp Zama, Japan in a few days and every night I went to sleep thinking about how I would tell him I wanted out!

Well, Sam arrived and I learned the reason I was in VietNam. The Marines were installing a 360 model 30 "up county" in DaNang, and none of the three SE's already in country were trained on one. I had experience having installed the first 360 (model 40) in Alaska at the University in Fairbanks. It seemed that I was to install the first 360 in VietNam as well. Fred Hodder, the third SE, was in Da Nang and they were having lots of problems getting the applications running on the new system. Well, I just couldn't tell Sam that I couldn't stay. I didn't relish the idea of being so far away from beautiful Saigon, with far fewer IBMer's around for mutual assistance. Not to mention the fact that I would be living with the Marines on their base at Red Beach in Da Nang

## The Technology (1967)

Just a brief note about the technology in general use during this period in VietNam and the U.S. Use of Unit Record equipment was still pervasive. Accounts with stored program computers were mostly 1400 series (1401, 1410, 1440, 7010), with a few accounts upgrading to the new 360 series that were all binary machines, far different from the 1400's that used Binary Coded Decimal. You technicians will appreciate how different these technologies were from one another. As a Systems Engineer, I had to understand all of these technologies in order to assist customers debug their application development problems. I had to read memory instructions and data in BCD when analyzing a problem. We did this at the console, tying up the entire system getting to the source of a problem.

Initial inputs were all from punched cards, which were then transferred to tape or disk for the stored program equipment. Key punches were everywhere and vital to all datacenters and user input sections. The keypunch was like a large typewriter, except rather than printing on a sheet of paper, it punched holes in cards using Hollerith code, which translated in memory to the Binary Coded Decimal system or Binary depending upon the processor in use. Unit Record equipment, also called Electronic Accounting Machines (EAM) all operated on cards: reading, punching, collating, sorting, and printing. Our fastest sorters, which rearranged the input card deck, ran at 1,000 cards per minute. Punched cards were everywhere.

## Up Country – Da Nang Marines

Things were pretty chaotic at the DPP 16, 3rd Force Service Regiment, 1st Logistics Command when I arrived at Red Beach, as the base was informally named. They had de-installed the 1401 that had been used to support their supply operation and installed the 360 model 30 in its place. They were having problems getting the new applications running that were written by the IBM Federal Systems Division (FSD) for use on the new 360. In order to keep the supply chain moving, they tried to run the old 1401 applications system in emulator mode on the 360. Two systems/programmer types from FSD were on site from Bethesda, Maryland for temporary support. Fred Hodder, whom I would replace, was on site representing IBM GEM. There were two well trained Customer Engineers who had setup the system and run hardware diagnostics. The

CE's initial job was done. The rest was up to the SE (me) to put the system into productive use.

Fred introduced me to the Marines of Data Processing Platoon 16 and the base commanding general. The General pointed out several cargo ships sitting idle in Da Nang Harbor waiting for data processing shipping and receiving documents. Our system was clearly the problem and the general was not a happy man, to put it mildly. I suggested that we stop trying to run two systems (the 1401 emulator and the new native mode 360 system) and go all out getting the new FSD application running perfectly. We did have two FSD techs on site and I didn't want to dilute our efforts de-bugging two systems. That meant we would not be running any supply cycles until we got the new system running. The general reluctantly agreed. I was to find over the next two years that the Marines were just as tough in the computer center as they were on the battlefield and would take chances with those they trusted. I loved working with those guys.

We were operating in a harsh environment: sand, dirt, unstable electrical power, and the new processor was 130 hours behind in engineering changes! Electrical power was provided by two diesel generators maintained by Korean civilian contractors. Each week they switched from one generator to the other to make sure the backup process worked smoothly. We had to shut down the system each time they switched generators. I hated this because often hardware or software problems would rear their ugly heads at power startup. When at all possible I liked to keep the system running 24/7.

The Marines had a saying: "12 on and 12 off, and every day is Monday". For those first few months we all worked a lot more hours than that. Of course, there was not a lot else to do on the base, other than drink and that tended to interfere with the working. After a few weeks we did have a running system processing the supply application. It was shaky, required constant monitoring and updating, but we were "cutting shipping mats".

The off shore winds from the South China Sea made it much more tolerable for me than Saigon. Da Nang , called Touraine in the French colonial days, is situated right on the coast. The air-conditioned computer room helped a lot too.

My next meeting with the general was concerning how "IBM has let us down, by under configuring our system". I promised I would analyze the installed system and see what could be done. The 24-hour daily supply cycle was taking around 30 hours! Problems found were: frequent disk errors, CPU errors, no checkpoints, a 100% hit ratio to the database, old 2411 disk packs and a data file far larger than the system was configured for. Fixes recommended and achieved were: machine Engineering Changes brought up to date, all disk packs replaced with new, 2411 read/write heads replaced, checkpoint/restart routines established, clean room procedures established, and the application re-written as a sequential rather than a random process.

## Random or Sequential?

The last performance fix as listed above was based upon the simple fact that for a large database with 100% hit rate a sequential processing approach is the classic solution. The data and input characteristics was now far from that provided by the Marines in their original RFP (Request for Proposal)

It was quite interesting to just observe the row of 2411's during a supply run. I could see them literally shaking with the comb access disk arm movement. The CE's showed me how to lift the cover on the unit so I could observe the pointer on the head of the rotator arm controlling the accesses without tripping the shutdown switch built into the cover. It was spinning back and forth rapidly jumping from one disk cylinder to another, each movement taking valuable system time. (We did not have very sophisticated diagnostic tools in those days). There were eight of these drives, all dancing with the rapid access movement across the logical cylinders of data.

I brainstormed some of these things with Marine Lt. Jim Russell who was commanding the programming section. The next morning, when I came in for "duty", I notice lots of Marine heads down programming in Lt Russell's section. When I asked what they were all busy doing, I was astounded to learn that they were implementing my idea to convert the application from random to sequential! These guys were fearless, I don't even think they had "asked permission". That whole group at DPP 16 was the best bunch I have ever had the privilege of working with.

The change to sequential processing proved very successful, I think we cut the daily cycle run time down to about 10 hours. The IBM account team who marketed to the Marine Corps HQ at the Pentagon was furious with me for suggesting this change. They had sold the system as the latest in computing technology, using *Random Accessing*. Once I explained that the system they proposed would have been fine had the application not changed radically before installation they cooled off a bit. Admittedly, it was a little unusual to use a bank of eight disk drives like tape drives. The 2411 had removable disks, a stack of six disks in an enclosed plastic box that could be placed into the unit through a top opening lid. We called these disks "6 Packs". Each disk drive unit was just below waist high and somewhat wider than a two-drawer file cabinet. So, why not mount disks in the same operational manner as tapes? The system became stable and dependable after a few months and DPP 16 could then process other applications, such as Personnel and Petroleum.

One night I was awakened in my hooch by the shift supervisor who told me they were having a serious problem with the system and they needed me right away. The 12 on and 12 off apparently did not apply to me. I guess I supported both "12's" at Red Beach. When I entered the computer room it was eerily quiet. Nothing was running yet I knew that they must have been fifteen or twenty hours into the "daily" cycle. Long faces all around. I looked first at the console typewriter for any system error messages and didn't see any. All I saw was the sentence, "Sgt so and so on duty at 20 hundred hours." I thought that was pretty nifty, they had discovered that you can take the typewriter off line and type on it. It was basically a selectric (the bouncing ball) typewriter after all. Then it hit me. Sure enough, the console typewriter was still in off line mode. The system had no way to communicate with the operator. Remembering that errors codes are placed in main memory locations 1 and 2 in hexadecimal when the system cannot communicate through the console, I dialed in location 1 on the console rotary switches and read the first two bytes of data. I asked the shift supervisor for the Messages and Codes manual and looked up the hex error code. The message was basically, "The console typewriter is out of ready". Normally we would correct whatever the problem was and type in the command to "retry". Since the error was displayed in memory, the response had to be entered into memory too. I switched the typewriter back onto system mode and entered the hex command to retry into memory location 2 and 3 and hit Start. The typewriter came alive immediately and typed out "mount tape so and so on drive such and such". The Sergeant mounted the requested tape and the whole system started up filling the computer room with the sounds of a busy, running system. I was so relieved, but not nearly as relieved as the Marine staff was that night. What they did not know was that I had had been drinking Chevas Rigal for several hours earlier in the evening at the officers club and was having trouble even focusing! Chevas Rigal cost only 10 cents a drink at the club!!.

## Problem Determination

During my "12 hours on", I spent a lot of time reading technical manuals when not attending some problem or another. That made me much better prepared for when there was a problem. I also read all the IBM "green letters" too, these were descriptions of known problems and fixes based upon symptoms. There were green letters for both software and hardware.

There was a saying, "If it's not broken, don't fix it" since it was not uncommon for the fix to cause a problem in another part of the system, known today as "unintended consequences". When things did not work as expected, I looked for known problems and then recommended a fix. Otherwise, it might be a new problem and those were more difficult. I would try to fix these myself or find a work around. Lacking that, I had to capture everything about the error that might be relevant and report it stateside, and then wait days for a possible answer with my fingers crossed. One had to decide where to concentrate the investigation, hardware or software, operator or user program. (or some combination!!). This became more and more difficult as the technology became more sophisticated. Having a thorough understanding of both how the hardware and software worked was invaluable to getting at the cause, and therefore the fix to the problem.

On many of the System 360's at the time, we were running DOS, a single program, single tasking operating system whose only benefit was a little IOCS and symbolic addressing when programming. Then along came MVT and MVS: 'Multiple Virtual Tasking' and 'Multiple Virtual Systems'. Wow!! How does one debug those? IBM decided that software and hardware systems problems were closely related they needed highly specialized personnel to diagnose and repair. They created a new CE position, one who had training for this complex environment. We had one in Saigon, good old Billy Banks, an outstanding technician. Finally, an expert I could call upon when I got stuck!

## Living Conditions

The GSA contract under which we operated specified that our military customers would provide quarters in remote locations when needed. For that reason, I lived on base at Red Beach for the first few months. The base was known as "Red Beach", since it was right at the 1965 landing point of the first Marine combat troops in I-Corps. When not working at the computer center, we slept in "hootches", just like the ones you see on "MASH" TV. These were lined up in two rows, sitting in the sand separated by a wooden boardwalk. There were thirty Marine officers housed there with one hootch set up as a shower. One water spigot in the center was available to fill our canteens.

The entire compound was situated on very sandy terrain which was so white that it sometimes appeared as snow in photos. A roadway ran down the middle of the compound connecting the datacenter at one end to the supply yard at the other. Constant truck traffic along this road kicked up sand and dust that we had to keep out of the computer environment. The datacenter consisted of a building within a building to help keep out contaminates. All who entered had to wash off their jungle boots in trays of water, then pull on fabric booties before entering the clean room environment.

An orphanage was located just inside the main gate and a large refugee camp sat just outside on one side of the road. A sign posted at the exit gate warned, "You are now entering the most dangerous highway in the world. Drive carefully". That was Highway One that connects Saigon to Hanoi and was called the "Road Without Joy" by the French colonialists.

Every night the Marines fired 105 Howitzer rounds into the surrounding countryside. They called it H&I fire - Hazard and Interdiction. The idea was to keep the VC away from the compound. Those 105's were situated not far from our hootches and they made a terrific noise and shook the ground we slept on! Occasionally a VC would try to breech the perimeter and get shot trying. One morning they found our Vietnamese barber, who worked on base, shot and tangled in the concertina wire.

"Whop, Whop, Whop", sounds of helicopter gunships overhead was common at all times of day and night carrying out missions and transporting men to active battlefields scattered around the countryside. This was definitely guerrilla warfare, something new to our troops. There was no simple battle line, rather lots of skirmishes, like little mini wars being conducted simultaneously. Today, when I hear sounds of helicopters overhead at my home in Walnut Creek, California. I always look up, with the comfort of knowing it's just the traffic monitor flying the freeways for the local radio and TV stations.

We all carried Military Orders issued by the Navy in Hawaii (CINCPAC) granting us GS13 rank, roughly equivalent to Lt. Colonel in the military. This gave us access to the Officer Club mess halls all around Viet Nam, as well as Post Exchange privileges. Our orders authorized us to fly in military aircraft, priority 2, and carry a side arm (I never did). I had a Top Secret security clearance that let me into most installations for support purposes.

The nearest Post Exchange was at Da Nang Air Base. They carried a wide variety of products, much like a supermarket in the U.S.: Watches, cameras, toiletries, diamond rings, and civilian clothing. We could even order fine Japanese porcelain dishware and Mikimoto pearls.

The food served in the clubs in and around Da Nang was outstanding, especially the Officers Club at the 1ˢᵗ Marine Air Wing, and the Navy Officer's club in the city of Da Nang. The food at Red Beach was also excellent.

Once the system at DPP 16 was stabilized, we decided to move into town where we rented a villa and an old Land Rover so we could service not only Red Beach, but other accounts in the vicinity. The other accounts were primarily Navy Covered Storage across the river at China Beach and the 1ˢᵗ Marine Air Wing at Da Nang airbase. It was also a blessing to get away from those big 105's! The general at 3ʳᵈ FSR was concerned when we moved off base as he was expecting around the clock service in support of his 24/7 operation. We agreed to leave one CE on site at all times and the CE's took turns doing this.

The first night after we had moved off base, Red Beach sustained a rocket attack. I was sooo glad we had moved into town. We did have random rockets lobbed into Da Nang from time to time, but no concerted efforts, until the 1968 TET offensive. The Admirals quarters were in town as was his headquarters building. That is probably the reason for occasional rocket shots, probably in hopes of hitting something important!

Da Nang was supposed to be off limits to military, however the Navy Headquarters was right in the middle of town, on the river. They had a fine officers club called the White Elephant just down the street from our first villa at 49 Quang Trung. Maybe the off limits was only for Marines. I know for sure they were not to go into town and for the most part they obeyed this regulation.

It was so much more interesting living in Da Nang town "on the economy", becoming more familiar with Vietnamese customs and culture than being stuck at Red Beach continuously. Our villa was surrounded by a stone wall topped with broken glass and concertina wire. We were right across the street from a civilian RVN radio station. Little old ladies in conical hats would squat on the roadside just outside our villa each morning chewing beetle nut (a mild narcotic) and exchanging gossip on their way back from the market. We could buy a delicious soup called "Pho" from street vendors. I got to try chicken heads and eel at local restaurants too. The local beer was "Ba Mui Ba" which means "33" in Vietnamese. It is actually a French beer, not very good, brewed in Da Nang. I have since had "Bier 33" in France and it is not very good there either!

## Navy Covered Storage

NCS was located in China Beach on the other side of Da Nang from Red Beach. It was the largest refrigerated storage facility in the world, serving the food needs of I-Corps combat troops and Navy LST's in the South China Sea. They had fresh produce from the central highlands of Dalat, Angus steak from New Zealand, fresh potatoes, tins of frozen strawberries and all things good. The Navy and Marines not only had fine food, but their chefs were outstanding too.

The NCS were running their supply system on a large array of unit record equipment, all punched card based. This utilized thousands and thousands of cards, all needing to be punched, sorted, collated, reproduced, run through 604 calculators then fed into 407 accounting machines. It was typical of many installations both in Vietnam and in the US at the time, even though two generations of stored program computers were readily available commercially from IBM and other manufacturers. Understandably, this processing system was overwhelmed with the volume it was experiencing and I told the officer in charge, a Commander Rixy, that they really needed a IBM 1401 stored program tape system. This was duly reported to the Admiral who "ran it up the flag". GSA just happened to have a 1401 in storage that was already owned by the government and it was offered to NCS on the condition that they could program and operate it without any headquarters assistance.

I assured them that I could teach their unit record board wiring personnel how to program and operate the 1401 as well as help them convert their unit record application to the 1401 on site at China Beach. In those days, System Engineering Services was free, so I could do this at no charge. While waiting for the system to arrive, I drew up plans for an air-conditioned computer building using the drafting facilities of the Sea Bees located in the Admiral's headquarters building. I specified connecting three Quonset huts in a tee formation, sitting atop three foot high concrete walls to provide the vertical clearance needed for the 729 tape drives. All electrical receptacle needs were identified. The building included a raised floor for the interconnecting cabling that was also used as a plenum for the air conditioning. I gave them the BTU requirements for air conditioning needed to keep the system running error free. The Sea Bees had everything built and ready to go in about a month, or maybe less!

The commanding officer identified a half dozen or so enlisted men to be trained in programming and I began the training a week or so prior to the system's arrival. I wanted them to test programs on the real system as soon as possible. I also included a little machine language too, as that is very helpful in understanding a system and how it works. How to operate the 1401 was integrated into their program assembly test activity. Within a few weeks I felt they were ready to begin developing the programs that would run their supply system. These seamen were sharp and very fast learners. In about a month they had the basic supply cycle converted with outstanding performance improvement over the prior system. The application design was simple; we just copied the unit record system but performed the operations on the 1401 instead of the array of unit record card equipment. This was exactly what my IBM instructors in 1401 training told us not to do. We were supposed to streamline the processing by making use of the superior capabilities of the 1401. Well, this was a war zone after all and we were working with newly trained programmers whose only prior experience was unit record board wiring so I make no excuses!

In order to assure that good operator messages would be included in the application programs, I set up the shop so that each week one of the programmers had to be the duty operator. They had to operate the programs they wrote. That made them combination programmer/operators. I had wanted to try that for some time in my customer assignments prior to Vietnam. Poor, or no, error messages were a constant problem for operational folks and my idea to combine programming with operating was intended to solve this problem. It did! Morale in that shop was very high, everyone involved was proud of what they were doing.

Some time later I received a Regional Managers Award for this effort from Ralph Pfieffer, an IBM Vice President and Manager of GEM Region. It was nice to be recognized since I was working alone, far from IBM direct support. I learned years later from my replacement in Da Nang (Graham Seibert) that this data center was hit during a rocket attack and the 1401 was extensively damaged. One of our CE's actually soldered new connections on the primary circuit board and had the system up and running in 24 hours!

## 1st Marine Air Wing

1st MAW at Da Nang Air Base was running a 1440 disk system and was eager for Systems Engineering support. When they learned I was nearby I received a call from the Major in charge. I must admit I was far more comfortable supporting 1401 and 1440 systems than the 360 at Red Beach, since I had several more years experience on these older systems.

This installation was very unusual as it was housed in what the Marines called a "bubble". The bubble was a portable structure that consisted of a series of inter-connected, inflatable pads that together formed a multi-purpose housing structure. Headquarters wanted to test this concept in battlefield conditions so they gave it to the 1st MAW datacenter for use and evaluation. What a joke! They spent a good deal of effort just keeping the pads inflated. During rainstorms the roof would collapse and had to be kept up with long vertical poles. The processor unit was protected with sheets of plastic on top. I worried about airflow through the unit – didn't want it restricted. Most of my support there was standard 'business as usual': providing manuals, answering a few programming questions, a little help debugging programs. The CE's took occasional trouble calls on this system, which by and large ran pretty well in spite of the "bubble".

The men were housed in old French colonial stucco buildings painted the old French yellow/orange color with red tile roofs. We heard that during the French/Viet Nam war, Viet Minh sappers entered one of these building and slit the throats of every man while they slept.

I did get involved in one interesting "bug" on that 1440. The application involved collecting data developed from interviews with F-4 Phantom Fighter pilots and aircraft inspections each time they returned from a combat sortie over North Viet Nam (Author's note: This was early 7th Air Force PIACCS as described in Chapter 4).This data was then encoded, sorted, and evaluated for the purpose of determining what additional armor was needed for future combat operations. The programmer analyst told me that at some point during the application system run about half of the data was lost. This application had been running fine for weeks until now. I spent several days studying the problem. We ran the data over and over again with the same, erroneous results. It did appear that the data was lost during one of the sorts.

I began thinking about how sort routines work, and recalled that when large chunks of data are moved or copied in memory the program logic uses the "move record" command. Move record begins the move at the address specified for the beginning of the data until encountering a "record mark/word mark" in memory. This stops the move and the record mark/word mark stays in memory for use in the next read or move operation. This seemed to me a possible explanation for what was happening but I then had to find out just how this bit pattern could have been placed in the "wrong" location in memory. The data was originally captured on punched cards so I asked one of the Marines to write a program searching all columns of every card in the input stream for this special character and "bingo"!! We found it on a card in the middle of the deck. It had been "multi-punched" by accident and that particular error produced the character in memory that stopped all subsequent moves of data collected. I really sweated that one out for several days. I had relied upon what we used to call "intelligent guessing", employed quite often before more sophisticated approaches were developed on future, more powerful systems

Thank goodness the application was not mission critical and a few days delay was not too serious. This led to my suggestion that the card input data should be verified after punching to avoid this problem. Verifying involves running the just punched cards through another machine and re-keying from the original input sheets. The verifier then matches the data on the card with that entered on the verifier. Cards that do not match are marked with a notch over the column that is mismatched. Yep, this involves keying input data twice but assures accurate input data for subsequent processing. This was standard procedure for applications like payroll and financial reporting in commercial applications. How archaic that all seems now!

## Transportation and Communications

When we three IBMers up country were just supporting one client, the Marines at Red Beach, we didn't need transportation since we all lived at the base and the datacenter was a short walk from our hootch, if we were not already on site. As time went on, other units in I-Corps heard we were available and calls began coming in for support through military communications. We felt obliged to help, and soon were fielding calls all around the Da Nang area as well as all across I-Corps. Our customers would provide transportation; cargo convoys, helicopters, or they would send a jeep and driver. We had to increase our CE personnel to include the additional manpower and provide skill sets needed to cover the broader range of equipment supported. These men were superb technicians, each one could fix just about anything, although the 360 at Red Beach was new technology so not all were trained for that.

Our maintenance coverage was stretched pretty thin, mostly because the time and distances were so challenging. It was not uncommon for a 30-minute trouble call on a simple key punch to take a day given the time to "commute" each way. Our service at Red Beach began to deteriorate, largely because of the extended travel time required for even simple fixes elsewhere. It was not unusual for transportation back to Red Beach to disappear as soon as the problem at the remote location was taken care of.

An extreme example of time to repair happened when one of our CEs took a call on a Navy ship in port. While on board the ship steamed to sea, docking next in Southern Japan! Our man had no money, no passport, and could not take civilian transportation back "home" because he wasn't even in Japan legally. The Navy did come through, though it was several more days until he was available in Da Nang. I explained to our Navy clients in Da Nang that their local service was severely impacted and something had to be done to prevent future occurrences. From that time onward, shipboard calls had to be coordinated through the Officer in Charge at NCS in China Beach.

Standard measurements used to evaluate the CE's in the U.S. made our guys service record look pretty bad and we began hearing from upper management in Honolulu about this. I tried to explain that you can not hold us to the same standards as those used in San Francisco. The general at Red Beach had also remarked to a visiting IBM dignitary that service was not up to his expectations and I was taking heat on this too. We were reporting that everything was going well, so this was not a welcome surprise for an IBM vice president to hear on his boondoggle to the war zone!

When asked the standard IBM Executive question "what can we do to help you do your job better?" I had a ready answer, fundamentals. We needed transportation of our own, and we needed "walkie-talkies" so we could communicate between ourselves. There were occasions when a CE would return from a remote site only to find that another problem was reported just across the road from the first trouble call. Another day lost! Had we been in communication, both troubles would have been fixed at the same time. The walkie talkies would have another important benefit: safety and security, more on that later.

Within a few months we got two 4-wheel drive Toyota Land Cruisers and everyone got a Motorola walkie-talkie. The Motorola's had a pretty good range and we could contact each other from most locations around

Da Nang. We would pass along trouble call requests and keep each other abreast of our whereabouts at all times. Now that we no longer lived on base, this was especially comforting. I think it was about this time (1968) that all IBM base locations in RVN also got Collins single side band radios. We could reach each other from Da Nang to Saigon, to Long Binh as well as Quy Nhon, NhaTrang, Bangkok, Subic Bay and sometimes even the parts depot in Okinawa. Our call sign in Da Nang was "Navy Dutch 5".

## Tet Offensive, 1968

Tet is an extremely important holiday in Vietnam. It occurs on each Lunar New Year and is as important in their culture as Birthday, Christmas, New Years, and Halloween combined is in our western culture. Everyone is a day older on Lunar New Year. All debts are paid and disagreements with neighbors settled. Gifts are exchanged and children get candy and "lycee" (Pronounced "lee see"), which is money placed in a small red envelope. The lysee is often hidden within the house, or outside, above a door jamb. Neighborhood children cooperate to dress as a long Chinese dragon, accompanied by a drummer and a humorous dancer dressed as a happy Buddha. The dancer searches for the lysee while the dragon points out possible hiding places, bobbing and weaving the whole while. The children provide delightful entertainment and are rewarded by finding the lysee.

Folks dress in their best outfits and visit friends, neighbors and relatives bringing small gifts of flowers and fruits. Tet is a special, reverent, joyful time. The war would stop temporarily, as most solders were home on leave and who would think of disturbing this joyous time of celebration and reflection? All day and into the Tet evening we heard firecrackers and shots fired into the air in jubilant celebration. Our CE's took this opportunity to "test fire" their AR16's they had been issued by the Navy. I didn't like this much but of course I was not as adventurous or flamboyant as the CEs.

Rifle shots fired into the night do not sound the same as those fired in your direction, we noticed late in the evening of the 1968 Tet celebrations. We also noticed that the shots were also very close together, coming in bunches that did not sound right for just a celebration, too many and fired too simultaneously. They sounded a lot like a firefight! The VC had mounted a ferocious attack on Da Nang. We tuned into Armed Forces Radio to find that a coordinated attack all across Vietnam was in progress. As the shooting outside continued unabated, we crouched on the floor against the concrete wall of our villa. Had we been at Red Beach we would have been in dugout sand bunkers but I don't know if we would have been safer or not. An enormous explosion rocked our villa and the overhead fan dropped from the ceiling onto the bed. The ammunition dump at Da Nang Airbase had been hit and the whole thing went up. Petroleum storage was also set afire we learned later. The Vietnamese radio station just across the street was taken by the enemy and held overnight.

Armed Forces Radio informed us of a 24-hour curfew for all civilians. This lasted for five days or so; we were not to leave our villa. Thank goodness for one of our 'adventurous' CE's, who took a quick trip down the road to the Navy Officers mess where they gave him a case of frozen steaks and a case of pork and beans. That sure tasted good for a while, but even that menu got pretty tiresome in a few days. At least we didn't go hungry.

The Air Base sustained a lot of damage. The old French barracks where the Marines we supported lived remained intact, however all of the clay tiles in the roofs facing the ammo dump shattered from the concussion and slid down onto the eaves and to the ground making a nice neat pile of broken clay. Naturally, the "bubble" housing the 1440 was riddled with holes and had collapsed around the system components. So much for battlefield testing! The computer equipment was largely undamaged and powered up with no problems when the bubble was resurrected. A piece of our unit record equipment in the Communications Center at Red Beach took a direct hit. When I reported this to IBM Administration (so leasing charges would stop) they asked me for a pencil etching of the serial number. I politely told them they were out of their minds.

The VC took the city of Hue, further north, very near the DMZ, and held it for three weeks in spite of fierce counter attacks and bombardment from the air. Hue had been the imperial capital for centuries. I was just sick to think of the beautiful and historic structures that were surely destroyed and I would never get to see them. When we finally re-took Hue, they found enemy soldiers chained to their positions, basically had to fight to the death. During the three weeks the VC held that city, they executed 3,000 civilians. We heard that a group of Vietnamese and their families had taken refuge in the Catholic Church. Years later I returned to Vietnam and met a man who was in that church with his family. He was 12 years old at the time and was our tour guide in Hue in 2004. It was fascinating to talk with him. His father moved the group from the church up to Phu Bai right on the DMZ, where they camped just outside the perimeter of the Marine base. He told me they could be shot just as easily by the VC as by the Marines, therefore by camping on the perimeter they would be safe from both. Smart move?

Politically, the VC scored in a major way by proving they were capable of a concerted, coordinated attacks across RVN. In spite of this, our military intelligence and CIA analyst continued to underestimate this formidable opponent, right up to the day Saigon fell in 1975. The VC, and by then the NVA (North Vietnamese Army), sustained terrible losses. History shows that this did not deter them however and they persevered against their cousins in the south. Their persistence in the face of formidable odds is still difficult for us Westerners to understand. Why did not the southern Vietnamese have this same stuff?

## Security and Safety

After the '68 Tet Offensive a 6pm to 6am curfew was instituted. Outside, anything moving after curfew could be shot on sight, our noncombatant cards notwithstanding! I spent a lot of time after hours reading technical manuals, and especially the GSA contract which had a number of interesting contingencies. Of particular note, to me, was the section that stated we did not have to take trouble calls if, in our opinion, our lives would be placed in excessive danger. I pointed this out to our CE's, and ask them not to hesitate after curfew to simply refuse. Another option, which they used fairly often, was to ask for an armed escort to and from the account. One night, when returning from a trouble call at Red Beach, the escort was engaged in a firefight in downtown Da Nang! The CE crawled under the "deuce and a half" until it was safe and was returned to his villa, badly shaken. The next day he asked to be transferred to Thailand for the remainder of his two-year assignment. IBM complied; after all, the assignment in Vietnam was strictly voluntary. Life in Thailand, by the way, was pretty sweet, compared to that in Vietnam.

At this point, I decided to ask for a weapon for use in protecting my villa. By now, I was "co-habitating" with a cute Vietnamese girl who worked in the keypunch section at Red Beach. I thought I would look pretty silly if a VC was running for cover, wanted to duck into our villa, and I would be totally unable to defend me and mine. The Marines suggested a sawed off shotgun, loaded with double ought pellets. They said just point it towards the closed door and fire. It would blow away the door and the VC on the other side too. My concern was that the recoil of the shotgun would simultaneously blow me out the back door! I settled on an old fashioned carbine, a fully automatic rifle with three 30 round banana clips. I kept it in the villa and never fired a round. I felt a little safer having it. The CE's decided on the latest combat weapon, the AR16 issued to them by the Navy. The Marines were still using older technology. However, the AR16 was infamous for jamming in dirty, wet, sandy conditions, which abounded in Da Nang. If I was going to fire a weapon, I sure wanted it to operate!

I occasionally broke curfew, with much reservation. When I did drive after curfew, I turned on the overhead light on the Land Cruiser so anyone out there could see I was a "round eye". My heart would be in my throat, as I knew a VC sniper could see me as well! I was never shot at, probably because the lone sniper would not want to expose his position while waiting for more important targets? One night I accompanied an IBM Vice President (Ralph Phieffer?) to dinner with the ranking officer in I-Corps, a Navy Admiral. This was an interesting evening, and of course the food was superb. After dinner drinks and conversation took us well after curfew so I asked the Admiral if he could arrange for a brace of Shore Patrol to escort the VP and me to the Da Nang airbase, which he did. We had to drive right through the center of town to reach the base, zooming down the main street, lights flashing and sirens blaring. I would have preferred a more subdued approach for safety and security. At the airbase we drove right onto the tarmac where the IBM Exec boarded an aircraft. The SP's mysteriously disappeared and I had to find my way back home with my dome light on! I guess the Admiral forgot to tell them the local IBMer planned to return to his home in Da Nang.

## Leisure Time

Viet Nam is blessed with a thousand miles of beautiful beach on the South China Sea. Several beautiful beaches were located near Da Nang and we enjoyed these when time allowed. The Marines at Red Beach had a "special services" group whose mission was to provide leisure activity equipment to wile away the "12 hours off". They had weight lifting equipment, badminton sets, and even surfboards! Several of us checked out a surfboard, but the surf was not that good, and this Midwestern boy had no ability at all to ride the waves! But, it was relaxing to try. The civilian beaches (some beaches were cordoned off for military use only) had numerous seafood shacks selling fresh fish, lobster, and other foodstuffs. at very reasonable prices. Then too, it was relaxing to momentarily escape from the chaos of war and just sit in the sun and smell the ocean's salt air.

My wife, Ngoc, and I (we married in mid-1968) sometimes took our landlord's children to China beach and let them play in the surf. We later sponsored the oldest boy into the U.S. and he, in turn, brought every one of his siblings to America. After curfew we watched armed forces TV, the favorite program, incredibly, was "Combat" with Vic Morrow. I read everything I could get my hands on, even a book on aerobic exercising my mom sent me!

## Drafted in Viet Nam?

Prior to Vietnam, I had joined the Air National Guard in Alaska while working there to avoid the draft; I admit it. However, my reason for not wanting to be drafted was based more upon personal ambition and income than any strongly held believe regarding the war. In fact, I knew very little about the war in 1967 when I decided to take the assignment and thought that this would provide insight and adventure, which it surely did. (well, adventure, anyway). Then there was the financial incentive too: a 75% increase to base salary, exemption from income tax, and all expenses paid. Obviously, our IBM leadership felt the need to provide seductive incentives to attract necessary talent.

The ability to attend my monthly National Guard meetings in Anchorage was going to be problematic, however I left Alaska without a solution to this problem. About six months into my tour in Da Nang I got a letter from the department of the Air Force informing me that I was being drafted and was ordered to report to Boulder, Colorado on a certain date! I had not been fulfilling my obligation of attending meetings, or the annual two-week encampment.

I had trained to be a qualified loadmaster on C124s, which I knew were being used within Vietnam and to and from Okinawa. I thought perhaps I could fulfill my obligation by taking a flight or two every month. With this in mind, I approached a Master Sergeant at base operations. The Master Sergeant explained that would be forbidden for a civilian in a war zone. Well, I reasoned, they could place me on active duty each time, just like they did in the National Guard. No good. He asked to see my letter from the Dept of the Air Force and found that he knew the Colonel who wrote the letter and knew him to be an intelligent and understanding officer.

With the advice and help from that Master Sergeant, I wrote a letter explaining my situation, included my orders from CINPAC, and said that I felt my work in Vietnam was far more valuable to my country than sweeping floors in Boulder, Colorado as an Airman 1st Class. I think I also included a letter from some IBM VP, arranged for by my Saigon manager, Bruce Thompson. It worked!! I was placed on inactive reserve status and "served" out my required 6 years time in the reserves, earning an honorable discharge with no obligation to attend meetings or annual encampments. So, strangely enough, **I narrowly escaped being drafted in Vietnam and sent back to the U.S.!"**

(Authors Addition: Curt also provided technical support to a few accounts in Thailand and in and around Saigon, including Long Binh. He helped install the first IBM 360 Model 20 Autodin tributary terminal in Southeast Asia at Korat Air Base. After his Da Nang assignment he transferred to Saigon with his Vietnamese wife (an exception to the policy) and made a major contribution to the design of the Vietnamese Print Train employed at USAID (see Chapter 5). He has passed along a few short stories).

After about a year in Vietnam I was contacted and told to proceed to the Air Base in Korat, Thailand where I was expected to install the first of the class 3 AUTODIN terminals in the global network, in conjunction with another early site at Ramstein Air Base, Germany. A seat was arranged from Da Nang to Korat on the daily South East Asia military courier flight, code named "ScatBack". Scatback was a four passenger, two engine jet aircraft used for sensitive military dispatches and to transport officers on critical, time sensitive, assignments. Well, I felt pretty important until we landed at Korat AB, and I was unceremoniously dumped at the end of the runway, along with the mail satchel, in a pouring monsoon rain. The pilot told me to hitch a ride on the jeep that was dispatched to pick up the mail and proceed to flight operations. He didn't even shut down the engines and started his takeoff roll immediately! Of course, I had entered Thailand "illegally", not having processed through Thai immigration and had no entry stamp in my passport. This presented problems later when I was bumped from the return Scatback by a general and had to return to Vietnam the normal commercial way, through Bangkok and Thai immigration.

Management in Saigon had discovered I was now married to a "local". It was decided that I move to Saigon to complete my tour. Moving to Saigon was truly moving to the "big city" even though Da Nang was the second largest city in RVN. Da Nang still had a number of unpaved streets, one of which we lived on. I loved it there, and remember it was much cooler than Saigon, although I had now grown more accustomed to the heat and humidity. Just as I remembered, Saigon was hot, humid, and dirty. Also, now there were many homeless who had moved into the city from the countryside to escape the constant warfare. They were encamped on the wide sidewalks on the boulevards in makeshift tents of canvas, scrap tin, and slates of wood. An IBM friend remarked that the peasants didn't care who ran the government; they just wanted to be left alone to make a living and raise their families.

## The Vietnamese print Train Project at USAID, Saigon

As part of Vietnamization, President Thieu's administration was implementing a land reform project called "Land to the Tillers" which transferred title of lands, then owned by wealthy land owners, to the peasants that worked them. Land ownership up to that time was much like that in a middle age feudal system. The transfer required printing land titles in the native language which USAID was doing on an IBM1403 printer, then "correcting" the title by hand, modifying and adding the letters and diacritical marks necessary for proper Vietnamese. This was a long laborious, awkward and error prone process.

## The Written Language

The written alphabet for Vietnamese utilizes a Romanized alphabet similar to English but with some notable differences. There is no "f", for example, the sound is created using the letters "ph". No "J", no "w". The problems arise when one examines the vowels. There are three distinct letters "a", for example, distinguished by marks above the letter. (two "e"s, three "o"s, and two "u"s)

There are also six diacritical marks used in conjunction with the vowels for pronunciation, which also serve to make a vowel distinct from another, changing the sound and meaning of a word as well as the alphabetical sequence. These "extra" vowels and tonal marks presented the challenge in printing and computer programming on a machine that was built for the English language. Correct vowels and tonal markings are critical to any legal document because the name with the "wrong" vowel or tonal mark could well be a different landowner!

## The Solution

There were three areas that would need addressing for the purpose of creating documents on the System 360:

1.  Creating source documents (punched cards) to represent the characters and marks not found in English.
2.  Storing these characters in memory and external storage in a manner that would allow sorting and logical comparisons (high, low, equal).
3.  Printing in correct Vietnamese alphabet at computer speed.

After several days of study, I developed a conceptual solution using the unique characteristics of the System 360 binary character configurations and a modified print train – yet to be manufactured in the US - for the 1403.

Punching data into the source document cards would need two character spaces for each letter that differed from English, then these two characters, when read into the computer, would be merged into a single memory byte that would automatically fall into the proper alphabetic sequence in the Vietnamese alphabet, including the tonal marks which also dictated sequence. The program would need to be written in Assembly language that allows bit manipulation within a byte. Cobol language could be used for the main program, with the bit manipulation accomplished in Assembler sub-routines.

*IBM 1403 Printing Land Title in Vietnamese*

Printing on the 1403 required the development of quite a few special type slugs that could be accomplished in our plant in Endicott, New York. I designed each new character on a special form made for that purpose. The 1403 utilized a spinning print train on which three sets of all possible characters were positioned and a hammer was fired when the appropriate slug was positioned in the desired location on the printout. Associating a character with firing hammer against a slug is done by comparison between the user's print line and a print layout table in memory. This then became a simple matter of loading up the layout table with the special characters we needed.

There was another problem to address in the printing that was due to the limitation on the number of slugs fitted in each of the three "spinning" character sets. I limited the number of special characters to those that would appear most often and relied upon printing each line a second time without advancing the paper for the purpose of adding the special marks to the base character already printed. Speed was sacrificed using this approach. Printing twice for each line that contained characters needing

233

additional formation made it necessary to develop a special print routine. The line had to be broken into two parts, the basic line, then another line that contained just the special marks for completing the letters for which we had no unique slug. Lots of fun, programming!

Overall print speed was dependent upon how often a character, for which no unique print slug existed, would appear in the final document; so I studied the Vietnamese dictionary with the help of our IBM Vietnamese secretary, Ba Phong. I needed to know which letters appeared the least in conventional writing, and these were the ones I relegated to requiring a second pass of the print train. Characters that appeared most often were included in all three sets on the train, and others only twice, some appeared only once.

My design materials were turned over to a co-worker, Graham Seibert, for detailed design and coding and I departed for the U.S. in June of 1970 before seeing any work completed. Six months or so later Graham sent me a printout in pure Vietnamese. It was beautiful! Of various accomplishments in my forty one year career with IBM, I am most proud of having developed this concept."

## Going Home

Curt departed SEA in mid 1970 via Hong Kong, Tokyo and Honolulu. Curt writes, "Exhausted that night after the long flight I sat out on my Honolulu hotel's balcony for several hours, but unable to sleep. I was unwinding after 3 ½ years of tension. I weighed only 135 pounds. The air smelled so sweet like Plumeria blossoms and I could hear the sound of the surf and Don Ho singing 'Tiny Bubbles' in a nearby nightclub. I knew I would be quite happy to never leave US soil for the remainder of my life." Curt moved with his wife Ngoc and young child to the San Francisco area. Curt re-educated himself in mainstream IBMese, was soon promoted to Senior SE and spent the rest of his IBM career as a leader on major San Francisco banking accounts. Retired now, he is writing his life story.

Curt concludes this portion of his story with the following proud but sad commentary:

## After the Fall

"South Vietnamese began escaping the country by the thousands, mostly by boat. Many of these boats were grossly over loaded and sunk, with most passengers drowning, including my brother in law (the husband of Ngoc's twin sister, Bao) and his son. Bao had remained in DaNang waiting for word that the husband and son arrived safely, before she too would escape. She died six months later, I believe from a combination of malnutrition and grief.

Our Saigon landlord's wife and son safely escaped by boat to a refugee camp in Indonesia. The Red Cross contacted us and I was able to locate her brother in Arlington, Virginia and he affected their entry into the US. Our landlord himself then attempted an escape when we informed him his wife and son had arrived safely, but was captured and interred in a "re-education" program. After a year, he escaped the camp, and was reunited with his family, setting up residence in Lodi, California. Ngoc and I visited them in Lodi, where he was attempting to learn English and find employment. This was proving very difficult, as he was already sixty-two years old, and seemed to lose heart. They were originally from Hanoi, but left everything to migrate to the South when Vietnam was divided, under the terms of the 1954 partition. He had his own construction business in Hanoi and a home, which had to be abandoned to start over in Saigon. Now he had to do it again, leaving a business, a home, and starting over but this time at an advanced age and with no money. He told me he wished they had not left Vietnam. It broke my heart to hear this, but I understood. I told him he left Vietnam not so his life would be better, but that his son's life would have a much brighter future.

Ngoc and I sponsored our DaNang landlord's eldest son and he lived with us while learning English and finding work. In subsequent years, he sponsored each member of the entire family into the US, except the father, who died before leaving and the mother who then did not wish to leave Vietnam without her husband. Every one of this family has thrived, became financially successful in the US.

One of Ngoc's brothers, a full Colonel and aid to Vice President Key, was sent to a re-education camp for five years. When released, he managed to obtain a Cyclo, where he earned a few piasters a day transporting passengers in the streets of NhaTrang. He was glad to have the work.

We lost track of our beloved Minh, who was bused to the countryside with others from her Buddhist enclave, where they were instructed to "farm". All of the churches and temples were closed, being forbidden by the communist regime. This was a typical occurrence in the south as the floods of refuges and those living in overcrowded housing were forcibly moved back into the countryside. Notification was provided one day in advance that they were being relocated and could bring with them only what would fit into one bag.

Within one year, all private enterprise was closed throughout the south, including the once thriving marketplace in Cholon. Goods and food once sold in this market were to be provided by government stores using ration cards to assure fair distribution. For several years after the communist take-over, times were extremely hard. Earnings averaged about the cost of one chicken, *per month*. Many lived at starvation levels, and food had to be obtained on the black market, as Government stores were often empty."

## Curt's Requiem

"Years later, I visited the Vietnam Veterans Memorial in Washington D.C. This memorial is so moving (more so perhaps than any other in our Nation's Capital), I could not restrain tears when walking by it – and even now. Names (58,282) of our fallen and missing are inscribed in a black granite wall, which becomes higher, rather deeper, into the ground across the timeline of the war, the number of dead ever increasing, then decreasing until the final withdrawal. A big, black gash across the landscape, an enormous tombstone for our fallen. Not a gallant, heroic monument, but a tombstone to tragedy. At last, a war memorial that fits the reality of war."

Note: The Vietnam Veterans Memorial is really three separate structures: the wall (1982), three servicemen (1984) and the Vietnam Women's Memorial (1993). These sit next to the Reflecting Pool near the base of the Lincoln Memorial. Is it a coincidence of location that Lincoln is known for our American Civil War and that what we call the Vietnam War was in the minds of North Vietnam, their civil war? There were no winners!

# Chapter 13
## Life In The War Zone By Stu Schmidt

"It was January 1968, and I needed to do something different with my life due to a broken romance and too much day-to-day routine. My IBM systems engineering manager called me into his office and told me that IBM was looking for qualified un-married systems engineers to go to Vietnam to support the war effort. I had been with IBM for about four years, had successfully completed the training programs and a couple of major computer installations. He said I was a prime candidate for the job if I was interested. I had no idea whether I was interested or not. I was in my mid-twenties and never been out of the United States. I accepted a trip to San Francisco to find out more about it. I interviewed with several managers and then returned to Denver. A week or so later, I was told by my SE manager that they were making me an offer and I needed to let them know, yes or no.

I didn't know much about Vietnam. Sure, I knew where it was geographically and knew there was a war going on, but I had very little knowledge of Southeast Asia and probably less about war and the U.S. Military. The work sounded interesting and it was an opportunity to completely change my life and save some money. The benefits were outstanding. I do not know if it was true or not, but I heard later that one of the reasons the benefits were so good was that IBM did not want to make any profit on the war.

I said yes. It would take a few months to get the paper work done, but I was committed. I started to pay more attention to what was going on. Television brought it right to me. Wow! The Tet offensive was raging. There was fighting in Saigon and our Embassy walls had been breached. Not only soldiers were getting killed but there were lots of civilian casualties. The famous photo of the Vietnamese officer shooting a Viet Cong in the head with a pistol was circulating everywhere. I wondered to myself, what did I get myself into? My friends and family asked me the same thing. Gradually I became more at ease with what was going on. In May, I received the word that they were ready for me to go. My house was not yet sold, but it was under IBM's moving policy so I did not have to worry about it. I did not have many possessions, and those that I did have were safely stored at my parents' house. I arranged a flight to Hawaii, where I would be staged until time to go to Vietnam.

Then came the next bombshell. The North Vietnamese and Viet Cong had successfully started what was known as the "May Offensive." Movement of support civilians had been temporarily suspended. However, since I had everything ready to go, I was told to go to Hawaii anyway. At the Denver Stapleton Airport, I ran into an old roommate of mine who had moved to Philadelphia. I was excited about my new venture, and proceeded to tell him about this wonderful opportunity. Then I asked him what he was doing there anyway. His reply stunned me. "I am just returning from home in Scottsbluff, Nebraska. We just buried my younger brother who was killed in action in Viet Nam. The sadness and apprehension that filled me was extreme.

I arrived in Honolulu with heavy heart and very mixed emotions. But, Hawaii!! Who would have ever guessed that I would be in Hawaii? I moved into the Ilima Hotel, My room had kitchen facilities and was near the International Market Place and two blocks from the beach. I anticipated that I would only be there a couple of days, but it took considerably longer.

In order for me to go from Hawaii to Vietnam, I needed Invitational Travel Orders issued by the U.S. military. Our sponsoring agency was CINCPAC (Commander in Chief Pacific). Every morning I would go to the IBM office on Ala Moana Boulevard and wait until our marketing representative returned from calling on CINCPAC HQ at Camp Smith. Day after day he returned with no travel orders. CINCPAC was busy with a lot more pressing issues than getting travel orders for me. I would leave the office around noon and enjoy afternoons on the beach. It was a great life, but I was anxious to get back to work and, besides, the financial benefits would not start until I was actually in Vietnam.

Finally, my travel orders arrived. I was given a one-way ticket on TWA and left for Vietnam via Guam. We arrived in Guam in the middle of the night, but I still remember how hot and muggy the terminal was. Hot and muggy - a prelude for what to expect for the next few years. Then we were off again – next stop, Saigon. Many hours later, the plane circled Saigon for what felt like an eternity and suddenly it dipped steeply to land at Tan Sun Nhut airport. Once on the ground, things proceeded smoothly. Immigration and Customs were a snap. I walked out into a mass of unfamiliar humanity and immediately recognized Bruce Tomson and Larry Pulliam in their white shirts and ties. They hustled me into Bruce's white Mercedes and we drove directly to an interim IBM rented villa; actually, just a large concrete house with several bedrooms and kitchen facilities. They dropped me off and casually said to get some rest and they'd be back to pick me up for lunch. I was in Vietnam!

The next few weeks were spent getting oriented - learning who our customers were, where they were located, what needed to get done and how I would participate. Also, I needed to find permanent housing and take care of transportation. One of the highlights of most days was what we did after work – a cutthroat sporty croquet game with my fellow IBMers. I soon learned that, it was more a game for burning off energy and work frustrations. Then, after croquet, we sometimes went across a dirt alley to the rooftop bar and restaurant and watch flares being dropped from fixed wing aircraft, followed by helicopter gun ships firing at Vietcong positions across the Saigon River. It was all pretty neat from the safety of that rooftop a few miles away.

There was also another orientation taking place with me. That was the discovery of the different sounds, tastes, smells and scenes of Southeast Asia. The sound and smoke of the Saigon traffic struck me immediately. Instead of two rush hours a day, there were four – the morning and evening, of course – but also the noon time and afternoon commutes. It seemed like most everyone went home for lunch, followed by a siesta, and then back to work. The traffic consisted not only of private and military vehicles, but interspersed everywhere were the smoking 50cc Honda motor bikes carrying as many as six or sometimes seven passengers, the Lambrettas (a mini pickup truck with as many passengers as could be squeezed in the back), the front loaded three wheeled motor vehicles, the myriad of little blue and yellow taxis, and even cyclos, a bicycle with an open passenger's seat in the front and pedaled by a Vietnamese driver, with whom you had to place your complete trust and future. This conglomeration backed up at traffic lights and squeezed into every available roadway space. When a stoplight changed, it became an "everyone for their selves" scenario resulting in honking of horns, numerous near misses and random scrapes. There were many other sightings, such as trash along the sides of the road, the "stinky creek" (a black oily slow flowing garbage dump) that we crossed every time we went into town, traffic shutdowns for political, military dignitaries or funeral processions and all other strangeness too numerous to mention.

Things were going well and I was getting adjusted and thinking that this assignment was going to be great. Then one night, I woke up to a loud THUMMMPP!!!. What was that? Then, another THUMMPP! I had no idea what was happening and no training on what to do, but I remembered somewhere in my past that in case of an earthquake, go under the sturdiest doorway in the center of the house. I did that just in time to hear several more thumps, I stood there, probably thirty minutes not knowing if that was the last one. The next morning I asked what happened. It turned out that the Viet Cong had indiscriminately and successfully fired a series of 122 mm rockets into Saigon and the closest hit was about four blocks away killing two civilians. That is when I first realized I was truly in a war zone.

Finding housing was rather straightforward. I moved into a two-bedroom apartment with CE Glen Marshall. Finding transportation was another matter. We were authorized to import one vehicle, but I did not want to wait. Plus, to buy a new car we needed to pay up front and I didn't have the cash. So, I opted to buy a VW Beetle from Maurice Brewster who was leaving to go to Germany. The VW was really great for maneuvering in the crowded city traffic. A friend sent a "THINK SNOW" bumper sticker from Denver and afterward the car was easily identified where ever I went.

One of the biggest benefits of being in Vietnam was IBM's R&R policy. It was patterned after the U.S. Military policy that allowed troops to visit such destinations as Bangkok, Singapore, Australia and even Hawaii. Since we were not authorized to use chartered military aircraft, we were given the equivalent airfare to Hawaii and allowed to go wherever we wanted within that budget limitation. Carl Odegaard and I decided to go to Africa together.

The first leg of our trip took us to India where we saw the exquisite Taj Mahal at Agra. From there we flew to Nairobi, Kenya where we went on a two-day safari to Ngorogoro Crater and the Serengeti Plain. At a rest stop along the way, there was a Masai warrior in full costume willing to pose for a picture with him for the right amount of money. I wanted a picture, but did not really want to pay him directly, so I challenged him to a spear-throwing contest. If I won, I did not have to pay. If I lost I had to pay. I threw first and he had no difficulty beating my throw. "Two out of three?" I asked. "No." So I paid for the picture I would have paid for anyway. When we arrived at the hotel at Serengeti, we discovered that they did not have our hotel reservation. After consulting with our driver (an elderly man with one ear lobe hanging down to his shoulder and with a gaping hole in it) he said there was no problem and took us to the hotel where a lot of the drivers stayed. We were given a room directly above the bar and there was music and dancing and drinking most of the night, but that was comforting because we really did not know if we were safe. Upon our return to Nairobi, we flew on to Entebee, Uganda and stayed in Kampala. Carl and I met a couple of girls who wanted to know if we wanted to go dancing, so we ended up at a dance hall somewhere outside of Kampala. We were the only white people there, but I never felt unsafe until later when I realized we were in Idi Imin's Uganda. This was my first and best R&R, but all of them that followed were welcome respites from the daily tension and rat race that was Saigon.

Two years in Vietnam passed rapidly and I signed up for a third year. As time went by and the war moved farther and farther from Saigon, life became less stressful and more enjoyable. There were, however, times of laughter, times of sadness, and times of fearfulness. I cannot tell you everything, but I will pass on some of the memories that I still have of those three years.

New Year's Eve 1968 was my first in Vietnam. It was almost like a new year's eve in the USA - until Midnight! We were on a rooftop when all of a sudden people everywhere began firing weapons straight up into the sky. Utter Chaos!! I quickly left the rooftop and made sure I was somewhere in the middle of the building. The spent shells had to return to earth somewhere, but not on my head. I spent two more New Year's eves in Vietnam, but never really got used to this type of celebration.

On another occasion, summer of 1969, I was again sitting on the same rooftop, this time with a Vietnamese girl who could speak English. I looked up at the moon and said something like, "You know, the Americans have a man walking on the moon right now." She replied, very seriously, "How long did it take to get there?" I replied, "I believe it took two to three days." "How long does it take to get to the United States?" she asked. This time I replied "Oh, about a day." Her surprising response was "Oh, so the moon is not that much farther."

One of the missions of the U.S. Military was to train some of the local Vietnamese to take over jobs performed by American personnel. I was given the task of training a group of six in programming and systems engineering. We started with programming. Boy, were they great!! The education system in Vietnam was and probably still is based upon learning by rote. Repeated over and over, you never forgot. If a COBOL program needed a decimal somewhere, they never forgot. Their programs would go through the assembler without an error. Systems design however was a completely different situation. I would give them a problem and ask them to develop a solution. "Give us the answer," they would say. The concept of having to analyze and create a solution was not part of their upbringing. Slowly, some of them got it; some never did get it.

The road from Saigon to Long Binh, site of Headquarters U. S. Army Vietnam, was crowded, noisy, dirty and dangerous. I drove it several days a week. I was getting tired of the strain of getting there so one day I decided to take a back road. I knew if I took this rickety bridge across the Saigon River it would get me on a road to Long Binh. However, it was actually Highway One west out of Saigon. I was surprised to discover how light the traffic was and finally realized that there were NO OTHER CARS. I smartly turned around and headed back to Saigon to discover I had made a wrong left turn instead of right turn. I later found out that I was on the road to Tay Ninh, and well past the now famous Viet Cong tunnels at Cu Chi and approaching the Cambodia border. A few other IBMers drove the same road, but I chose not to push my luck and never again deviated from the tried and true roads.

Wherever you went on Army installations, there were telephone poles. They provided seating at the on base softball fields. They provided stability for ground that tended to erode during the heavy monsoon rains. They were useful for construction projects. But, the real question was, "why was there so many of them?" An investigation was made and it was discovered that a supply clerk who needed to order telephone poles thought he was ordering board feet when in fact he was ordering each (previously discussed).

Cam Ranh Bay was a beautiful natural inlet in the central coastline of South Vietnam. I went to Cam Ranh Bay with Paul Senior from Computer Sciences Corporation and several Army officers to look at a data processing site for a new supply depot. I traveled on a C-130 for the first time. No seats, just netting against the side of the plane and noisy, noisy, noisy. The facility was great and ready to operate. I went back for technical support several times. There was not much to do there after work, so one night I decided to go to an outdoor movie. Yes, the seats were all telephone poles.

I started talking with a GI who had just returned from a two-week patrol in the jungle. He told me, "We can see the VC and they can see us, but if we are lucky we just keep passing each other and nothing happens. On the other hand, if someone starts shooting and we call in air support, all hell breaks loose and there are lots of casualties." This may have been an exception, I didn't know. It was a strange war. He also told me they were restricted from shooting into the rubber plantations (reportedly a common and secure resting place for the Viet Cong) because the Army was required to pay the French plantation owners $195 for each damaged rubber tree. I had no way of verifying the accuracy of this comment either, but thought it made an interesting story.

Close to the end of my assignment I went to Qui Nhon, which was about half way between Cam Ranh Bay and Da Nang, and a gateway from the coast to facilities in the Central Highlands. The Army was building another depot to support 'Highlands' supply requirements. Ground transportation inland from Qui Nhon was dangerous (one stretch of road in the highlands along Route 19 was known as 'ambush alley') so this time I was most fortunate to travel "in style" in a U21 Ute, the Army's equivalent of the turboprop Beechcraft King Air. However, there was no landing strip so we were supposed to land at the Air Force facility about 40 miles north and helicopter in. After a very rough landing in the middle of a typhoon, we were told that the helicopters would not fly because of the typhoon, but that they had provided an armored gun truck for us. We started out with just our small party, but soon started picking up other soldiers who were trapped by the rising waters. I was sitting in the back next to a GI with a machine gun and several clips of ammunition. He was dressed in his full combat uniform, pack and all. I had on my white shirt and tie and briefcase, but they did provide me a helmet. What a contrast!

It was a slow dangerous drive with lots of vehicles off the road because of flooding. We made it and spent the night at the BOQ (Bachelor Officers Quarters). If this was how traveling officers lived on the road, I could only imagine the facilities for enlisted men. The next morning, however was sunny and bright. The new depot was located a few miles away in the Long My valley. We drove to the facility and I helped ascertain that "all was ready for data processing occupancy." I learned later that the land on which this depot was built was owned by my future grandfather-in-law. He paid income taxes to the South Vietnamese government after sale of his land, but refused to also pay more taxes to the part time controlling Viet Cong. Subsequently, he was killed by the Viet Cong while sitting in his rocking chair at the age of 93.

The farthest north I went was to Phu Bai, northwest and across a mountain pass from Hue and almost to the DMZ. There was an Army Division (101st Airborne, I think) based there. We were continually getting complaints that their unit record machines (key punches, sorters, collators and accounting machines for punched cards) were constantly down. While IBM did not have responsibility for maintenance in such remote locations, we did train GIs to do self-maintenance and someone decided to have me go take a look. The facility where the equipment was located was not the best, but adequate and they had plenty of spare parts. So I asked the officer in charge if I could talk to the maintenance personnel. Oh no, he said, they are out on patrol and won't be back for several days. How, I asked him, could you get the equipment fixed if they were out on patrol? He understood and agreed, but said he had no choice because everyone was required to participate in patrol and guard duty. I do not know how that got resolved, but I did take the message back to USARV headquarters at Long Binh. That night in Phu Bai was a rather sleepless night with flares lighting up the skies all night and the boom, boom, boom of outgoing artillery to accompany them – all a part of the job!

Off the coast of Vung Tau was a Navy hospital ship. It had IBM equipment aboard so I was sent down to make sure they were getting the support they needed. I boarded a helicopter at Hotel One and as we departed I noticed what a great country this could be without war. Rice paddies everywhere, farmers tending their animals, and lots of greenery. I'm not sure how high we went but the view was outstanding, and the flight smooth. Upon landing on the ship, I was met by the OIC, had a great lunch on board, made sure they knew how to reach us if they needed maintenance and boarded the helicopter to return to Saigon. This time I noticed we were cruising along the Saigon - Vung Tau highway, and not at a very high altitude. I also noticed that the GI manning the machine gun by the door seemed to be a lot more alert and tense. I asked him what's going on and why were we flying so low. Oh he said, rather nonchalantly, "We are flying under the artillery trajectories."

I received a letter from my mother one day who told me that my good high school friend was in Vietnam and I should look him up. We had not seen each other since high school about 14 years prior. Sure, Mom, I thought, there are only 500,000 troops in Vietnam and they are scattered all over the country. One day, I entered the computer room at Long Binh and lo and behold there was my high school friend mounting tapes on the tape drives. We exchanged contact numbers and promised to get together later to catch up on things, but there was no time then because they were running a supply cycle. Maybe more telephone poles? Every requisition for military material went through the Long Binh depot and every moment counted in getting one cycle done so they could move on to the next cycle. There was no time to connect with old friends, even good ones, who you had not seen in 14 years.

As my three years in Vietnam were coming to an end, I had a time to reflect on the changes that I had seen. I arrived right after the May 1968 offensive in which street fighting occurred in Saigon's outskirts. We were told going to Cholon after that was dangerous, which we did anyway and regularly for the many excellent Chinese restaurants. One Sunday before I left, I suddenly had a desire to see more of Vietnam. I decided to drive through Cholon down Highway 4 to My Tho, a city about 60 miles south of

Saigon in the Mekong River delta, and a popular tourist destination today. I did not go farther because that would require a ferry across the river and I was doubtful about getting back. As I drove past quiet farms and villages, and people casually going through their daily routines, it occurred to me this was as peaceful as it gets anywhere in the world, at least that day and in daylight. I am convinced we won the war on the ground; we gave it away at the peace table and in Washington D.C. My heart goes out to all of the Vietnamese and Americans who made the ultimate sacrifice for others, only to find out that it was all in vain.

It was finally time to go back to the United States. Part of the agreement for going to Vietnam was that my old IBM office would accept me back when I returned. That, however did not necessarily mean they had a meaningful job for me. I spent a couple of months in Tulsa working with marketing representatives teaching them to use new on line financial tools. They were all busy trying to make sales quota, so while what I was teaching them was probably beneficial; it was probably also a burden. I did other myriad jobs, but did not have anything that was particularly challenging

I also noticed that things had changed. Actually, things did not change; I had changed. Denver Broncos, Nebraska Cornhuskers, and Colorado Buffalos, while still of interest, did not stir up the fanaticism that they once did. I used to enjoy going to parties and meeting new people but noticed that conversations often died around me. They were interested in movie stars, local social activities, and, quite frankly, needless gossip. I was interested in international affairs, and found most of my friends lacked the knowledge to participate. One particularly annoying comment I heard over and over was, "Why are we fighting that war? The peasants in Vietnam could care less what kind of government they have." I knew better. So, I was getting antsy again.

Then I received a phone call from Bill Doody, the old Honolulu Branch Manager, who was now with IBM in Washington D.C. He wanted to know if I was interested in returning to Asia Pacific. Our representatives, Bob Colley in Okinawa and Rob Moore in Thailand were due to rotate home. Bill knew that I knew the territory very well and was comfortable with living overseas. Would I? Yes! In a heartbeat!

So, in June 1972, four years after my move to Vietnam in 1968, and one year after I returned to the United States, I was on my way to Okinawa. Okinawa was a major support location for the U.S. military in Vietnam as well as a major parts depot for IBM machines in SEA. Peace talks were in progress in Paris, and the U.S. Military in Vietnam was well into the draw down. Containers after containers were arriving daily in Okinawa with "who knows what machine things" inside of them. We installed a separate computer program just to keep track of this entire returning inventory.

One of my first assignments was to return to Saigon and meet with the Military people at DAO responsible for IBM equipment in country. I also met with Jack Ewen, General Manager of IBM WTC Vietnam. I needed to understand and help manage what would happen to IBM GEM assets (remaining computer systems) if a peace agreement were reached.

Also, from Okinawa, I was planning a trip a few months later to see our customers in the Philippines. Then came the edict from Clark AFB – all nonessential travel was to cease immediately. Something big was about to happen, and speculation was that the Paris Peace Conference was about to conclude with the signing of the Paris Peace Accords (signed January 27, 1973). To great fanfare, it was done. We were about to get out of the war, with dignity. I remember being glued to the television watching a live broadcast of C141s arriving at Clark AFB from Hanoi with our POWs. I was proud to be an American as the former POWs deplaned and kissed the earth as the background scene was filled with fluttering American flags. These men were showing the world how much freedom meant to them. It was exhilarating and I felt that in my own very small way I had helped our country in these difficult times."

Author's comments: Stu's story, working for IBM on foreign assignment in Okinawa and Southeast Asia, continues for another three years. What follows is a condensed version about the remainder of his assignment and a marriage.

The U.S. Army Depot in Okinawa was a major facility supporting the duration of the war in Vietnam. They had a large computer installation and were Stu's main customer responsibility on the island, He also provided both technical and marketing assistance to the DAO in Saigon as that organization continued to manage data processing support to a much-diminished military advisory function for the ARVN and VNAF forces. He also called on the U.S. Air Force installations in Thailand – principally the data processing function transferred 13th AF at Nakhon Phanom.

During the course of multiple weeklong trips to Saigon, Stu meets and falls in love with a Vietnamese young lady, and his intermittent trips, to the city he knows so well, become much more than just technical advice, marketing paperwork and liaison between IBM GEM (the domestic US company and IBM World Trade Corp). Stu writes the following:

"Each time I saw Therese, I decided I wanted to know her better, so we started dating. But it was different than dating, as we know it in the United States. We would meet for tea or soda, but never really go "out". There was a good reason for this. Therese still had her local Vietnamese friends, her school, and her job at a lawyer's office. I do not think she wanted to be seen with an American as she might experience some resentment or worse from that side of her life. Slowly but surely I was getting myself involved."

Stu's IBM responsibilities continued: "In January 1975 I flew back into Vietnam, maybe for the last time, with the resolve to ask Therese to marry. She didn't say no, so it became, "what do we do now?" I had come prepared with my own passport, birth certificate and proof of baptism and confirmation. But in developing countries like Vietnam, you don't just ask for a passport and leave when you get it. In order to get Therese a passport, we needed a valid reason for travel. There are many good reasons for this restriction, one of which is being married to a foreign citizen. There was a major problem, however – we were not yet married. Which came first, marriage in the church and then legally married in a civil ceremony or vice versa? Fortunately, we chose the latter.

The next morning we went to a government office. I do not know if it was a federal office or a provincial office, but I remember filling out some paper work and then waiting with Therese and her father. An official called us into his office, put some papers on the desk and said, "sign here". It was all in Vietnamese, but I signed them and he said, "You are now married". Wow, that was quick!

We also needed to plan for what was to happen next. In order for Therese to leave the country, she needed a passport and exit visa from the Government of Vietnam. Since I was still living in Okinawa, Japan, she needed a visa to enter Japan. I also suggested that she get visas to enter Taiwan and the United States. That would give us flexibility in destinations. We also set the date for our church wedding. We were to get married in her church in Vung Tau in the latter part of April. That gave her almost three months to get the necessary travel documents.

At the same time, there were rumors that the North Vietnamese were beginning to infiltrate thousands of troops into South Vietnam. We were not too concerned because this happened every year during the dry season before the summer monsoons arrived. But that was before the signing of the Paris Peace Accords that supposedly ended the Vietnam War.

Soon it was March 1975. South Vietnamese President Nguyen Van Thieu had declared that his country could not defend the Central Highlands from the invading North Vietnamese Army. The rout was on. It was only a matter of time before the entire country would be overrun. But, how much time? Did we have time to wait for our wedding in late April? That thought kept going through my mind. Every day on the television news there were pictures of the panicking people picking up everything they owned and scrambling for safety. Out of Pleiku and Ban Me Thout -- into the cities of Da Nang and Nha Trang and Saigon. Finally I had seen enough. I needed to get Therese out of Vietnam. So, at the end of March I flew back into Saigon and talked with Therese. We agreed to try to wait because she really wanted to get married in her own church, but also agreed that I would stay in country until we married. Fortunately, I worked for a great company and had a very understanding (remote) boss.

I went to IBM Vietnam and talked with General Manager Jack Ewen. He suggested we get married immediately and get out of the country. He had already sent his family out and was leaving the next day for Hong Kong (See the last chapter). IBM management in Hong Kong wanted Ewen out of the country temporarily, but confidentially he told me that he would probably never be able to return. On that accord, he was right."

(Author's comment: History will show that IBM WTC left the entire company without any American leadership or a valid rescue plan for the employees who wanted to escape the immanent communist incursion).

There follows a very funny and almost tragic two days in which Stu and Therese' hastily arranged Catholic wedding takes place; then walking through the empty streets of Saigon, no spare clothes in which to change, her father spending the wedding night in their hotel room:

"You are getting married tonight!" I will never forget those five words – from her best friend Nga.. It was early on the morning of April 3. The day before, Therese's father had come into Saigon from Vung Tau and the approximately 70 mile trip was treacherous with multiple military check points that would only get worse if the situation deteriorated. There was no point trying to wait until the end of the month to get married in Vung Tau. There was no point in waiting at all.

Her father left early in the morning to go back to Vung Tau to get her wedding dress and bring her mother and brothers and sisters back to

Saigon. Therese had an even messier and more difficult task. The day before, her cousin had been shot in the back by one of his own troops (probably a secret Viet Cong). I found out later that she didn't just have to go and identify the body, but that she had to look at multiple bodies until she found him. It was a gruesome thing to have to do on her wedding day.

Finally, her dad showed up, but none of her family was with him. The travel from Vung Tau was so difficult and dangerous that they decided not to chance all of them coming and then try to return home. He did have the wedding dress.

The wedding was scheduled for 7 P.M. The chapel where we were to get married was not far from her apartment. So Therese put on her wedding dress there and I my one good suit and we went down stairs to catch a taxi. What a surprise! There were none. In fact there wasn't any traffic at all. There was only a lot of people milling around and talking excitedly. That was the afternoon a Buddhist monk decided to protest by setting himself on fire - just up the street from Therese's apartment. So we walked the couple blocks to the chapel, in our wedding clothes, to the applause of the milling throng.

The Catholic priest, Father Robert was French, but also fluent in Vietnamese and English. He had forgotten about our wedding and had to be summoned from a secret meeting (the Priests were discussing what they would do in the event of a Communist take-over). A good friend, Nga, did the readings in Vietnamese. Although Therese could have done her vows in English, Father Robert chose to do them in Vietnamese also. When it was time for my own vows, he got out the English version and I repeated my vows in English. It was not a huge wedding. There were only six people present. In addition to the priest, there was Therese, her dad, her roommate, and me. Her landlord made six and had been invited to take photographs, but his camera did not work. Thus, there are no pictures of our wedding.

After a fine wedding dinner at a nearby almost empty French restaurant on Tu Do Street, we left to walk to my hotel. It was not yet 10 o'clock curfew, but the streets were totally empty. We got to the hotel, and they had already lowered the metal barricade that most businesses used for security at night. We knocked on the barricade, and a member of the hotel staff came and opened the door. We walked in and immediately the guests who were still in the lobby began to cheer and clap when they saw our wedding clothes. It turned out that the Government had changed the curfew to 9 o'clock. Things were tightening up.

So, now, here we were in our hotel room on our wedding night, Therese and me - and her dad. Suddenly, Therese looked at me and started laughing. She said, "I don't have anything else to wear". I found a shirt and pajamas that she could wear and the three of us talked late into the night. What would her family do if the North Vietnamese took over the country? Her dad assured us that they could see the ships off of the coast of Vung Tau, and if it looked like the country would fall, they would hopefully be on one of the ships, as refugees. That didn't happen.

The next morning, her dad left to go back to Vung Tau. Therese and I went to the travel agent's office and fortunately were able to book a flight to Taipei for the next day. They checked all of her documents and determined she had everything necessary to leave the country. So we went to her apartment and began to pack up her few things; most of her personal things were still at her home in Vung Tau. For her, like so many others, this was truly a break from the past into an unknown future.

While we were at the travel agent office, there was a lot of scrambling and anxiety. It turned out that on that same morning, a C-5A Galaxy crashed in a rice paddy twelve minutes after take off from the Ton San Nhut airport. It was the initial flight of 'Operation Babylift'. 138 people, including 78 children, 35 DAO personnel and seven adoption volunteers were killed. Rumors spread that the plane had been shot down. It wasn't, but this was just another indication of the tenseness and prevailing negative atmosphere that consumed the entire nation. (Reports indicate that approximately 1200 children were evacuated from TSN following that C-5A crash, including 40 of the crash survivors – source: Wikipedia)

Finally, April 5 arrived. We did not know what to expect at the airport so arrived very early. We went to the counter, checked our bags, got our boarding passes and headed for the departure gates. In order to leave most foreign countries, passengers must go through the exit procedures. When we arrived at the immigration, there two lines – one for foreigners and one for Vietnamese. The Vietnamese line was almost empty and Therese cleared through in two minutes.

Although I was in Vietnam on a multiple entry/exit visa, most of the foreigners were not. Some were on work visas. Some of them were French citizens whose families had lived there for decades. Others were Americans who had worked for the U.S. Military or were civilian contractors, some were married or with girlfriends, and were now bailing out. There was also a smattering of Australians, Chinese (Taiwanese,) Koreans, and Europeans.

The common denominator for all of them was that in order to leave the country, they needed to have a certificate from the Government that they had met their tax obligations. Some had the papers, but many did not. Some were allowed to leave; others were not. I am not normally a suspicious person, but in this case, I imagine there was a bit of money trading hands while the paperwork was completed right there on the spot. Finally, it was my turn. I presented my passport, got my exit stamp, and we were on our way.

As we boarded the plane, I held my breath and thought for the first time that we were really going to make it. Therese, I am sure, was saying a prayer of Thanksgiving and concern for the rest of her family. The flight was uneventful; we arrived in Taipei, and sped through customs and immigration. From Taiwan we planned to fly direct to Okinawa, which was to be our first home. After a few days delay, we took an alternate route via Tokyo and were finally on the ground in Naha. I owned a small cement blockhouse in Awase, cement construction to survive the multiple typhoons that hit the island every year. We arrived safely and in the traditional fashion, I picked Therese up and carried her across the threshold into our new home. She said to me, "You know, this is the first time in my life I have entered a house and there was no one inside."

Stu and Therese remained in Okinawa through the year 1975 and then transferred to a new home in Hawaii to continue Stu's IBM career, and raise a family. His initial two-year assignment lasted almost eight years. Stu continues his narrative:

"Therese became a U.S. citizen that same year of 1975. One of the questions she was asked during her exit interview was which amendment to the Constitution is your favorite? Her answer was #19. Next question: Why is that your favorite? Answer: it gives women the right to vote! After several aborted attempts, her two brothers, Peter and Joseph, made it to the United States in 1980 after fleeing in a boat, picked up by a British freighter, dumped off in Singapore and six months in a refugee camp in Malaysia. They became U.S. citizens as soon after their arrival as possible.

Therese's father, mother, sister, and brother in law came to the United States in 1990 as part of an orderly departure program designed to unify families. Her father became a U.S. citizen as soon as eligible. When asked why he wanted to be a citizen he replied, "A man is not a man without a country; the United States is the greatest country on Earth."

Her mother, who speaks practically no English, was required to wait longer to qualify for citizenship in her native language. When asked whether she would take up arms to defend her country, she started to say "Oh. No, I couldn't shoot anyone." Therese's sister, present as an interpreter, said "Mom, just say yes." She did and is a proud citizen as well.

As I write this, 36 years later, I am still amazed at the grace and strength that Therese carried throughout the whole episode. South Vietnam fell on April 30th. We left on April 5th. In the course of a month, she got married, left home without saying good bye to her mother, sisters, and brothers, buried her cousin, moved to a totally new way of life, and saw her country fall. She displayed a determination to make her new life the total success it is today. We have two daughters, both professionals in their own right and we are living happily in Arizona. I retired from IBM in 1991 after a 27-year career. Thank you IBM Corporation!"

# Chapter 14
## The General's Boat Trip

FOR MORE THAN TWO YEARS I lived in a fine Saigon home on Cach Mang Street. The property was larger than most in the area and was walled with concertina running along the top of the surrounding stone walls. At each corner there were platforms and sandbags that had served as machine gun emplacements, which I didn't need but which had been in use when U.S. Army General Goodpaster and his staff had lived there a few years earlier. A large black steel double gate opened to a paved circular drive around a green lawn and the drive also extended down one side of the house under a large porte-cochere and down the other side of the house to a double side door entryway. There were a few large trees, some banana plants, bougainvillea and nice flower gardens along the walls.

*My Home in Saigon*

The white stucco house was two story and had four bedrooms, three baths, large living and dining rooms, a bar area and a huge kitchen at the rear. The ceilings were 12 feet high and almost every room had the classic electric fan. In back of the house on one side were several outbuildings where our maid and houseboys lived. There was extra parking to the rear. On the other side sat a large diesel generator used for backup electricity, if needed. Architecturally, it was French traditional, attractive to look at and was most comfortable during my residence.

The house did double duty; it was intended that the IBM Location Manager live there as sort of a perc, and the house could also provide a comfortable guest room for visiting stateside executives and serve as a meeting place for our office personnel. Fine business dinners were served for guests and fellow employees at the large dining room table. Many visiting IBM managers from DPD, FED, FSD and WTC enjoyed good meals, drinks and our hospitality in that house.

The property was owned by a retired Vietnamese General, to whom IBM paid a reasonable monthly rent. The General was a real gentleman and we became friendly tenants and also befriended a few of his family members. The General was born in 1917 but looked older, when I knew him, than his 58 years. Bruce Tomson found the house originally in 1968 and IBM occupied it up until our withdrawal in 1973. We took good care of the place and always paid the rent on time with a large paper bag full of piasters. Early on, the General was offered rental payments made to a Swiss bank account so he would have money there with which to educate some of his family; however, he turned the offer down. The General was a very honorable man and he and his family looked upon IBM as some kind of friendly benefactor. Out of that relationship came a plea for help a few years later, as related in a letter dated July 10, 1975 and addressed to his old friend Bruce Tomson who by then had become IBM Thailand's General Manager. The letter is written in English in a legible and neat handwriting; it is reproduced almost verbatim below:

Vietnamese Refugee Camp Vayama July 10th, 1975
Sattahip Naval Base
Sattahip, Chonburi (Thailand)

"Dear Mr. Tomson,

It is a great pleasure for me to receive, today, your letter of July 3rd; everyone in my family almost have the tears in their eyes as your letter is read aloud. A glance at the name below your signature immediately brings back to me all the memories of the 1969, 1970 period and I could easily figure out who is writing to me.

The memories that fill now my mind is not only those between lessee and lessor! They are much more than that, they are those created by a profound feeling of former friendship, of close human relationship between you personally and the other IBMers using my house in Saigon, and I and my whole family.

Thinking back of those days, I sometimes wonder whether my family, while offering our house in Saigon to you had behaved in a good manner enough vis-a-vis the IBM staff members. I even dare say that not only we were proud of our house but also proud of the IBM representatives, by their behavior and exemplary personalities, during the time they used it. I am glad you mentioned in your letter your appreciation of my 'taking care of the IBMers' using my house in Saigon. Please be assured that we did appreciate the relation my family had with the IBMers too.

Really, your letter recalls me a lot of wonderful souvenirs, including those family-styled lunches or dinners we had together in Saigon downtown, those nice talks as the sun set down on the flowered lawn of our house at 253 Cach Mang Boulevard.

However, everything is now gone, forever! Only the memories remain. In fact, before the fall of Saigon, I hardly thought that I would be loosing so many precious things with such a suddenness, in such a pitiful manner!

In fact, early enough in April, I wrote a letter to the US Embassy in Saigon, requesting for the evacuation to and resettlement in USA of my family. Subsequently I was assured that my case was OK'ed, my family was on an active file and I was given a place and time of departure. But on the morning of the 29th of April when we went to the rendezvous, there was no person, official or not to meet us. Meanwhile, Tan Son Nhut airport was becoming a chaos (remember my eldest son is an Engineer in Civil Aviation) because of the heavy VC rockets shellings, and North Vietnamese and VC troops were fighting at every Saigon gates.

I took the decision to bring my family quickly home, to re-arrange our luggage, caring only for the very minimum en-route needs and to flee immediately the trapped Saigon. Like fish in a tightening net, we fought our way through the crossfires, through the barbwires, through the unsecured roads and succeeded finally in reaching a small village on the seashore. During the process, my daughter was lost out of sight, together with her husband and two children.

That night was a ghostly one and our lives and the few belongings we brought along were about to be taken away by a horde of robbers, it was fortunate that we could win the deadly fight and save our own lives. Early on the next morning, we hastily rent a fishing boat to sail to the high sea with the hope of being rescued by the US vessels we know awaiting offshore. Unfortunately, the boat was too fragile to support the sea waves and we could only follow the shoreline, sailing south. By the time we changed to a bigger fishing boat, it was too late when we overheard on the radio broadcast that all the US vessels were terminating their mission and heading for Subic Bay.

After a seven day-and-night journey, sailing 24 hours a day, assuring our navigation by the most rudimentary instruments and maps, after suffering from hunger, thirst, sea piracy and sickness (my wife is 58 and my daughter-in-law is pregnant); after our boat was about to sink, we finally boarded the land at Sattahip Naval Base, where we were taken in charge by the Thai Navy authorities (now transferred to the Ministry of Interiors Department of Public Welfare). At least we found Freedom and we breath the air of Peace, our sufferings are temporarily ended, we are now waiting for another peaceful but lengthy exodus: that which will bring us to a final resettlement in USA to restart our lives from zero.

We have spent more than two months in this camp, hygiene and feeding are the minimum ones. Meanwhile, my daughter-in-law gave birth to a wonderful but prematurely born baby girl, bringing the total numbers of the family to 12 persons."

The same letter goes on:

"Dear Mr. Tomson,

I am a retired General, Former Director of Military Security, Minister of Information and Vice Prime Minister. When I retired, in 1965, though taking the decision to put an end to my political career, I continued to keep myself up-to-date with the current developments of the overall situation in Vietnam. I had no political activity but writing articles, published on Vietnamese newspapers, trying to draw the attention of the politicians and others on the way to keep South Vietnam in the Free World. My spare time was used for reading, planting flowers, educating my children, taking tea and writing my memories. All my life, I have wanted - and succeeded - to be uncorrupted, honest (this is why I have rented my house as the only way to financially support my family living, instead of thrusting myself into the more or less 'dirty' business of those retired or acting generals and politicians of Saigon corrupted world). And now, I have lost everything. Nobody will take care of the tombs of our ancestors, all my career, my houses, my relatives, my most precious personal library, my daughter with her husband and children (for whom my wife is now crying every night), my

beloved country, my companions and friends.... all these precious belongings of a man's life are now left behind, maybe forever, with no hope for retrieval!

Yet, I have and am known by some of the well known American personalities such as former Ambassador Henry Cabot Lodge, Generals Paul Harkins and Westmoreland, Mr. Colby now head of the CIA, General Taylor and some others. But all these gentlemen belong to the political world, but I don't want to commit them by seeking their assistance, into any kind of engagements, which may have (by side effects or misinterpretation) harmful consequences to their career.

My family and I are deeply touched by the kindness, frankness and the friendship you express in your kind letter. Far of our mind any intention to create any sort of disturbances to you, however we know you are the right person whom we can count on, during these difficult times. Therefore I am sincerely begging you to help us facing the present and near future problems.

In principle, my family belongs to the 'category 2' (among 3 categories of Vietnamese refugees in Thailand, already approved by Washington to be resettled in the USA) because I have a 'close relative already admitted in the USA'; in fact, one of my sons, Mr. -------, his wife and their daughter, have already been evacuated to Guam, to Camp Pendleton then, and now temporarily resettled at Hope Village, Weimar Medical Center,

Weimar, California 955376. The process is reportedly (by Mr. Meinheit, US Embassy, Bangkok) underway. Pending a formal approval from and by Washington, we will be moved to U-Tapao USAF Base, and from there airlifted to USA. We are expecting thus to leave this camp in one week or two.

If we are airlifted to USA, we are lucky as compared with our compatriots and relatives left behind in Vietnam. Nevertheless, we will be facing many problems once in America, the most urgent would be of material order, in other words we will have to find out sponsors to get us out of the camp, to bring us into the everyday normal life and to find jobs to financially support ourselves in order not to constitute a long and heavy load to our potential sponsors (and we won't have no house for rent once in America, even if the IBMers wanted to!).

So, we are asking your assistance in two fields: Sponsorship and Employment."

This lengthy emotion filled letter goes on to propose that the General split up his family into three smaller sponsorable groups so as not to be too heavy a burden on any one sponsor. It also discusses the qualifications of each member of the family for use in finding jobs and a request to work for IBM is made. The two sons were both well educated and graduate engineers from schools in France and a daughter was trained to be a high school teacher of English; they were all multi-lingual. The letter closes, as follows:

"Dear Mr. Tomson,

While you are in Bangkok and intending to pay a visit to us, we are wondering whether we should ask you to bring us some things we badly need due to the very limited facilities available to us here.

- a baby carrying bed for a 2 month old baby .... and some dozens of disposable diapers.
- some mentholed filtered cigarettes
- some canned fruit cocktails and vitamin C tablets.

Please do not hesitate to 'forget' any or all of the above items if you consider that we are abusing your goodness, your kindness, we will understand that despite your willingness you could not do so."

*Dan E. Feltham*

"Dear Mr. Tomson,

How could I ever express enough my joy and my family's at the receipt of your letter. How could I ever thank you enough for your kind attention and your spontaneous willingness to help.

For all this, my family and I wish to express verbally our appreciation and deepest grateful feelings during your coming to visit to our family here.

Warm personal regards,
General ------------------"

Bruce Tomson did follow up with the U.S. Embassy in Bangkok, but to no avail. He also visited the Sattahip refugee camp several times in order to help the General and his family through their ordeal and provide them with some of the things they needed. The General was the senior Vietnamese officer in the refugee camp and as a result was given the only tent site with a cement pad. The rest of the camp lived in the mud and squalor of the summer monsoons. Status helped a little. During one visit Bruce helped the General pen a plea for help to then Secretary of State Henry Kissinger in Washington, D.C. The reply said that the General's file was missing and there was nothing they could do. Bruce went back a second time to solicit aid from the U.S. Embassy--same result, nothing. Never one to give up, Bruce then enlisted the help of the Department of Labor in Washington, who helped him contact CIA Director William Colby, who knew the General. Colby was shocked that the General was still in Thailand and things began to happen. The General's family received approval to travel to California in late July, and while the General's file was being re-created, Bruce obtained permission to move the General to his IBM General Manager's quarters in Bangkok. Approval for California finally came through and in late September, the General finally flew east to join his family. Tomson paid for the airline ticket. How helpful can you be!

I have reproduced this letter and the General's story for two reasons:

1. A copy of the letter has been in my possession for many years, and

2. The story of the General's escape from Vietnam is one of many thousands like it and represents a very touching and soul searching example of what the South Vietnamese people had to experience in order to flee communism and retain their precious freedom.

The emotions within the letter give good insight as to the love of family, an inner strength, determination and instinct for survival of these Vietnamese who were forgotten in the last days of April 1975 by our country's faithless diplomats. Nevertheless, they were willing to endure indescribable hardships and believed in our American ways strongly enough to risk everything to come to our country. These strengths have made most Vietnamese outstanding U.S. citizens.

# Chapter 15
## Vietnamization & De-Escalation

We were in Vietnam to do a job - assist the U.S. military with information processing and maintain the equipment, but we couldn't help but have personal feelings about the war and some of the strange military decisions being made. We did not understand what was going on back home, especially those of us who had been in SEA for a couple of years. Why didn't the American people want us to win this war and come home victoriously like we had always done in past wars? What was happening with the Paris Peace Talks, and what political deals were affecting our ability to wage war correctly (i.e. – Al Davis, "Just Win Baby!") Where did the idea and term 'Vietnamization' originate and why was it all of a sudden U.S. policy? The new policy was to turn the war over to the Vietnamese military forces and stockpile additional supplies and equipment for their use. While we IBMers were working and playing hard, what was really going on? There were many questions and few answers. I have since read that the credit for coining the term "Vietnamization" went to Melvin Laird, President Nixon's Secretary of Defense, at a meeting on March 28, 1969, and a few weeks later Dr. Henry Kissinger, Nixon's National Security Advisor, issued a directive that "All agencies of the government work to achieve Vietnamization." Was this to be our winning strategy?

One day Cach Mang Street was cleared of normal traffic, security forces were put in place along this main artery into town and a cavalcade carrying President Richard Nixon drove by my house as I watched from my upstairs balcony. It was July 30, 1969, and Nixon had recently met with President Thieu on Midway Island on June 8th, so something was up. My general feeling at the time was that Nixon had a pretty good handle on what was happening in Vietnam and that he wanted to end the war with a victory by conquering the Viet Cong forces in the South and then invade North Vietnam, or, at least, bomb them into submission. I felt, along with many others, that the idea of a Haiphong ship blockade and a massive airdrop of American troops into Hanoi after many B-52 missions could stop their war machine and attain the desired results in short order. It seemed obvious to me that Nixon could direct such a victory. How idealistically naive! President Nixon had promised disengagement from the war when he was running for President in 1968 but he wanted **"peace with honor"** and was in Saigon to discuss U.S. troop withdrawal plans with Thieu.

By the end of 1969, population control in the countrysides rose to a reported 90%, versus 67% for the period prior to the January 30, 1968 TET offensive. Enemy troops were switching over – defecting - to South Vietnam and more than 1.5 million Vietnamese civilians were resettled or returned to their native villages. However, about 40% to 50% of the population lived in the cities (versus 15% before the war), and most of them were in Saigon and Cholon, with a large portion subsisting at a refugee level. The Vietnamization process was beginning to work, at least on paper in Washington, D.C.

In early 1970 the level of concern for the safety of Saigon rose a notch. Curfews were earlier, more American and RVN troops were on alert, more barbed wire was put in place throughout the streets of Saigon and sandbagged gun emplacements were increased around the city. Rumors of a huge buildup of North Vietnamese regulars along the western border, but still inside Cambodia, were discussed daily, and too many men and supplies were coming unchecked down the Ho Chi Minh Trail. Our military friends on the bases were suggesting that perhaps we IBMers should buy and store extra water and food in our respective civilian villas. Military and civilians alike seemed to be more tense, and an air of deep concern prevailed throughout Saigon, a city preparing for a siege. More uncertainty. Why had we permitted such a buildup in the Cambodian sanctuaries, were the rumors true and when would there be an enemy attack?

On April 29, 1970, the ARVN (Army of the Republic of Vietnam) entered Cambodia. On April 30, 1970, President Nixon announced in a U.S. national television address that the combined forces of U.S. and

South Vietnamese ground troops had crossed the border into Cambodia and attacked the communist sanctuaries. They found and destroyed massive amounts of weapons, ammunition and supplies brought there courtesy of the *neutral* Cambodian trails. These sanctuaries had been the staging areas for the NVA's limited incursions into South Vietnam and were probably the staging areas for an imminent major NVA invasion. Our allied invasion aroused more anti-war protests in the U.S.A. and precipitated the May 4th Kent State University killings of four student protestors by U.S. National Guardsmen. However, Nixon's announcement and subsequent local rumors of our counterattacks gave those of us in Saigon a great uplift, a sense of relief; our homes, livelihood, friends and all of Saigon were finally being protected. I didn't know about the protests at home but I have always respected President Nixon for taking that timely action. The Vietnamese military gained confidence from their Cambodian success and they controlled their own country for the remainder of 1970 and through 1971. Still, I also naively wondered why it was OK to invade Cambodia but not OK to cross the DMZ and invade North Vietnam. The sandbags and concertina remained in place throughout the city streets, but the military presence in Saigon relaxed, the curfew returned to a later hour and the threat of attack receded from Saigon by a few dozen miles. American troops were withdrawn from Cambodia in July and in December 1970, the U.S. Congress voted to restrict the President's power as Commander-in-Chief, in the middle of the war. Perhaps for the first time in our history, a President could not direct his military; he was forbidden to introduce American ground troops into Laotian trails, route of the enemy supplies. He was forbidden to take the action that many believed could win the war. However, there were no restrictions, at that time, on the air war. What the hell was going on?

This was about the time that the Senior Master Sergeant at MACV called me and told me to have our fifty M-2 rifles back to MACV within two weeks. The idea within our military was that they were going to arm the ARVN with M-2s instead of M-1s and our fifty rifles were part of the plan. This meant to us that part of 'Vietnamization' was that the South Vietnamese soldier could now be trusted to shoot more than one bullet at a time; real progress! As explained earlier, I said "No" to the sergeant, "We prefer to keep the M-2s". He didn't understand the word "No" and escalated the order to our sponsoring MACV Colonel, but we held out for another six months. There was something comforting about those M-2s. Our IBMers, especially those men upcountry, didn't want to give up their authorized defensive weapons.

Also, about this time as tension was building along the Cambodian border, we had just completed several highly successful computer installations. Our successes reached the attention of upper IBM management and personnel awards and recognition letters for a job well done were forthcoming. I received a phone call from my manager in Honolulu that some special recognition would be coming my way too. Sure enough, a week or so later a letter from the Office of the President, IBM Data Processing Division in White Plains, New York, arrived saying that I had been selected as the top Marketing Manager in the GEM Region for the month of January and that I should come to New York the following week in order to have lunch with the President of IBM's Data Processing Division on Friday, April 2. There would also be a product briefing and dinner that evening, again with the DP President. The letter went on to say that I would be contacted shortly by their 'Special Activities Department' regarding final arrangements. It concluded with, "Again, my congratulations and I look forward to seeing you on the 2nd. Sincerely, R.A. Pfeiffer Jr." At first, I thought this was an April Fool's joke someone was playing on me, but it was confirmed by my manager and his manager who both encouraged me to go. I actually thought about it - for a few minutes; "Wow, a rare opportunity to receive marketing recognition at the highest level at IBM's Corporate Valhalla." I then sat down and wrote a letter thanking the Data Processing President for the thought, but that my place was in Saigon and it was not logical to fly half way around the world to have lunch for simply doing my job. I went on to explain - two pages if I remember correctly - that we had more important things to do and that the circumstances in Saigon were extremely tense and required my presence rather than me flying away on what seemed to be a boondoggle (perhaps I used a more polite term, but I am sure they got the message). "Thanks very much, but no thanks." I did receive a telegram from the so-called 'Special Activities Department' on the afternoon of April 2 which said the following, "Arrive in New York no later than April 1 evening, proceed to St. Regis Hotel where room is reserved, first event Friday morning (April

2) at 1030, lunch and go to meetings with R.A. Pfeiffer, dinner with Mr. Pfeiffer, return to New York 9:30, Saturday free if you intend to remain through Sunday or have interest seeing Broadway shows, please advise. You are one of four managers and their wives attending." (Note: name of telegram sender is withheld to protect the stupid!). I worried about my decision, but thought the invitation was really dumb! They never said so, but I believe that my Honolulu management was embarrassed for letting that inappropriate award process go as far as it did, and "Guess what? I never heard back from IBM HQ and never received any recognition what-so-ever." In fact and in retrospect, I was never invited to New York again for the rest of my career! Maybe it really was an April Fool's joke, but I didn't bite. I also guess refusals were not acceptable at that level in IBM, even if they didn't appreciate our critical situation in Vietnam. I would certainly do the same thing again.

Apparently, I made the right decision - at least from my customer's point of view. A letter on MACV stationary, dated 23 June 1971, was sent to my manager in Honolulu. It read:

"Dear Sir (name withheld):

As I prepare to finish my tour as Chief of the Data Processing Agency at the Military Assistance Command in Vietnam (MACV), I would like to pass on to you my appreciation for the outstanding support I have received from your local representatives. They have been cooperative, informative, and available at all times, and they have helped me complete a successful year of providing computer support for our military operation in Southeast Asia.

None of this would have been possible without the excellent management of Mr. Feltham. Therefore, I hope you will pass on our appreciation to him and his staff. You can be assured that your company has been well represented during the past year at this agency."

Sincerely,

(Name withheld)

Colonel, USA"

From time to time, IBM executives from our Regional Office in

California and from GEM Headquarters in Bethesda, Maryland would come to Saigon for a few days to review our welfare and to make high-level customer calls. These executives had the ultimate responsibility for our presence and wellbeing in Vietnam and had to determine, first hand, whether we were being effective. Also, in view of the political turn-around within the IBM Company and the U.S.A., they had to determine how to correctly remove our operation in concert with the military's de-escalation. IBM management was not only concerned about our safety but also concerned about becoming over committed to what was becoming an increasingly unpopular cause. We were asked to put together an escape plan and jokingly my initial thoughts went to our three rickety 16-foot ski boats, but I admitted that we would probably have to rely on a military or Embassy sponsored evacuation in the event of a North Vietnamese incursion.

The executives would arrive and expect General Officer calls to be established and scheduled to fit their two or three day visit. This was not always an easy task. Generals of the Air Force, Marines or Army had their own agendas and usually did not want to be bothered by a social, fact-finding or computer business call by someone who they thought probably shouldn't be in country and who probably didn't understand how busy they were. However, we were persistent and knew that we had better set up meaningful appointments for our important visitors, who needed the visibility back home, whose support we needed and who could have such an effect on the success of our Vietnam operation. Our IBM executives had to return to the States and be able to say that they had called on so-and-so general and had had some important face-to-face discussions. Military protocol had to be followed, and we asked our data processing officers to assist with these appointments. They usually agreed because they too could benefit through our comments made at such visits.

During one such IBM Regional Manager's trip to Saigon in October of 1970, I was able to arrange appointments with six stars and an Ambassador. In two days, we called on four 7th AF and USARV generals - two Major Generals and two Brigadier Generals - and finally we paid a visit to Ambassador Ellsworth Bunker at the U.S. Embassy. The purpose of the General Officer calls was to assure the military that they had our full support, to make sure that the military knew we were there (as originally requested by Tom Watson), to help determine a time frame for our IBM departure in conjunction with the U.S. military's ultimate departure, and to say, "Thank you for the business" to some of IBM's best customers. The purpose for the call on Ambassador Bunker was to establish an Embassy point of contact in case of any emergency with our personnel or operation. I have saved the following letter:

> "Dear Ambassador Bunker:
>
> I enjoyed meeting with you last month and appreciated your consideration in affording Dan Feltham a point of contact at the Embassy.
> I would like to express best wishes for success from both the IBM Corporation and myself in your vital work in behalf of our country.
>
> Sincerely yours
> (name withheld)
> IBM District Manager"

In point of fact, the Embassy only paid lip service to setting up a point of contact with our local GEM office, but fortunately we never needed their assistance. On the other hand, that was a good IBM executive visit.

I am much tempted to add here and will, that all these high level IBM executive trips to Nam also provided them ample opportunities for shopping sprees on their way through Honolulu, Hong Kong and/or Bangkok.

For some reason the number 540,000 has stuck in my mind as representing the high water mark of U.S. military personnel physically in Vietnam at the peak of the military buildup (my research places the actual number somewhere between 541,500 and 543,300 in April, 1969 with an additional 65,000 allied troops in country – those allies being Australia, New Zealand, South Korea, Thailand and the Philippines). President Nixon began troop reductions as early as June 1969 and by that December U.S. troop strength declined to 475,200. The reductions continued steadily for the next three years. I had graphed the military buildup and reductions on a chart for an IBM management briefing that tracked equivalent increases and reductions in IBM personnel and company assets. Both sets of data showed classic bell curves, with our manpower curve trailing the military's by 10 to 12 months. IBM-GEM probably had close to 100 American men in Vietnam and Thailand at the peak of our support, including Data Processing Division, Field Engineering Division, Office Products Division and Federal Systems Division personnel. By 1970, it had become clear that we too should start reducing our personnel headcount through '71 and '72, although the 'how many and how fast' was debatable. By July 1972, U.S. troop strength had been reduced to 45,600 and we knew we should get the hell out - and soon! (see Chapter 12 for more detail).

The early IBMers who had arrived in-country in 1967 and 1968 had more than completed their two year assignments and many had already rotated home. A couple of the men, who wanted to continue the grand adventure, had been re-assigned to positions in Bangkok where they could help coordinate sales and SE support in Thailand bases like Sattahip, Korat, Ubon, U Tapao, Takli, Udorn and NKP. A year's assignment in Bangkok was not too tough! The point is that we too were feeling company vibrations all the way from IBM HQ that this war was becoming highly unpopular and that we should hop on the Vietnamization bandwagon as a graceful way out. We didn't understand it - or didn't want to - but we began adjusting our longer range support plans. Several sources have since told me that the attitude within the higher echelons of IBM paralleled the general "Let's get out of Vietnam" attitude that was becoming prevalent throughout the U.S.A. The almost total lack of recognition for our efforts there over the years that followed have certainly confirmed the fact that IBM did not want to be accused of being a war-mongering mercenary company or perceived as making big money at the expense of a failed war effort. Our Saigon office may well have been one of the most profitable branch offices of comparable size in all of IBM's Data Processing Division during the years 1969 through 1971, but I am sure that those figures have been (purposely?) lost forever.

The next couple of years saw our operation trying to scale back, but growth has inertia. Obligations to maintain computer systems at an already established high level of excellence had to be met, older generation computers and unit record equipment was being replaced with more powerful S/360 systems, two year overseas assignments for our personnel had been promised (at least the 510 days out of 18 month tax free period had to be met), and many of us enjoyed what we were doing and did not yet want to return home to a normal career environment. Initially we began cutting headcount by becoming more efficient and curtailing non-essential services. For instance, our office was assigned two headcount slots for Office Products CEs (actually, four OP CEs, in total, served in Vietnam over time). The military had shipped literally thousands of IBM Selectric typewriters, a few big Selectric machines called Composers and some dictation equipment to Vietnam and they needed regular maintenance. There were typewriters everywhere, and the two CEs were constantly on the run trying to keep up with the number of service calls around Saigon and up country. They would receive calls like, "This is Captain so-and-so; can you get up here to Pleiku tomorrow and fix three typewriters?" Somewhere along the line, we changed policy and asked the military to begin taking care of their own typewriters or else bring them into our main office where our Field Engineering CEs could do a best efforts repair job whenever time permitted. Our typewriter maintenance contracts were phased out.

At other times, when a manager, CE, SE or administrative employee rotated home and we could rationalize the loss of a certain technical talent, we would not replace that person. Eventually, in mid 1972 we cut back to just one sales person in Saigon, a handful of CEs and two managers. However, it was difficult to just start sending men home at a time when we were all working in excess of 60 hours a week to support the ever increasing sophisticated level of the computer systems and the urgent needs of our good customers.

Early in our customer relationship with USAID (mid 1968), the need and an opportunity to give more responsibility to local Vietnamese was envisioned through a special computer training program for USAID sponsored Vietnamese students (refer back to Chapter 5). An IBM executive told our Saigon management that Corporate IBM was somewhat embarrassed because the U.S. IBM Corporation (IBM-GEM) was the major provider of computing equipment in Vietnam. He asked if there was a way for our organization to begin thinking about extricating ourselves from such a dominant position. An agreement was made between USAID, the local IBM WTC Saigon office and our own IBM-GEM office. It went something like this: Our stateside trained American SEs would train the USAID students in the principles of computer operations and several programming languages like COBOL, FORTRAN and Assembly Language. After a certain level of proficiency had been reached, the top 10% of the students would be given Systems Engineering jobs at the local Saigon office and the other 90% would go to work at various Vietnamese military installations. The arrangement had the blessing of the American Embassy and MACV, and the program that began in the fall of 1968 was certainly one of the first examples of what was later called "Vietnamization".

The USAID training had to be converted to what became known as Systems Engineering Services (SES) Contracts when IBM unbundled sales from technical assistance in 1969. Why IBM insisted on making us un-bundle in a war zone I never did understand. Yes, we were a part of the Data Processing Division, but an exception in a war zone could have been made if anyone higher up had argued the case. That policy change caused me to convert, overnight, four or five especially talented Systems Engineers to Marketing Representatives, because, according to the new IBM rules, SEs could not be on customer premises without billing for their time but our Marketing Reps could come and go as they pleased. We suddenly had a few new technical salesmen who continued to teach COBOL and FORTRAN as needed during their new, perhaps unwelcome and temporary careers (previously discussed in Chapter 5).

Another process of Vietnamization that had some merit was the transfer of certain computer applications from U.S. military control to RVN military control (e.g. command and control, intelligence and supply). There were two ways within the IBM business process that this could be accomplished: 1. The computer equipment could be transferred from MACV or Air Force or Army use, IF, in fact the asset was already owned outright by the U.S. Government or if our government wanted to buy it first. Most equipment was being leased or rented from IBM and the purchasing of equipment would have required complicated and lengthy procurement processes back in the U.S. which were not supported by any budgetary planning; or, 2. New equipment could be procured

by the Vietnamese Government (using USAID channeled funds? See *
footnote) from IBM's WTC's Saigon office. After initial installation and
testing, the application software and data would gradually be transferred
and the maintenance and technical support would then be provided by
IBM Saigon's Vietnamese personnel. This procedure would in turn free
up the U.S. military machines for return to either the IBM Company or
to their stateside military installations. This game of musical chairs with
computers took planning and cooperation and a few of the changes were
successful. The accompanying computer training and education for the
Vietnamese military and the WTC personnel in the 1971-74 time frame
greatly enhanced their technical proficiency. We began to work more
closely with World Trade's IBM Saigon personnel so that Vietnamese
CEs and SEs could improve their expertise with the more complicated
equipment. In today's world, this training and transfer might be called
'Nation Building'.

I recall a day in 1969 when we received a panic "we need your help"
call from IBM's downtown Saigon office. There was a 407 listing machine
installed at a local Vietnamese government office which had a 'unsolvable'
problem and we dispatched one of our American CE experts to assist in
a repair. He returned in about 30 minutes and reported that new power
cables had been ordered for the machine because rats in the building had
eaten clean through the existing cables. The IBM Vietnam CEs and their
customers were going to have to do better than that to meet their future
challenges!

The Paris Peace Accords were finally signed and MACV was closed
in March 1973. President Nixon authorized an expanded role for the
Defense Attaché Office (DAO) in Saigon to provide further assistance
to the South Vietnamese military. DAO was initially commanded by
Major General John Murray and from June 1974 to the fall of Saigon the
next year, Major General Homer Smith was in charge of the DAO. This
organization played a vital role in the transfer of IBM data processing
equipment from U.S. to Vietnamese ownership.

* Footnote: The US Agency for International Development (USAID)
was created in 1961 by Congress and President J. F. Kennedy. Its
mission was to adopt programs assisting foreign countries in economic
development and internal/external security. In addition to loans and

grants, AID assigned American specialists abroad and by the end of 1962 had 5000 employees overseas and were training 8000 foreign nationals. By 1965, AID was spending $2 billion a year and was operating in 70 foreign countries with 15,000 employees. Most workers were assigned to projects in agriculture, education and public health. In Vietnam, AID became involved in anti-Communist programs - public safety, civic action and rural and community development. Its 1967 budget exceeded $550 million. AID's image became somewhat tarnished in Vietnam when its ties to the CIA were revealed. In 1975 they assisted with refugee resettlement programs.

IBM provided products and services to the U.S. Military and to the U.S. Embassy and government contractors under provisions of a contract with the General Services Administration (GSA) in Washington, D.C. The GSA Contract was our operational bible and clearly defined rental, lease, purchase and maintenance prices. It applied to all U.S. Government Agencies world wide, but there was a special section in the back of the contract that applied only to Southeast Asia and the Vietnam War. (Sometime in 1970, I went to Washington, D.C., made a presentation about our operation in SEA and helped clarify and negotiate some of the terms of that special section). For instance, it addressed our in-country logistics support and the fact that we were entitled to such privileges as access to the military PX, commissary and eating facilities with officer-level GS equivalent rankings, it provided for transportation on military aircraft if we had appropriate travel orders, it stated that we could ask for military escort in cases of emergency repair travel during dangerous hours or conditions, it limited the type of machines that could be brought into Vietnam so that our maintenance service could be somewhat specific and coordinated with the level of our training, it specified the military bases in SEA where IBM maintenance and SE support would be provided, and it provided for a maintenance service surcharge which was double that normally charged in the United States in order to cover our extraordinary costs of operating in the manner we did in the war zone.

Each year, the GSA Contract was re-negotiated in Washington, D.C. and was made more specific in its applicability to our Southeast Asia operation, and each fiscal year IBM and GSA haggled in pure beaurocratic fashion which delayed its issuance and forced us to operate on the previous year's obsolete contract. Because the Contract was late, we could not collect rental, lease or maintenance fees and our accounts receivable were always months in arrears. Our Government could fight in the war, but they couldn't pay their bills on time!

Sometime in the summer of 1971, I was at our Saigon office doing manpower planning, reviewing installation schedules and writing reports when there was an unexpected knock on the front door. Two well dressed American civilians walked in and asked for the general manager. I offered them fresh coffee and asked for identifications. They produced some documents stating that they were from GSA in Washington, D.C. and were on a fact-finding trip. I said, "Welcome to Saigon and what can I do for you?" After some unimportant chit-chat, they asked to see our financial records. I asked, "Why?" and they mumbled something about it being time to institute more accurate accounting principals now that the Vietnam buildup was over and the war was being turned over to the Vietnamese. I wondered what that had to do with me and why they hadn't at least called for an appointment, after all we did have telephones! I politely said that all IBM equipment being utilized by any and all American military organizations had to go through formal procurement procedures at Stateside Headquarters locations and Washington, D.C. and that they should already know that and also that "No, they could not see my records because we didn't have any here in Vietnam, and that they should go make their inquiries at IBM National Federal Marketing offices in Bethesda, Maryland." They left shortly after without shaking hands and I decided that part of 'Vietnamization' involved U.S. procurement agencies doing some independent 'CYA' accounting on where all the material and money went. I never heard from them again and have always wondered what those two stooges were really doing, whether they were lost or whether it was just another overseas boondoggle. Maybe they had come to buy some of the famous Vietnamese ceramic elephants or visit a few local massage parlors?

IBM's Vietnamization process was successful. One way or another, our computer and data processing equipment was smoothly transferred to local Vietnamese control. The last U.S. ground combat unit departed Vietnam in August 1972, and an artificial feeling of peace settled over the

City of Saigon. Much of the ground war moved into Cambodia. The last American IBM Customer Engineer, Doug Weidman, departed Saigon in mid 1973 and amazingly enough, the remaining computers just kept on running for the next couple of years under the able care of World Trade's IBM Vietnam company. However, I retained a haunting doubt about the success of our U.S. Government's *Vietnamization* process - which some of you may say is 20 - 20 hind-sight, but which I believe was partially based on the following hazy principle: "When you give something to someone, it doesn't have nearly the value as it might have had, had the person really worked for and earned it from the beginning" (unless it is love – an entirely different problem).

We Americans tried to give Democracy to South Vietnam, but instead it turned out to be capitalism and materialism. We gave the Vietnamese people radios, TVs, cars, jet planes, computers, a navy, rifles, drugs, prostitution, agent orange defoliation and sickness, land mines, ammunition, thousands of illegitimate babies, our way of fighting and many other things they could fight over, but not fight for. In Saigon, there were always more things to acquire from the Americans and if it wasn't given to them, they could always steal it. This depressing suspicion seeped into me because I worked and lived in Vietnam for more than just a two-year tour. When you live on the economy for several years, and are not isolated in someplace like Washington, D.C. or confined to a military base, you begin to understand the emotional and social makeup of the people around you. Many young adult Vietnamese were still like children (or maybe they just seemed that way because we treated them so?).

Granted, as a result of the Geneva Accords in 1954, approximately one million people had bravely fled the North and made new and better lives for themselves in order to retain their religious freedom, but life in the South - before the Americans or before the Viet Cong or NVA occupation - was relatively easy. In my opinion, the South Vietnamese people were more emotional and more artistically talented than their geographic cousins to the north. I found that most South Vietnamese people also had a strong work ethic as well as a marked innate intelligence. However, as a collective nation, they were not wise; greed, graft and jealousy were all too pervasive.

Americans are raised competitively with a spirit of aggressive teamwork (e.g. football). From grade school up we are taught sportsmanship and to compete and win fairly without cheating or bribery. Play by the rules! We are taught to never quit ("Don't start something if you are not going to finish it!"). America gave all right! American fighting men gave 58,183 lives and many many thousands of wounded, and our government promised more and then finally reneged on those promises. Without their own national teamwork or pride, the South Vietnamese could not handle the job without our help. The ARVN and the South Vietnam political leaders did have some minor victories during 1973 and 1974, but they were not going to win against the fanaticism of the North - no matter how much we gave them! In the end, without our help, South Vietnam simply gave up! *Vietnamization* was a solution to an American problem and provided an apparent graceful and early way out, but obviously Vietnamization was an eventual failure and our country has suffered a national anguish ever since.

As I update this writing in 2012, I truly hope that in the years ahead the same remorse won't be true with respect to our missions in Iraq, Afghanistan or elsewhere? Like the old Pete Seeger song says, "When will we ever learn? When will we e-v-e-r learn?"

# Chapter 16
## Send The Computers (And The IBMers) Home

I COMPLETED MY IBM ASSIGNMENT and left South Vietnam in September 1971. Our IBM operation was rolling along smoothly, but the handwriting was definitely on the wall. The best technology, best troops and best fighting equipment in the world were being wasted. More computers, better guns, faster aircraft with more bombs were not going to help turn the tide of Communism in South Vietnam without the continued resolve of the U.S. military and political leaders in Washington DC. Vietnamization was fine in theory, but would it work? It was time to make a graceful departure and it was also time for IBM to start cutting back on our manpower and maintenance support in Southeast Asia.

However, unlike most of the IBMers completing their assignments and returning home, I was not going to leave my professional role of providing technical and marketing support to the military. I was returning to Honolulu where I would continue as IBM's Federal Marketing Manager with continuing responsibilities throughout the Western Pacific and Southeast Asia. My new job was to help IBMers in Saigon and other Far East locations with the Vietnamization transition and to help close our offices there in an organized and timely manner. My job over the next couple of years was to literally work myself out of a job. I was filled with a deep satisfaction about what we had accomplished over the past few years but I was also filled with a deep disappointment about what was happening to our military establishment and our IBM team of computer experts. I was not looking forward to my career in 1972 and beyond, but it was a job I could do, and do well, and there were many benefits to being able to live in beautiful Hawaii again. As I sit here many years later, I can still feel the extreme frustration of dismantling an operation that I had helped build and that was working so well, but it had to be done, (didn't it?).

My memory of my IBM responsibilities during the years 1972 through 1975 is dulled by a certain lack of enthusiasm for what I was doing or lack of positive purpose, as in my previous Vietnam years. I was to help tear something apart and I didn't want to. I didn't think corporate IBM knew exactly what it was doing in those years either (ignoring the fact that they were under heavy pressure of Anti-Trust Divestiture). They kept trying new organizational arrangements, such as the General Systems Division (GSD) with its competing and often inferior products, Field Engineering Division previously had been split away from the Data Processing Division and our District and Headquarters locations kept changing personnel and locations. I remember one of my fellow marketing types saying something to the effect that he had been through 5 Marketing managers, 4 Branch Managers, 7 District and Regional Managers and 5 Headquarters re-organizations during a period of about 8 years and that he had never moved from his desk!

I was also measured and paid on a 'sales achievement quota', but since my job was to help remove machines from the military marketplace and send them back to various IBM plants, the quota system didn't make much sense. "Fat chance of ever making the 100% Club!" IBM's Federal Marketing organization invented a process called 'federal sales relief' (or some such term) which granted quota relief for every piece of equipment that was being returned from Southeast Asia. In spite of that, our then small Honolulu based federal sales team put up with much criticism from headquarters locations for sending the Vietnam machines back. IBM loved it when the business was going well in Southeast Asia, but couldn't take it when the war was phasing business out. IBM was trying to grow, in spite of the antitrust suit and our Vietnam situation was not helping. Our mission in Southeast Asia in support of the Vietnam War was soon to be forgotten and brushed aside. I did my job conscientiously, but I threw my real energies into after-hours pursuits including house investments, Hawaiian girlfriends and racing sailboats. One event on Guam, in 1975, brought it all back and refocused attention on Vietnam at the highest levels within IBM and I became deeply involved. But, that is the subject of a later time and will be told in the concluding Chapter 17, "The Last Phone Call".

Meanwhile, there were still a few hardworking IBMers in Vietnam, Thailand and the Philippines who were continuing to support the U.S. military to the best of their abilities. One of those dedicated men was a lanky young bachelor from Florida by the name of Rob Moore. Rob had volunteered for duty in Vietnam as a marketing representative and had arrived in-country in July of 1971. I was privileged to work with him there for only two short months before my departure, but my responsibilities in Honolulu kept me in contact with some of the Vietnamization duties and equipment reduction processes that Rob handled. Rob helps explain the environment in Vietnam during the remainder of 1971, 1972 and 1973 by contributing much of the remainder of this chapter. I will rely on his younger and excellent memory and use most of his words that follow:

## Rob's Story

"By the summer of 1971 President Nixon's Vietnamization program was well under way. It had reduced U.S. ground forces to the point that the Army was returning data processing equipment to the U.S. in avalanche proportions. The large inventory control system at both Da Nang and Cam Ranh Bay were soon to be powered off along with vast numbers of card sorters, key punches and other varieties of punched card equipment that had been spread across South Vietnam. The Long Binh depot remained in operation for some time though and continued to keep a few of our CEs employed at both the depot and at the Army's Inventory Control Center - Vietnam (ICCV), co-located at Long Binh. The Army's data center (AMMC) at Tan Son Nhut that provided parts inventory management support for a vast fleet of helicopters remained in operation for many more months as well. The Air Force also reduced its in-country bases but continued to operate from Da Nang, Cam Ranh and Bien Hoa as well as from eight air bases in Thailand, as well as the B-52 base at Andersen AFB on Guam.

Soon after the Cambodian invasion in the spring of 1970, Saigon had ceased to have its almost nightly rocket attacks and during the summer rainy season of 1971 the war seemed to be at a comparative lull. However, with so many GIs still in Saigon and military vehicles clogging the streets, it was evident that the war had not yet ended. B-52 strikes were easily recognized in the evenings when, in rapid succession, you heard your windows rattle three or more times. The last group of 'replacement' IBMers arrived that summer; one marketing representative (me), two systems engineers, two administrative persons and a new location manager to replace Dan Feltham. The camaraderie that had been shared among so many IBMers up until that time began to wane with the decreasing number of employees and de-escalation of the war. Villas were still shared but were reduced in number. The Hawaii Bar across the alley from the office continued to be an after-hours watering hole. Its pool table was well used by many of us while the bar girls called us 'Cheap Charlies' because we kept our own company and did not cater to their ceaseless thirst for expensive 'tea'. Memberships at the Club Nautique and Circle Sportif were no longer in vogue though some of us joined the golf club and played regularly. One villa is remembered for it poker games, but I was not a gambler and preferred watching or playing pool with the card player's girl friends. During that fall some enterprising American expatriates opened casinos in two nearby villas. They had obviously not bribed all of the necessary officials because they were closed within a few weeks.

The custom of 'DEROS' parties did continue and at such events the standard gift for departing IBMers was a plaque displaying a facsimile of a black-pajama-clad Viet Cong holding a rifle with the departing recipient's name inscribed beneath the caption "VC Dodger". This was recognition that an IBMer had been successful in avoiding harm from the Viet Cong. One such party continued all the way to the airport and I vaguely remember a contest to knock geckos off the ceiling of the airport restaurant with corks from champagne bottles. Some of the parties for the departing CEs were more formal ten-course banquets at the My Le Hoa restaurant in Cholon. The food was so good that by the end of the seventh course, few of us could eat even another morsel. At one CE's going away party, the departee was served 'Hot Dogs Flambeau', either because he savored or detested hot dogs, I cannot remember which. Two other CEs left their joint departure banquet celebration and continued to drink heavily at almost every Tu Do Street bar that was still in operation. Their thirst extended beyond their funds and they were unable to pay their bill at the last bar. They left their IDs with the bartender as collateral and promised to return the following morning to square the bill. On their way home, weaving up Pasteur Street, they misjudged the dogleg left turn to go back over to Cong Le Street when suddenly out of the night a monstrous oak tree leaped out in front of their Toyota Land Cruiser and caused considerable damage. The White Mice came to investigate and quickly determined that our friends were not only drunk but that they were missing their driver's licenses and all other forms of identification. The two CEs spent their last night in Vietnam in the 'monkey house' feeling no pain.

Jack Higgins, another CE, also had a rough last few days. One of the burdens we all bore at the end of the assignment was to sell our car. It was not a simple process because the seller was responsible for paying the import duties on the car. Jack coordinated his efforts carefully with our U.S. Embassy liaison officer and with Vietnamese customs and did all that the law required. Somehow the Vietnamese paperwork was mis-processed and Jack's name was placed in the 'To-Be-Detained' book at the TSN airport. When Jack arrived at the airport, fully expecting to begin his homeward journey, and started through immigration, he was arrested and whisked away to the monkey house. Even after IBM management intervened by involving our Embassy and the needless confusion was finally settled, Jack still had to pay a $100.00 bribe to return to the airport a free man.

Major Vietnamization programs were well under way with both the civilian government and the military pursuing efforts to automate their information systems. The USAID data processing manager, Jack Pruden, had persuaded the senior ministers of the government to build a new computer center to meet the basic needs of South Vietnam and enable them to compete with other developing Southeast Asian nations. The center would require extensive renovations to an existing building, including new power, air conditioning and raised floor, as specified for System/360 computer installations. A pool of young Vietnamese technical talent was available, as a result of previous years of IBM training, to support the project (see Chapter 5).

The ARVN also had its own computer installation at the old French military headquarters compound near Tan Son Nhut, In such a crowded city, this compound seemed like an oasis and had enough open space to make most college campuses envious. The American advisor, Colonel Vince Powell, worked with Colonel Hue's staff to establish an effective information system to support supply requirements for the South Vietnamese Army. The IBM computer in use there was a S/360 Model 40 that was rented from IBM WTC Saigon. The U.S. Army helped by supplying the ARVN with punched card equipment that was installed at their depots that was being rented from IBM/GEM. The move required stateside IBM plants to provide kits which would convert the U.S. supplied machines from 60 Hz power to local power of 50 Hz.

One of the local nationals, a Chinese woman named Miss Kinh, whom we had trained to program at the center at Long Binh, eventually transferred to this site to be their chief systems programmer. Whenever I called at this site, I noted that she was always standing at the computer console politely telling the operator, a young Vietnamese soldier, what to do. Normally computer operators did not require such supervision, so I asked her privately why she was always standing watch. She was surprised I had to ask and said that all the Vietnamese soldiers who worked at the computer center were the sons of wealthy families who had bribed ARVN officers for their son's soft, non-combat jobs. Many were ill suited for the work and thus required Miss Kinh's supervision. (Twenty-two years later Miss Kinh became a programmer at NASA's Goddard Space Flight center involved in the Hubble Space Telescope program.)

One interesting event that happened that fall of 1971 was the official exchange rate for dollars and piasters suddenly adjusted from 275:1 to 400:1. This matched the approximate black market rate - a sad event for all the black market money dealers. It changed several more times before I left in March of 1973 continuing to reflect the relative buying power of the two currencies. (Author's note. During the 1969 - 1971 period when I was there, the exchange rate was fixed at 118:1, but the relative buying power of the two currencies was actually 400:1. No wonder there were considerable illegal exchanges always in progress). A month or so before the so-called Peace Agreement was signed, it became legal to use U.S. greenbacks in Vietnam and the use of military script was suspended.

In late 1971 the workload for an IBM marketing representative diminished to the degree that the three SEA countries of Vietnam, Thailand and the Philippines could be handled by only two men. I was assigned Thailand and the other salesman, John Leussler, was assigned to market to our Philippine accounts. We continued to live in Saigon. However, I happened to be in Bangkok on Christmas day and was pleasantly surprised to find that this predominantly Buddhist nation seemed to be recognizing our Christmas as a national holiday. (Again, author's note: It may have seemed like Christmas to our American, but I have been told that in actuality the Thais were celebrating a series of special days that December - the King's birthday, December 5th; Democracy Day, December 10th; the Queen's birthday December 12th. Rob continues to insist that Christmas Day was being celebrated.)

Things continued to muddle along through the first quarter of 1972 without any memorable events relative to the war, our customers or the office environment. As more of our military customers left Vietnam, workload for our field engineers (CEs) continued to dwindle and many of them returned home or sought other adventures around the world. In April however, war fury once again fell upon South Vietnam. With American ground forces gone and its air power reduced, North Vietnam's General Giap gambled once again on the prospects of an all out victory, similar to his achievement against the French in 1954 at a place called Dien Bien Phu in the mountains near the Laotian border west of Hanoi. The northern provinces were invaded and Quang Tri captured. A similar gamble had failed during the '68 TET offensive, but that was when American military presence was at its height. For the first time their strategy was one of conventional warfare with front lines, artillery, tanks and all the rest. When the offensive began, President Nixon recognized that he could not reintroduce American ground forces, but he directed the use of all the air power that the U.S. could muster to stop the communist offensive and it was effective.

Before this new offensive began the Air Force was flying 200 - 300 sorties per day. During the offensive, that number increased to more than 1100 per day. The IBM computer systems that the AF used to establish, coordinate and report these missions (PIACCS and Seek Data II) were pushed to the maximum. B-52s and F-4s often waited at the ends of runways for target information from the Tan Son Nhut based systems. Our Navy's offshore carriers were beehives of activity too, and the Marines moved their entire Third Air Wing from Iwakuni, Japan to Nam Phong, a remote airfield in northeast Thailand. (Within thirty-six hours after receiving their orders, the Marines were flying combat missions out of Nam Phong, three thousand miles from Iwakuni - that's moving out in true Marine fashion!). Fortunately, the ARVN ground forces fought back successfully and withstood General Giap's offensive. By mid-summer the North Vietnamese effort was spent and it was thought by many that this defeat changed North Vietnam's attitude toward pursuing a peace agreement with the U.S.

As the level of American ground forces in Vietnam continued to dwindle, the IBM Branch Manager in Honolulu, Bill Doody, began to feel the burden of responsibility for the safety of his Vietnam based employees. The U.S. press reports gave the impression that South Vietnam was teetering on the brink of disaster and would be overrun. Bill stayed in touch with us on a daily basis and soon came to visit. Most of the NVA's offensive was well to the north of Saigon so we convinced Bill that there was no immediate danger. In fact, the only change that did take place in Saigon was that the nightly curfew was once again enforced rigidly and observed faithfully. On his return trip to Honolulu, Bill stopped at Hong Kong and made a contingency plan with Pan American to send a charter flight to rescue his IBMers if the need arose. He had to give Pan Am a $10,000 deposit that was queried by one of IBM's senior executives, Dean McKay. When McKay asked Bill for an explanation, Bill said, "Dean, don't worry, if we ever have to use that plane, we will look very smart!" (Author's note: In my last chapter, "The Last Phone Call", it would appear that lack of similar advance planning by World Trade Corporation management for a similar contingency in April, 1975, cost many of their employees dearly).

In the summer of 1972, I became the last Saigon resident IBM-GEM marketing representative covering our accounts in Vietnam and Thailand. John Leussler returned to the U.S. after serving three years in Vietnam and Stuart Schmidt covered the Philippines from Okinawa. It became a busy time for me, and I barely had time to do more than answer phone calls. Occasionally IBM had opportunities to serve its customers in unusual ways and sometimes our customers did likewise. There were many small things such as delivering something to someone or giving someone else a ride to a base. Our customers normally served only one-year tours and usually seemed to rotate during the summer months. Consequently we found that we were the ones providing much of the operational continuity. Questions such as "When did such-and-such happen?" or "Why did so-and-so do such-and-such?" were frequent, especially right after rotation season.

A bizarre opportunity to help occurred one evening in Da Nang. Two IBMers (a guy named Ron and myself) were cruising through town and came upon a brewing argument between four GIs and a throng of belligerent Vietnamese. Each time the GIs tried to board their jeep and leave, the Vietnamese would close in and force them to stand and defend themselves. Ron and I watched the cat and mouse game for a while, and then Ron decided to "run interference" for them, like a pulling guard on a football team. We rolled up our windows and Ron put the Toyota Land Cruiser in four-wheel drive. We turned toward the crowd with horn blaring and the engine racing in first gear. As we approached, the crowd parted in a manner that would have made Moses proud, and the GIs were given just enough time during the confusion to jump in their jeep and race with us high tailing it out of there. I guess we were lucky that it didn't amount to much more than that.

On another occasion, a Criminal Investigation Division (CID) detective phoned me and asked whether I could help identify the source of some printing on a form. He was especially interested to know whether the form had been processed on an IBM printer. His office was next door to the Long Binh jail. I was scheduled to go to Long Binh the next day and told him I would stop by. When I arrived, we looked at a preprinted form that had been completed on an automated printer and sure enough, it was an IBM 1403 printer. He then went on to explain more about his investigation. The form he showed me was a Material Release Order (MRO) that Army personnel would normally present to a depot clerk when drawing supplies. However, this MRO was bogus. Someone who worked in the Long Binh computer center who had access to these forms had written a simple program to create this (and other) bogus MROs in order to steal supplies from the depot and sell them elsewhere on the black market. The detective called me several times later to clarify a few points, and I learned sometime afterward that he had arrested an Army Captain who confessed to the MRO crimes. I also noted that the Long

Binh jail was quite large and still had a full to capacity problem. (Author's note: Apparently that Long Binh MRO scam had been around at least since 1967, since a reference to the same procedure appears elsewhere in this book's Chapter 9).

Customers helped us too in unusual ways. I had the privilege of being involved with the adoption of a little girl from a Catholic orphanage in Qui Nhon by a family in Ann Arbor, Michigan. Processing her adoption paperwork, passport, visa, etc. was a month long process that finally ended on December 21, 1972. The little girl, whose name was My Linh, was living at my villa under the able care of my maid. When we received word that the paperwork was complete, I was on vacation and out of the country, but my marketing manager, Larry Saslaw, took it upon himself to arrange her passage to her anxious new parents in the U.S. But more than that, he was committed to make it happen by Christmas, four days away. Larry was a driven man if there ever was one. He spread the word among military customers who might be going home for Christmas and who would be willing to lend a helping hand. Thanks to divine providence he found one of the Department of Army civilians, a Nick Lind, who was not only going home for Christmas, but was also going to the Detroit airport that serves Ann Arbor. Nick was the father of eight children so he was the perfect volunteer. Larry now faced the challenge of booking the same consecutive flights that Nick had, but it was Christmas time and all flights were certainly filled. Larry contacted the manager of the Saigon Pan Am office who found a seat on Nick's flight to Los Angeles. Next, Larry called the branch manager in Honolulu who had a friend there who worked for American Airlines; the correct onward flight to Detroit was booked. Nick Lind then made the thirty-hour flight half way around the world with the young My Linh in his care. Thanks to Nick, Larry and the others involved, My Linh arrived into the arms of her new family on Christmas Eve.

During the summer and fall of 1972, Henry Kissinger and Le Duc Tho were busy negotiating the agreement that they hoped would finally end American involvement in the war. In November both men made premature announcements that peace was imminent. IBMers began making definite plans to leave Vietnam no later than our own military's final departure. Two of our remaining SEs began working on plans that would enable Vietnamese system programmers at USAID to assume full responsibility for their own operating system software. Our local management began to transfer our customers to the World Trade office. Everyone made plans to sell his car and liquidate other assets that were better left in Vietnam. There were also uneasy thoughts about whether the South Vietnamese felt that the U.S. was betraying them and might take retribution on the then remaining Americans. All of us became far more circumspect in our public behavior.

Despite the initial euphoria following the peace announcements, a peace agreement was not forthcoming. The South Vietnamese government had not been included in the private negotiations and balked at the agreement. The hoped-for peace agreement began to unravel. Events became more sinister on the morning of December 6th (1972) when the VC launched a rocket attack on Tan Son Nhut. A total of thirty-six rockets fell that morning, but there was little damage. However, it was a grim reminder that peace was not at hand. When I arrived at work that morning, I discovered our secretary under her desk and one of our Hawaiian CEs running around the office with a handmade Japanese flag attached to a broomstick shouting, "Tora, Tora, Tora!" He was a day early for Pearl Harbor's anniversary, but we got the idea.

On December 13th, the Paris peace negotiations broke down completely and President Nixon resorted to retaliatory air power. The B-52s flew! The U.S. launched the "Christmas Bombing" raids (Linebacker II) into North Vietnam, believed to be the heaviest in history, dropping over 100,000 bombs in a little over a week. As a result, peace talks resumed and on January 27th, 1973 the United States, South Vietnam, the National Liberation Front and North Vietnam signed the Paris Peace Accords which provided for an end to military action, the release of U.S. prisoners, the withdrawal of U.S. and other allied troops within 60 days and recognition of people's right through free and democratic elections to determine the fate of South Vietnam. (Approximately 20 percent of South Vietnam territory was in Communist hands). That meant we too had 60 days to leave Vietnam and we began to spend considerable time with our customers preparing for the eventualities.

Our customers were divided into three groups - those who would simply pack up and leave, the Air Force customers who would move to

Thailand, and those who would remain in Vietnam. This last group was the toughest because we had 60 days in which to make them independent of the IBM assistance they had come to rely on. This included USAID and a number of small military customers who were absorbed within the Embassy's Defense Attaché's Office (DAO). The IBM S/360 Model 50 that the MACV Data Management Agency had leased for many years was purchased from our IBM-GEM organization and given to the ARVN Headquarters computer center. Another S/360 Model 50 that had been leased by the USAF at Tan Son Nhut was purchased and given to the civilian government for use in their new data center. The DAO continued to use the same building that had been occupied by MACV HQ up until March 29th to meet their data processing needs but they reverted to using old punched card equipment once again rather than more modern computers.

Transferring maintenance services from IBM-GEM to our local IBM WTC Vietnam counterparts was not easy. The U.S. government adamantly negotiated with us in Saigon, Honolulu and Washington, D.C. They wanted to continue to have American trained maintenance expertise. Bill Doody was then our manager in Washington and was in such a negotiating meeting at the Pentagon when IBM was accused of abandoning its commitments. Bill replied, "We are simply climbing into the same truck you are." That brought an acknowledging chuckle from an Army General who recognized the obvious truth of Bill's statement. Our IBM Vietnam counterparts had been maintaining all the types of equipment that our customers were planning to continue using in Vietnam, so we did not anticipate any major problems except for the two S/360 Model 50s that had just been given to IBM Vietnam customers. In the end, we agreed to leave one American CE in Saigon to help with the transition. The lucky CE was Doug Weidman who moved into the big villa at 153 Cach Mang (Author's note: the residence described in Chapter 13) and he stayed another six months.

Several procedural problems arose during this computer asset transfer phase that illustrated a new level of bureaucracy and accounting red tape that normally does accompany a transfer of responsibility at the end of a project or mission. The DAO data processing center was on Tan Son Nhut Air Base and in order for IBM Vietnamese CEs to service the equipment there, they would need base passes. DAO was made responsible for the acquisition of these passes, but normally passes were not given to Vietnamese citizens without "fragrant grease" changing hands. Weeks went by with no money changing hands, no passes and no computer maintenance. Eventually the Embassy intervened and the passes were granted, but the delay was somewhat amusing and even gratifying because the DAO was consistently delinquent in paying their IBM bills.

The transfer of the USAID account to IBM-Vietnam was complicated because it eventually required the U.S. domestic IBM Company to sell its S/360 Model 40 to IBM Vietnam so that USAID could rent from IBM Vietnam. It was particularly awkward because it required that the S/360 system go through normal import procedures even though it had already been in Vietnam for several years. We finally accomplished the sale using USAID's own Commodity Import Program. The process lasted for many months and among the U.S. Government, the government of Vietnam and IBM, the most bureaucratic of all was IBM (Author's note: possibly because there was no sales commission or quota points available to IBM Vietnam with this type of transaction. I recall several discussions, that took place with IBM Vietnam in which every possible alternative except the direct transfer of the existing S/360 was preferred).

When we learned that a Command and Control 7th Air Force function would be transferred to Thailand, it was not immediately clear where they would establish their new command post. At first we thought they would move to Bangkok, but instead they wanted a location with a much lower profile. Next we thought it would be Korat because of the large communications hub located there. Not so. They decided to move to NKP because of the IBM S/360 Model 65 system located there (the old Igloo White project which had been phased out) with its then excess capacity to handle any incoming workload. Tape drives and other S/360 components and an 1130/2250 system were also moved to NKP. The 1130 had suffered a system outage just prior to shipment and was accompanied by an IBM CE to NKP on board a C-130. The move went well, and IBM personnel received compliments from the NKP data center CO. Eventually, the 360/65 processor was crated and sent back to the U.S.A. and the Air Force continued to process on a 360/50 that had been sent from the U.S. mainland.

Those last days in Saigon were busy ones as we handled the asset and application transfers and also helped prepare all the equipment for shipment that was heading stateside. Each machine and cable set needed to be moved, packaged and crated in preparation for the long trip back to an IBM plant. The CEs worked hard and long and their dedication and professionalism certainly earned my lasting respect. Our managers were scheduled to return home also, and I would move to Bangkok to continue marketing support to our Thailand and remaining Vietnam customers. After seeing Saigon during a time of heavy American presence, it seemed eerie to watch it change into a relatively inactive and quiet city as the agreed upon sixty days ticked away. There was no feeling of impending doom, only a sense of quiet peacefulness that I had not experienced there before. Perhaps it was the best glimpse I had of Saigon in its early French colonial days when Somerset Maugham sipped gin and tonic at the Continental Palace's porch bar. Even during morning, noon or evening rush hour, there was simply no hustle or bustle among the populace. Had peace really settled over the land?

During the last week of the sixty days evacuation period there was only a handful of IBMers in Saigon and our up-country personnel had already departed. Things began to mysteriously disappear from the office. It was not clear which of our local national employees was stealing things, but what we had remaining at the time were items that Goodwill would have easily refused. It became comical to watch. We did actually sell some of the furniture to the locals and even our longtime and faithful maid, Ba Bai, bought a few chairs. On the fifty-ninth day our two remaining managers gave me a ride to the airport, and I boarded China Airlines for my new home in Thailand. When the managers returned to the office, they found the compound's guard shack gone along with the guards. Theft seemed to be the Vietnamese national pastime. The two DPD and FED managers left the next, the 60th day. Branch Office 562 (fondly remembered as Pacific Operations South) was officially, and yes sadly, closed!

Much of the next few months involved helping the new Air Force tenants at NKP settle in. One of the computer applications that was transferred there was something called the Bright Lights file. It was a database of all the information that the U.S. military had for our MIAs. I persuaded the AF to put that data base on-line so that they could quickly answer questions coming in from the Special Forces search teams that were allowed under the terms of the Peace Agreement to begin searching for crash sites. While visiting the two AF captains who managed that data base, I asked whether there was any success in recovering the remains of any of the servicemen from the crash sites. The answer was a dismal "No." When I inquired further, they told me that the only sites that were safe to search were those in areas controlled by the South Vietnamese. They went on to say that a Special Forces search team had recently found a site and collected what they could. Whatever they found was insufficient for identification purposes so they were told to return and look again. Unfortunately, they were unable to find that same site again. Such was the challenge, even then, of finding our MIAs.**

I returned to Saigon several times during 1973 to call on USAID and the DAO's office. I stayed at the 153 Cach Mang villa and found Saigon to be as quiet and as peaceful as a small American town on a Sunday afternoon. There seemed to be no threat of war or danger of any sort. The American presence that had driven Saigon's economy for so many years simply did not exist, and there was no significant industry to support such a large urban population. I suppose many of the refugees had returned to their villages. (Perhaps USAID's 'Land to the Tiller' program had helped in their return?) A couple of months after our last CE, Doug Weidman, departed, I spent several days with Dan Feltham in Saigon. He was amazed at the quiet that had settled over the city. It was December of 1973. We were there to make final arrangements with Jack Ewen, IBM Vietnam's Country Manager, for his people to assume full responsibility for our few remaining customers. We also called on DAO in order to persuade them to pay past bills, and it appeared that they were bogged down in administrative paperwork. Dan was able to carry a first-hand report on the status of asset transfers back to Honolulu. Stu Schmidt, who was still resident on Okinawa, assumed responsibility for our customers in Thailand and I returned to the U.S.A. in January, 1974." (Author's Note: Many thanks to Rob Moore for having provided most of the history contained within this chapter).

** On Easter morning in 1995, while waiting to sing in my church's choir, I overheard a fellow choir member say that he had been in Vietnam twice in the last couple of years. I was obviously curious so asked him why. He said that he had been a member of an MIA search team that had been sent to Vietnam by a Joint Services task force (Central Identification Laboratory for Full Accounting) based out of Camp Smith in Hawaii. His team's mission was to try and locate crash sites and then use aircraft debris to try to identify the aircraft types and their serial numbers. If this could be done the flight crew that had been on board at the time of a particular crash could be identified and that would then hopefully enable them to pursue the remains of any of the individual crew members that might still be in that area. He said they used data stored in lap top computers but that one of the problems was that the data was 25 years old. Was this the same data, referred to above, that we had recorded on the S/360 Model 50 system at NKP in the early 1970's? Could be, it is a small world and data is data no matter how old.

# CHAPTER 17
## The Last Phone Call – The Fall Of Saigon

IT WAS LATE APRIL, 1975, and I was on the island of Saipan, about 200 miles north of Guam in the western Pacific. I was now a Senior Marketing Representative and was working with the Trust Territories Government coordinating the installation of an IBM System/360 Model 30 computer that replaced an older 1401 system. The Trust Territories was then an unincorporated territory of the U.S.A. and was made up of thousands of North Pacific islands in the Marianas, Marshalls, Gilbert and Caroline Island Groups spread over a geographic region roughly the size of our lower forty-eight contiguous states. The Government organization, which was my customer, had the responsibility of administering to the diverse and complex mix of Micronesian peoples. They were modernizing their computer applications and I had been on Saipan for a few days. I was staying at the new Saipan Intercontinental Hotel not far from the government's Administrative Headquarters and in my off hours had been enjoying the beach and bar in front of the hotel (the unique bar happened to be built within a converted concrete gun emplacement left over from WWII days). The previous afternoon I had been to see the sea cliffs where hundreds of Saipanese and Japanese had jumped to their deaths in 1944 rather than be captured by the "barbaric" Americans. I had a few more days of work to complete with the Trust Territories people, but that was suddenly interrupted. At 5:30 a.m., my hotel room phone rang and a faint voice on the other end changed my plans.

"Hello, is this Dan Feltham?" "Yes it is, who is calling?" "Are you the Dan Feltham who works for IBM in Honolulu, and are you on Saipan near Guam?" said the voice. "That's correct, who is this?" "Dan, this is Terry Lautenbach, IBM Corporate Vice President, and I am calling from

Poughkeepsie, New York, and it is 8:30 p.m. here. What time is it there?" Well, that's nice I thought for a VP to call me all that way and tell me what time it was in New York, but I sleepily said it was 5:30 Friday morning. Mr. Lautenbach then asked, "Can you drop what you are doing in Saipan and get back to Guam this morning?" I said, "Yes, I probably could, if it is necessary. There's an early morning flight, what's going on?" "Well", he said, "It looks like Saigon could fall in the next week or so, and we need some people on Guam to help handle the Vietnamese IBMers who will be airlifted from Saigon. I would like you to go to Guam as soon as possible, tie up ten or so rooms at the Guam Hilton Hotel and set up a 'war room' environment there so that we can receive our people and start placing them into new homes and jobs around the world. We are expecting 130 World Trade Corporation families, and they should be there in the next couple of days. You will be joined by other IBMers, but I want you to get it started as soon as possible; will you do that?" "Yes", I said, "I'll try to leave within the hour". The adrenaline started pumping as I realized this was serious. He said, "Fine Dan, thank you, we are counting on you," and hung up.

I sat there stunned and then, forgetting what time it was, started to pick up the phone again to call my Trust Territories customer and tell them I would not be in that day or even for a few days. The phone rang before I could dial and a new voice said, "Dan, this is Bill Kerr in Honolulu, did Terry Lautenbach call you?" "Yes", I said, "It looks like I am going to be out here longer than planned." Bill Kerr was my Branch Manager in Honolulu, and he was calling to confirm that I should go to Guam, that I would have all the support that I needed from the IBM Guam office and that I should stay on Guam until the job was finished. "Don't worry about expenses and keep me informed", he concluded, "And good luck!" Wow, my mind started reeling as I flashed back to Saigon and to the faces of some of the Vietnamese IBMers whom I had known while there. I wondered whether they were in trouble, but it sounded like they were going to be rescued and taken care of. Little did I know! I made a couple of early morning calls, packed, checked out of the Intercontinental and drove to the airport to catch the short 8 a.m. flight to Guam. All of a sudden I was on another plane and heading for another adventure. It was a Friday and the date was April 25, 1975.

I will set the scene to help with the events that follow. Guam is the southern most and largest of the islands in the Mariana chain and is volcanic in origin. The climate is tropical with temperatures averaging around 80 degrees F with a high relative humidity. The average annual rainfall of 80 to 100 inches occurs mainly from May to November, and typhoons usually hit the island yearly. Guam is 30 miles long and 4 to 8 miles wide; its area is 212 square miles and its permanent population in 1975 was around 100,000 persons, a large portion of who were U.S. military personnel and their dependents. As a Territory of the U.S.A., its people are U.S. citizens and they have wanted to become our 51st state for many years. The people elect their own government except for the Governor, who is appointed by our U.S. Presidents. Most of the residents are of Filipino decent, but about a third are natives of the island and are Chamorros or Chamorros mixed with various other ethnic groups such as Filipino, Spanish, Mexican and some European and Oriental strains. The language is English and Spanish with some older Chamorros words thrown in. Most Guamanians are Roman Catholic, a heritage of their earlier Spanish rule. Guam was discovered by Magellan in 1521 and it belonged to Spain until the Spanish American War (1898) when it became a U.S. possession along with the Philippines. Its strategic location in the western Pacific makes it a highly valued American asset. It was occupied by Japan early in WWII and recaptured by the U.S. in August 1944. Most of the population lives in or near the capital city of Agana. The face of Guam was about to change.

I rented a car and arrived at the IBM Guam office by 9:30, called a meeting of all personnel to explain the situation and started making the necessary arrangements for the days ahead. We would need things such as radios, signs, cars, money, secretaries and the hotel reservations. Yes, the Hilton could help us and would cooperate to the fullest, but they didn't realize what was going to hit them soon. I had an old IBM friend from Honolulu who had taken an assignment on Guam for a couple of years. His name was George Winter, and he and I decided to start visiting the refugee camps that were suddenly sprouting up at various military bases around the island. The map of Guam, reproduced here from an April 28th news article, shows the location of these camps. We first drove to Asan, the new camp closest to Agana, and immediately found IBMer

Mr. Chang and his family and told him we would be back with things he needed. George and I naively thought this was going to be easy. We then drove to Barrigada Camp, then to Andersen AFB and North West Field at the northern end of the island. That was the first time I had ever seen rows of the awesome eight engine B-52 bombers that close. Their drooping wings were painted black and they looked menacing and lethal, as indeed they were. At these refugee locations, we left IBM signs, called out on the public address systems and gained some information from the military as to what was really happening but did not find any more IBMers. Mr. Chang had somehow been the first.

*Guam Refugee Camps*

We moved quickly that first day - went back to the Hilton, then to the IBM office to meet a high level IBM Far East executive, Charlie Swift, from Tokyo whom had arrived on Guam at 3 p.m. We returned to Asan and Mr. Chang, then went to the Hilton again and then to the airport to pick up Jack

Ewen (Country Manager for IBM Vietnam who, with his wife, had been called away from Saigon by his IBM Americas/Far East headquarters a month earlier as part of IBM's emergency plan for expatriates. Jack had gone to Hong Kong, Singapore or Indonesia to wait out the situation until conditions became safe for his return) and a Frank O'Keefe. Finally, we returned to the Hilton. Around 8 p.m. George and I went over to the arrival area at the Naval Air Station (NAS) where all the transports were arriving with more than full loads of Vietnamese. I dropped George off at his home at 10 p.m., then went back to the Hilton to talk with Swift and Ewen and then returned to NAS until 2:15 a.m. Saturday morning. I stood in one of the hangers there to watch the big transports come and go, holding an IBM sign, and was thankful that I had a hotel room and that it was a warm night with a full moon. I reflected on my experiences in Vietnam, the good friends I had made there just four years earlier and the tragedy that must be unfolding in the streets, homes and offices of Saigon. The Guam IBMers had been most helpful throughout the day. We had made some progress by developing a search and communications strategy, learned some base refugee camp procedures, displayed our signs and found one family.

The incoming Vietnamese were unusually quiet, subdued, clean, but dreadfully tired. Many stood patiently in lines to complete necessary paperwork. They accepted food and drink and queued up for bus rides to the new camps. Some looked worried and others worked hard to help others where needed. The reception and processing centers were well organized and there were a great many American military and civilians assisting the new arrivals. What a day! Somewhere along the line, I had consumed too much coffee and not enough food. I returned to the Hilton before 3 a.m. to catch what sleep I could knowing the next day would start early and be just as hectic.

I was up by 6:30, canceled my Pan American reservation home, wired my Honolulu girl friend that I would be delayed and finally had a wonderful Hilton breakfast. It was then that I started making the notes that enabled me to write this chapter. Somehow I felt that I would want to remember the details. The newly arrived IBM executives had called for a 9 a.m. meeting at which time an organization would be established and assignments given to all IBMers that might help us locate our IBM refugees. Charlie Swift took charge as the senior executive and things were organized as follows:

## IBMer Assignment

Charlie Swift: Commanding officer and interface to IBM HQ in New York.

Frank O'Keefe: Clearance procedures & keep IBM Hong Kong informed.

Matt Ash: Relocation plan, rehabilitation, I.D.s and outside help.

Ted Robinson: Personnel administration and IBM logistics, personnel, control charts, attributes and futures of the refugees.

Jack Ewen: Vietnamese interface (they were his personnel).

Dan Feltham: Base and refugee interface (I think that meant "runner")

George Winter Asan and other refugee camps (runner #2)

Bob Mayishiro: Administrative office services, hotel rooms, food and medical (from Guam Branch Office).

Steve Tanaka: Accounting, banking and funds (Guam Branch Office).

Other IBMers: Part time branch office assistance, as needed.

Regular meetings would be held at 8:30 a.m. and 6 p.m. each day. During the last hour of this first meeting, concern developed that certain critical Vietnamese IBMers would not be allowed to leave Saigon because of the maintenance of computer systems belonging to the South Vietnamese government, and word was received that the expected number of IBM evacuees should be revised downward. At 11 a.m. Charlie Swift, Jack Ewen and I drove to Asan to talk with Mr. Chang. We wanted to learn how he escaped Saigon so quickly and others did not. He told us that he had a sister who had married an American journalist and that the journalist had sponsored the whole family's departure several days earlier.

We also talked to a U.S. Army Colonel, a chaplain and a Marine Captain. We needed real information. That afternoon I drove out to Andersen AFB again; checked in at the Military Airlift Command (MAC) terminal and gave an IBM sign to an AF Colonel and received a quick briefing. Flights from Saigon had become less frequent and the Andersen refugees were being transported to other camps around Guam.

I made a public address broadcast to the refugees at Tin City, which went something like: "I am an IBM Corporation employee and am looking for any IBM World Trade Vietnamese who might be listening. If you hear and understand me, please come to the main office so that I can help you, etc. etc." The World Trade Vietnam IBMers all spoke English and we made this type of broadcast at every refugee camp on Guam. There was no response, so I went to NAS again and learned that flights into Guam were being purposely delayed because there was no more space for the refugees at that time. However, refugee flights were continuing past Guam to the individual islands of Wake, Midway and Saipan. I made another broadcast and then went to Barrigada and the Black Construction Company camps and made more broadcasts. I talked to some of the Vietnamese, to some nurses and to some military men. The Vietnamese families were huddled in small groups clutching their meager belongings. They had small black suit cases which contained a few personal effects plus any gold, jewels or other valuables they had grabbed on their way out of Saigon. Finally, I dropped by George Winter's small Columbia 23 sailboat, tied in its slip in Apra Harbor and relaxed for awhile talking with George and sipping a well earned beer.

Back at the Hilton, the 6 p.m. meeting covered status reports from each team member. We discussed health, food, security and immigration concerns and asked that more IBM help signs be made. A plan was being developed within IBM that would selectively place our Vietnamese refugees in acceptable countries where homes and jobs could be provided once they were free to migrate. (Some countries had specifically stated that they did not want to have anything to do with the refugees). IBM intended to sponsor each employee to countries like the U.S.A., France, the Philippines, Thailand and Indonesia. IBM HQ was even considering a rehabilitation center at San Jose, California with follow on relocation from there. But first we had to find them! Time was running out. No one mentioned that President Gerald Ford had given a televised speech on 23 April, declaring an end to the Vietnam War and all U.S. aid.

At 9 p.m. we received a call from Bruce Tomson, IBM Thailand's General Manager in Bangkok. Bruce had new facts that placed our IBMers behind 10,000 other Vietnamese in the "staging queue" and he said there was a high likelihood that they would not escape Saigon at all. Bruce knew what he was talking about and was intimately involved. He said that he was in contact with a Mr. Jim Oshida at DAO to evaluate alternate evacuation plans, such as sending in a chartered TWA 747 with people who knew Saigon and with money to buy our Vietnamese out. This began to sound more positive than the present plan that was "use the present system and hope." Permission to send in a 747 was being requested of DAO and of Ralph Pfieffer in New York. Bruce also told us that 15 Vietnamese IBMers wanted to remain in Saigon and that the remaining WTC Vietnamese Manager, an experienced man named Quan Trung Nghia, had re-established priorities for those departing so that 315 people divided into three groups would leave over the next few days. Our people were classified with Saigon's general business population. Mr. Oshida had more than he could handle and was ranking IBMers lower on his list. Those of us in that small far away Hilton hotel room began to agonize over what to do next and what to recommend to IBM HQ in New York, which was trying to make the best decisions. We began to learn something of the tragedy in progress and that the original estimates of people trying to escape from Saigon had increased drastically. We realized that the facilities to handle the evacuees on Guam were even more inadequate than judged earlier.

At 9:25 p.m. Charlie Swift phoned Ralph Pfieffer in N.Y. and gave him an update on the delays in Saigon. Pfieffer was President of World Trade's Asia Pacific Corporation, and he was located in Tarrytown, New York. It was said that the four-day cease-fire might end Monday night and that "the Embassy is suggesting we send in a 747 to rescue our 315 people and others. It is not known whether permission and arrangements to charter the 747 can be made". Charlie was very succinct in his explanation to Pfieffer. He explained the revision to the departure personnel list, based on the fact that the maintenance of the IBM computers was considered a Saigon critical industry and that our IBMers might be further delayed to the point that they might not get out at all. He said that Air Vietnam, China Airlines, Air France and Singapore Airlines were still scheduling flights into Tan Son Nhut, but that Pan American was not and that buses were still running in Saigon and that it was assumed that Oshida could arrange transportation for the IBMers out to Tan Son Nhut Airport. The call ended at 10 p.m.. We all sat quietly, wondering what decision would be made. *What would happen to our people?*

At 10 that night, a young Vietnamese woman called me to the Hilton lobby. She said her name was Nhu and that she was the wife of Bob Sada, one of our IBM GEM CEs who had worked with me in Saigon. Nhu had been a programmer at Long Binh in 1969 and 1970. She told me that Bob had gone to Hong Kong and was trying to fly to Saigon to rescue her family. She simply wanted me to know what was going on. The next day I received a call from Bob who had just landed at Andersen with three of Nhu's immediate family. Bob had gone to Saigon, made it through the streets to rescue his in-laws, signed the necessary paperwork as their sponsor and returned within two days. I gave him Nhu's number at the hotel and she and Bob left for Honolulu the following day. Some heroic individual rescue efforts were proving successful.

At 11 p.m. we received another call from Bruce Tomson in Bangkok. He said there might not be a 747 rescue attempt since our people were considered "critical industry" providing essential services to the South Vietnamese government, along with the telephone, water and electric company plus Honeywell at USAID and a few commercial banks. Tomson had talked with Oshida again and Oshida was going to escalate our problem to Denny Ellerman in the U.S. Embassy's Commercial Attaché Office.

At 3 a.m. on the 27th I received a telephone call from Gene Murdock in Rochester, Minnesota. Gene had also been a CE in Vietnam a few years earlier. He gave me seven names of his extended Vietnamese family who had arrived on Guam and said they were in one of the ten refugee camps there, ages ranging from 3 to 55. "Could I look for and help them?" Gene and I talked about the situation and he said he would call another one of the old IBM-GEM CEs. At 7 a.m. Randy Keeler called me from Chicago and asked for help and advice. He gave me the names of twenty-one American IBMers who had worked in Vietrnam (for our old IBM-

GEM office) and who had families in Vietnam. He also asked me to find and help four Vietnamese - if they arrived on Guam. I described the Guam situation and gave him Bruce Tomson's name and number in Bangkok. Randy was extremely disappointed with the U.S. Government's lack of action and what he described as "continuous white-washing" of his persistent requests for assistance. I told him there was nothing we could do in Guam for people still in Saigon, but for him to go ahead and call President Ford and ask to have the cease fire extended. What else could he do?

Meanwhile, the Hilton Hotel was starting to fill up, but we continued to hold a couple of extra rooms. I didn't know what was going to happen as a result of the phone call to IBM HQ the previous night. They were seriously considering the 747, but would it work? The thought went through my mind, "I knew the territory. Would I go back into Saigon if the opportunity presented itself?" The morning papers of Sunday, April 27th, were filled with refugee stories. The morning TV stations carried the following: "Guam Memorial Hospital volunteers are collecting children's clothing, toys and other items for the refugee centers. Persons wishing to donate may deliver the items to the lobby of the hospital" while some background music was appropriately playing *"Bridge Over* Troubled *Waters"*.

Another call came in from Bruce Tomson who told us the following:

1. Aircraft were still flying into Tan Son Nhut and that TSN base operations would assist with a quick turn-around if the Pan American 747 standing by in Manila were to be committed; 2. The remaining WTC Field Engineering manager, Nghia, had notified 100 IBMers that they could leave that very day, but that the fate of the remaining 200+ is dependent on our ability to convince the U.S. Embassy that a few CEs could maintain the essential computers and that someone should make a presentation at the U.S. Embassy; and 3. Nghia had lists of non-essential and essential personnel. Tomson also told us that the standard operation in Saigon was that there were two types of notices from the U.S. Embassy: A. first alert, which meant that people would leave in 48 hours and to prepare immediately; and B. second alert, which meant, go to location X in two hours - and presumably you would be picked up by buses and somehow

evacuated. He also said that the consensus was that Ambassador Graham Martin was calling the shots in Saigon as to the departure priorities and not our government authorities in Washington, D.C. It was becoming all too evident that without an on site American dealing with the Embassy "eyeball to eyeball" an evacuation for our employees had little chance for success. Tomson closed by telling Swift that he should leave Guam and come to Bangkok.

What we didn't know was that a frustrated but determined Bruce Tomson was also trying to arrange a backup plan. Bruce had been the IBM-GEM Location Manager in Saigon, prior to my replacing him, and definitely knew the territory. Bruce was also someone who could squeeze an amazing amount of use out of a telephone. He had contacted a quasi-military source and arranged for an Air America DC-4 to fly into TSN, pick up the IBMers and fly them to Bangkok. The second half of their flight to freedom would be provided by an Air Siam Airbus, which would ignore Thailand immigration requirements and take the refugees to Guam. Bruce even called an IBM government liaison office in Washington to obtain permission for the Airbus to fly through Philippine airspace and refuel at Clark if necessary. He also had located a bus in Saigon to carry the IBMers to TSN. There was one catch; he was probably going to have into fly to Saigon himself, buy the bus from a U.S. Air Force Sergeant for an exorbitant sum, and he knew he would need additional contingency money for various payoffs along the way through the chaotic streets between the IBM office and TSN - not an easy or welcome task! There was a high probability that the bus would be demolished crashing the TSN gates. He called Chase Manhattan Bank in Bangkok, and they filled a large bag with small denomination US dollars worth $75,000 which Tomson planned to carry with him. Another fact that this author recently learned was that another alternate plan was being discussed. Wil Derango, then General Manager of IBM Malaysia, had offered the Thai Government five IBM System 360 Model 50 processors (a huge amount of computing power for such a small emerging nation) in exchange for any Thai aircraft that could fly into Tan Son Nhut to rescue our Vietnamese employees. The Thai government was indeed interested but could not obtain the proper approvals in the short amount of time remaining. It's probably a good thing too, since Derango hadn't the slightest idea of how he was going to provide the five large processors.

At 10 a.m. a call came in to Charlie Swift from Ralph Pfieffer in New York which said that an alternate plan was being considered to evacuate our Vietnamese to Manila and that our U.S. State Department in Washington D.C. said that all 315 IBMers would be going to Clark Air Base. Back on Guam, we had grave doubts that such a plan had any real chance for success. Washington and New York were out of the loop and definitely out of touch with reality.

Sometime that morning, we learned that IBMer, Mrs. Vo Kim Thoan, with nine dependents, arrived at Clark. The Red Cross at Clark sent a wire to the Red Cross in White Plains, New York who notified IBM HQ in Armonk. Vo Kim's father had worked for USAID and the family had departed Saigon via a good and successful USAID evacuation plan.

At noon, we called the IBM Philippines office and talked to a Mr. Malabanan who described the situation there. Our local executives decided that Jack Ewen, Frank O'Keefe and Charlie Swift should go to Manila that afternoon. Someone told us that a cable had been sent to the Saigon Embassy from Washington, D.C. for them to send the 300 plus IBMers to Clark. We felt that there was a strong possibility that the Embassy couldn't or wouldn't comply.

We then had a call from Bill Stafford, IBM SEA Regional Manager in Hong Kong, with new information. A WTC Field Manager named Antonio and some IBM Vietnam personnel on Vietnam military leave would stay in Saigon. Nghia had briefed the Embassy and needed $34,000 and that Nghia was now talking evacuation for his groups by the end of the next week. The $34,000 represented the amount of money in IBM's retirement fund designated for those employees who were volunteering to stay behind and would be used as their separation pay. Something did not add up! And, the latest on the 747 was that we could not obtain one to fly into TSN, but that we could charter one elsewhere when we needed it for the peaceful airspace between Clark and Guam. Big help! Then, of course, Charlie Swift called a Bob Jones in Agana to set up the Royal Taga Hotel in Saipan for a refugee center and said he could have Pan American fly our refugees there.

I needed to get away from all the crazy ideas and haphazard plans that were filled with wishful thinking. It seemed to a few of us that a better escape plan and understanding with the Embassy should have already been in place. George Winter and I drove to Orote Point, west of Agana, where a huge tent city was being built rapidly by Seabees or Army Engineers, or both. The progress was amazing, a tent city to accomodate thousands of people was being erected in a matter of days. Bulldozers were removing rocks, leveling irregularities and smoothing what had been just a thick kiave or tangatang brush covered landscape. The dust was thick and everywhere, but straight dirt roads were being bulldozed and long lines of large olive drab tents were being pitched in record time. Some of the tents had signs that said things like "Immigration" or "Latrines" or "Red Cross Station" or "Cafeteria." along with their Vietnamese language counterparts. Trucks were offloading cots and other supplies. We were really impressed!

Back at the hotel, Bill Stafford phoned again from Hong Kong and said that 34-year old Denny Ellerman told Nghia that he didn't know when the IBMers would be going. Great! Then Bruce called from Bangkok again and talked with Charlie Swift for one full hour. I thought Bruce was trying to put together some kind of plan that might have had a chance for success (I found out about the DC-4 plan much later). Out of that conversation came the following: a few of us would maintain our Guam watch; one man would go to Manila; Charlie Swift and Jack Ewen would go to Bangkok and set up a command post in Bangkok; and finally, Bruce and probably Jack Ewen would go to Saigon to negotiate the evacuation of most of the WTC IBMers, minus a few critical technical people who would volunteer to remain behind.

At 10:30 p.m. on the 27th, a call was placed to Ralph Pfeffer in N.Y. The following information was passed along the line, I quote from my notes: "1. The Guam situation is the same; flights will start again tomorrow at 9:30 a.m. Guam will be the clearing point for all Vietnamese prior to going to the U.S.A. 2. A bank transfer of the $34,000 via the Bank of Indo China and Franceis Commercial has been made to Nghia in Saigon; 3. The contact between Nghia and the U.S. Embassy can be netted out as follows: the U.S. Consulate has not bought our withdrawal plan and no IBMers can leave. There is no cable from Washington, D.C. (Author's note: There were, in fact, at least two telegrams as reported in

David Butler's book, *The Fall of Saigon*, the texts of which appear below and which when read would seem to indicate that earlier telegrams were also sent on behalf of IBM to our U.S. Embassy which were either lost in the shuffle or summarily ignored). Our Vietnamese IBMers are <u>hostages</u> of the U.S. Embassy! Apparently the Embassy believes that if we evacuate some of our employees along with the families of those who stay behind, then the others will quit their computer maintenance responsibilities and also leave. The Embassy has interpreted Nghia's presentation in a negative manner and has said 'No' to any IBMer leaving. (Author's note: I learned later that when Nghia was asked in the briefing whether he could guarantee that the critical CEs would not flee even if their families were allowed to leave, Nghia said something to the effect that he couldn't lie or give positive assurances on the behalf of other employees. He was the acting IBM Country Manager but he was also a good Buddhist first and had not learned our questionable western style of negotiating). 4. Ambassador Martin is in charge and is backing the retention of essential services (critical industry personnel) and is firm on the point. Martin has made the decision with Denny Ellerman's support."

Since that time, with the help of some reliable correspondence, I have been able to better reconstruct what was happening in Saigon from IBM Vietnam's point of view. On April 10th, Nghia had hand delivered a list of all IBM Vietnam employees and their immediate dependents to the Embassy's reception desk; it was addressed to Mr. Wolfgang Lehmann, Deputy Chief of Mission, U.S. Embassy, Saigon. This list was to have formed the basis for an Embassy sponsored evacuation. The political and military situation was rapidly deteriorating, so Nghia went to see Jim Oshida, Commercial Attaché, U.S. Embassy a week later, April 17. He learned that Ohida had not seen the list and also that Oshida needed a sponsorship letter from IBM outside of Vietnam, which would state that IBM would take full responsibility for every person on Nghia's list. Nghia returned to his office, sent a duplicate list to Oshida, and called Jack Ewen in Hong Kong. He outlined the need for the sponsorship letter. Ewen was trying to return to Saigon on April 22, but was refused by his Asia/Far East HQ management.

A sponsorship letter and another complete list of Vietnamese personnel who should participate in an evacuation was sent to the U.S.

Embassy, Saigon via diplomatic pouch from the U.S. Consulate in Hong Kong. Nghia received a copy of this same list and letter via friends at Air Vietnam and called Oshida for an appointment. At the meeting with Ashida on April 24, Nghia was able to show his copy of what had been sent via diplomatic pouch and Oshida stated that it was the first documents he had ever received from IBM on the subject. (Smell a rat?) Oshida then told Nghia to have his 315 people ready to leave on a two hour notice and that he would be informed as to the pickup point and time. Nghia had successfully negotiated with IBM A/FE HQ to include employee parents with the evacuation group, and upon Oshida's recommendation had split his 315 evacuees into three groups, each of which would depart in priority order. Ten employees, including Nghia, had volunteered to remain behind, without their dependents, if necessary. At this point, everything looked organized and all they had to do was wait for instructions from the Embassy.

On April 26, 1975 Nghia called Oshida and asked for a status report on the evacuation. Oshida told him that all the paperwork had been completed and he was waiting for an approval from his boss, Denny Ellerman. Oshida also told Nghia that it looked like all 315 might go together since IBM was planning to send in a Boeing 747, and that people from Bank of America and 3M might join them. The next day, April 27, Oshida asked Nghia to come to the Embassy and meet with Ellerman. Denny Ellerman told Nghia that he could not let IBM personnel go (orders from Martin?) because the highly trained IBM technicians were essential to Vietnam's future government. He said something like: if he allowed Nghia's people to leave, it would jeopardize the backbone of the structure that would support the new government's efforts to reconstruct the country. Nghia tried to explain that a certain number of technicians had already volunteered to remain and that all the others should be permitted to go now. Nghia said that he felt like he was being interrogated by Ellerman, but that at the end of the meeting Ellerman eased up and promised to reconsider IBM's case. On the morning of April 29, Nghia heard the attack on Tan Son Nhut and was told that all airport fixed wing air traffic had ceased and he realized that his air evacuation route was cut off. Nghia tried to call the Embassy but couldn't get through and he also tried to walk to the Embassy but could not even approach it safely because of the mobs trying to storm the walls. He had to sit and wait.

*U.S. Embassy, Saigon – 1970 Photo*

My notes go on to say that late on the 27th the U.S. Embassy's assessment of the situation in Saigon was that things were better than they thought and that there were several positive signs to bear this out: there were discussions between the French Government and Hanoi, that the ARVN were not being challenged, there were only minor riots at the TSN airport and that the police were controlling those and that the situation was stable. It was apparently believed by Ambassador Martin that if the essential services were left intact then the NVA would agree to enter Saigon peacefully. Martin naively believed that a political settlement could still be reached. On the down side, ex-President Thieu had fled the country the previous day, Tran Van Huong who had been appointed President six days earlier stepped down and was replaced by Duong Van "Big" Minh, there were some rockets fired on Saigon, Bien Hoa was under attack and people there were being evacuated; and finally, if Bien Hoa fell then give Saigon about two weeks!

A new plan within our little Guam group was finalized. Charlie and Jack would go to Bangkok as soon as possible since our Embassy in Thailand had contacted the Thai military and said they would help if needed. "Some one, or two or three, must go into Saigon in order to convince the WTC Vietnamese employees that we should evacuate all but the essential people, and that if a collapse was imminent, then the 20 or so who would remain could be rescued also." Whoever went into Saigon would have to know the streets and alleys of Saigon. They would also have to convince the U.S. Embassy that we had a good plan and that we would not abandon the essential computer services. The tone of this last plan was one of discouragement but it was hoped that they could pull it off. My notes actually say that the Embassy would arrange for a military aircraft. Our executives optimistically ended the meeting with, "I think the Embassy is trying to help and that Ambassador Martin is sincere." And, "The general feeling is that if we don't cooperate, the Embassy will forget us, but if we do cooperate, we will have their support. The margin of safety seems OK and the Embassy will assist." (History has, of course, proven much different and Tan Son Nhut was useless to fixed wing aircraft as of the 27th). O'Keefe went to Manila, Swift and Ewen went to Bangkok and I remained on Guam to continue doing what I had been doing – looking for refugees.

At the same time, Bruce Tomson hired a TSN based twin Beechcraft that was to be available after its crew took video clips of "Big" Minh's swearing in ceremony. The Beechcraft was to return to Bangkok with the film and then be available to take Tomson, his bag of money, and one other in to Saigon. Departure for Tomson's charter was scheduled for 0900 on the 29th. None of us knew at that time that the NVA was launching its final assault on the capital and there were only two days left for a free but panic stricken Saigon.

The next day was Monday, April 28th. Things had quieted down, at least with regard to my responsibilities, because those of us left behind on Guam didn't have ten new IBM executive plans every half-hour. I met with some of the Guam IBMers around 9 a.m. and explained what was going down and later went out to NAS to post another IBM sign. A photographer came by and took my picture as I was standing in a receiving area hanger holding the IBM sign and the picture appeared in a well known U.S. news magazine a few weeks later. The refugees flying in

309

at that time were coming back from their temporary stay at Wake Island. That afternoon a news reporter came by the office and wanted a story on Vietnamese companies. I asked her not to comment on IBM World Trade. She would not have understood what was happening to our people because I knew I didn't. I went to Asan again to check whether the listings of new arrivals had been posted. They weren't, so I then went to the camp at Andersen AFB. I checked the Air Force's refugee listing there and found the names of Gene Murdock's family and George Miyashiro's sister-in-law. I worked with a Family Center set up by the Red Cross, which was helping to find people. Back at the Hilton, there were a couple of messages from hotel personnel who said they could help us with additional rooms. Sadly, I didn't really think we would need them. I had a refreshing dinner at George Winter's home that evening. George's house was on a bluff overlooking the end of the NAS runway, and we watched and listened as the aircraft continued to arrive, one after one after the other. Back at the Hilton, I was asleep by 11 p.m. and dreaming of refugee camps and one of IBM's good looking Guamanian secretaries whom I had befriended during the past few days. Thank GOD I was born an American!

Bruce Tomson later told me that sometime during the 28th, he called Ellerman's office in Saigon to update him on the new plan and to confirm his arrival for the next morning. Ellerman's secretary answered the phone and in a trembling voice said to Tomson, "Don't come!" and hung up. He then found out that the video-tape Beechcraft never did depart Tan Son Nhut for Thailand and that TSN was unusable to fixed wing aircraft. The videos had been taken out by helicopter. Additionally, the Air America DC-4 that was planned for the evacuation of the IBMers suddenly became unavailable. It was one of two DC-4s that had been used to fly President Thieu and his entourage out of Vietnam, and the plane had been detained in the Philippines. Tomson called Ellerman that night with the hope that he could still help. Ellerman was emotional and confirmed the fact that Tan Son Nhut was not usable and that Tomson definitely should not come to Saigon. Things were falling apart and fast.

At 7 a.m. on the 29th, I called my office in Honolulu and said I would be in Guam only a few more days and that things didn't look good for the World Trade people. I didn't know at the time that this would be the last day of freedom in South Vietnam for many years to come and that panic and heroism were running side by side through the streets of Saigon at that exact minute. I continued to visit the various camps throughout the day, hoping but not expecting to find a few more Vietnamese on our lists. At some point in the day, I called on a high level officer at COMNAVMAR that had overall responsibility for military affairs on Guam. I was gathering as much information about what was happening in Saigon and on Guam as possible and during the course of the conversation, I asked the officer what his most urgent concern was. I thought perhaps he would say food and clothing for the refugees or too many incoming flights or a possible concern about disease or an epidemic in the tent cities. But no, he surprised me and said, "Right now there is a major typhoon about 150 miles east of Guam with winds over 100 miles an hour and if it hits here I don't know what we are going to do about those 100,000 people in the tents. We're sure watching it and praying!" Fortunately, that typhoon passed to the northeast of the Marianas. Curiously enough though, exactly one year later to the day (I checked because I was living in Hawaii) a typhoon bearing up to 200 knot winds struck Guam with devastating force and left a major disaster in its wake.

For some reason my detailed notes stop on this most important of days, perhaps out of discouragement. I didn't know that Saigon's U.S. Armed Forces FM Radio station had played *White Christmas* that morning at 10:51 a.m. to signal a massive helicopter lift – <u>Operation Frequent Wind</u> - for the final evacuation. It was said to be the largest helicopter evacuation in history. (Nghia later told me that when he heard *White Christmas* played in Saigon that morning he thought to himself, "How strange to play such a song at the hottest time of the year, then again with Americans you can expect anything, even the craziest." He too didn't know it was the evacuation signal). I continued to search the camps, use the public address systems, check the arrival lists, post signs, talk to new arrivals, ask questions and watch the hundreds of C-141s and other overloaded aircraft land and depart as the last refugees continued to arrive throughout the day from Clark. Somehow I knew our people would not be among those arrivals. I talked to Tomson in Bangkok sometime during the day and he said that they were not able to fly into Saigon; it was too late! Tan Son Nhut was a shambles and under heavy attack. He was tired and dejected.

This is probably the best place to quote the actual text of the telegrams referenced previously. At 10:11 p.m. April 29, a telegram was received by the Embassy which said "For Martin from Brown (former Ambassador Dean Brown who had been brought out of retirement to head up a task force for the evacuation and planning for the resettlement of Vietnamese refugees), IBM Headquarters reports its personnel still in Saigon and is most disturbed, Do what you can." And at 11:06 p.m. a message came into the Embassy from President Ford's Chief of Staff: "To Martin from (Don) Rumsfeld, I understand that 154 IBM employees, including their families, are still awaiting removal from Saigon. I further understand that they are standing in front of the IBM building awaiting instructions where they should go for evacuation. I ask that you do your utmost to see they are evacuated with the current helicopter lift." According to Butler's book, this was just minutes after Martin had received a message saying "Defense promises 30 CH-53s (Chinook 53 helicopters) on the way." Martin and his staff had done nothing to help and did nothing more for the people he had seemingly held hostage. Many others, more knowledgeable than I, have spoken of this shameful unconscionable act of betrayal.

Late that night, I was in the IBM office and a call came in from Saigon. It was Nghia on the line and the conversation was fatalistic. He said that the IBM families comprising a couple hundred men, women and children had all packed their barest essentials and gone to the nearby Ben Bach Dang Navy docks. Apparently a last minute effort to get them successfully evacuated by barge down the Saigon River had been arranged by the Embassy (Ellerman had called Nghia around 3:30 p.m. and told him that a barge had been scheduled to leave from near the #5 warehouse at 6 p.m.) Hopes were high that freedom was yet possible. The large group was quickly organized and they arrived early at 5 p.m., the designated barge was there but it was deserted and un-motorized. After inspecting the unmanned barge they waited and waited nearby in the dark for directions and hoped for a towboat or another barge.

There were many other boats but they were all over-filled. Two IBMers tried to climb up the side of a large Navy vessel but were repelled by gunfire. (A Mr. Ton Trong Kiem and a Mr. Truong Thanh Van and his family did manage to scramble aboard a departing boat bound for Subic Bay, Philippines.) Eventually the rest became frightened and disillusioned with the situation around them and finally around dawn returned to their IBM office. Nghia went on to say that the families again waited in the street but no one from the Embassy or with any authority to guide them ever showed up. The IBM office was only about four city blocks from the U.S. Embassy. After a couple of hours, they realized there was no hope. They feared for their safety and finally knew that they had been left behind.

Other faithful groups were suffering similar fates. Some IBMers went home to await the communist take over, but most of the families stayed in the IBM offices until 11 a.m. the next day. He (Nghia) was in his IBM office and had decided to make *One Last Phone Call* to our group on Guam to let us know of their luckless fate. He said he would eventually send everyone home, turn off the lights, lock the office door and go home himself. He finally gave me an emotional "Good-bye" and the line went dead. "Chao Ong and good luck," said I. Ambassador Graham Martin left the Embassy rooftop at around 4:40 a.m. that next morning in a CH-46 helicopter, the *Lady Ace 09*, and the last 11 heroic U.S. Marines left the roof in a CH-46 at 7:58 a.m. April 30, 1975. How many other friends of America had our politicians in Washington and Martin and his staff in Saigon left behind?

Bruce Tomson was the kind of guy that never gave up and as soon as he found out that our employees were still in Saigon, he called Frank Cary, IBM CEO, in New York. Oddly enough, Bill Doody, previous Branch Manager in Honolulu, was in Cary's office making an executive presentation when the call came in. Tomson asked Cary to contact Brown and Rumsfeld and have them order Martin to help evacuate our employees. Cary apparently threw Doody out of his office and then put a call through to Hong Kong to John Throckmorton, past General Manager of IBM Thailand and IBM Vietnam, newly appointed General Manager of IBM's Southeast Asia Region (Stafford's replacement) and a good friend of Tomson's. He asked who this guy Tomson was and that Tomson should call the Center for Evacuation at Nakhom Phanom in Thailand and ask for their help. By then it was probably realized that there was nothing IBM HQ could do in New York. Meanwhile, Tomson was trying to persuade the stranded IBMers to use a helipad within

Saigon's Alliance France compound, which was just next door to the IBM office, but was told that it wasn't available for our rescue helicopters even though some helicopter rescues had already been made from there. Bar girls, hustlers and politicians were airlifted out, but skilled technicians and data processing professionals were left to their fate, victims of our final betrayal.

A telex connection had been established weeks earlier between IBM Saigon and IBM Hong Kong. Apparently Nghia did remain in his office after he called me in Guam, because he was still in his office and using that telex from Saigon up until almost noon on April 30th. Some of the above information has been "remembered" as a result of those telexes. At some point during the day, it was agreed that the telex service should be discontinued and the hard copy telexes themselves should be destroyed in order to protect the future of the IBM employees under Communist domination. Even the Vietnamese telex operator that had remained on duty in Vung Tau through the 30th encouraged the IBMers to disconnect and to destroy the copies. I have been told by two IBM American executives that their copies of those telexes were later stolen from their desks. (Huh?) A last minute attempt was made to sort and then burn sensitive correspondence that might have compromised IBM, such as the Defense Administration Office customer (DAO) files. All the System/360 computers were captured intact during the next few days and the security lists, payroll information and other military data contained within their files was never used against the IBMers.

On 30 April 1975, VPA troops overcame all resistance, quickly capturing key buildings and installations. A tank crashed through the gates of the Independence Palace and at 11:30 a.m. local time the NLF flag was raised above it. Saigon's surrender marked the end of 116 years of Vietnamese involvement in conflict either alongside or against various countries, primarily France, China, Japan, Britain, and America, plus their own people.

On May 1, a North Vietnamese businessman by the name of Mr. Duong Ky Nga arrived at the IBM main office and told the employees there that he was their new General Manager and that his wife would be the lead telephone operator. He was a representative of the new Provisional Revolutionary Government of South Vietnam and had been assigned to manage IBM. He was friendly enough initially and just moved in. However, he knew nothing about managing a data processing business and had been trained earlier as a tanner in Czechoslovakia. During the following years, it was determined that no IBM Vietnam employee had any contact with the Communists and contrary to some people's suspicions there were no internal spies or threats to the organization.

I have been told, again by a reliable source, that life for the IBM Vietnam employees became rather grim after "The Fall". On meager salaries, adjusted to conform with that of civil servants, they worked ten to twelve hour days six days per week, attended frequent political education classes and waited in long lines to buy food. They spent the seventh day at a communal farm ten miles from town being "rehabilitated" by learning the value of physical labor while also hoping to produce additional food to supplement their meager rations. The technically experienced IBMers were asked to train new employees from the north, who considered the computer a novelty. Many of the old IBMers were then arbitrarily laid off. At the same time the northerners tried to foment distrust among the remaining old employees in order to gain control of the company. (*See note) North Vietnam approached IBM France requesting that they re-establish an official IBM presence in Vietnam but they were denied. Technical training and spare parts availability must have become a severe problem but other private sources have said that parts were acquired in Phnom Penh, Cambodia that had originated in France. As IBM Vietnam employees arrived at refugee camps in Malaysia and later the U.S. and France, IBM made great efforts to help with their daily needs, help with their resettlement in the United States and give them a new start on life with new jobs.

* The communists incarcerated approximately one million South Vietnamese in remote areas under severe conditions for their "re-education". About 240,000 remained longer than six years and 60,000 died. The last were released in the early 1990's (source: San Diego Union Tribune 2/13/94). It is not known whether any IBMers were treated in such an extreme manner.

As for me, I sadly helped close up our insignificant Hilton Hotel operation a day or two later and tucked away my memories of Guam's refugees and the failures in Saigon for twenty years, until the initial writing of this book. I was 41 years old and unlike the millions in Southeast Asia, I had a free and blessed life to return to in beautiful Hawaii. IBM had done everything possible under the circumstances for their Saigon employees, **or** had they?

# Epilogue

THE PRECEDING CHAPTERS MAY HAVE left some questions in the minds of readers about what happened to this or that or to whom. I hope so, because there are a few loose ends. I will attempt to wrap some things up, but not all. Unfortunately, a few of the pieces of the 'IBM in Vietnam' jigsaw puzzle have been lost through the intervening years. This section also gives the author an opportunity to make a few last comments about his own experiences during the Vietnam War.

One of the major problems IBMers encountered within our military customer set was the one-year Vietnam rotation tour. Quite often our most important contribution to a data processing installation was providing operational continuity. It seemed that we were continually retraining military personnel or answering questions about "What happened before?" and "Why was this done?" By the time I left Vietnam, I was working on – and for - my third set of military customer personnel.

The GEM office compound and villa at 115 Ming Mang Alley served us well from 1968 through 1972, and many of our collective memories are about things that occurred there. When I arrived in Saigon, the office was well established and was running smoothly and when I departed the same was true. The curious thing about it was that we were never billed by anyone for its use while I was there and to my knowledge IBM never paid a cent for the rental of the property. I sometimes wonder if that compound – and the hotel/restaurant/brothel across the alley – are still in place?

*Ming Mang Alley, to Office*

The General Services Administration (GSA) Contract specified that the U.S. military was responsible for providing our operation with an office and that IBM in turn would reimburse them for it. Thus, MACV rented the villa on our behalf and simply discontinued rental after the last IBMer shut the front door on his way to the airport. I suppose that the property was returned to the landlord, but I do not even know who that was. Some years later an IBMer who probably knew the facts told my source of information that neither MACV nor CINCPAC ever billed IBM for the villa and that IBM never brought that fact to anyone's attention. Who would have handled such a transaction anyway? We ALL, military and civilians alike, bailed out.

Some IBMers were so entranced by life in Southeast Asia that they either remained at the end of their assignments to pursue other interests or returned after brief encounters with life in the States. One CE became a part owner in a Bangkok Bar. Two FSD employees converted an old rice barge and operated a successful riverboat restaurant on the Chao Phraya River in Bangkok. Two employees that worked for me in Saigon migrated to Singapore and began a successful service bureau business using their IBM acquired experience and knowledge. Other IBMers found that they were best suited for overseas assignments and volunteered to work with IBM's World Trade organization in Korea, Japan, Germany, Okinawa, Saudi Arabia, Brazil and elsewhere. I took a management position with IBM Saudi Arabia during 1976 - 1978 and was lucky enough to work with two other Americans there who were also with me in Saigon.

Bruce Tomson returned to Thailand as IBM's General Manager, replacing his good friend John Throckmorten, for two years after 'The Fall of Saigon' and helped that country develop into a modern data processing based economy. Throughout the later 1970's, IBM's overseas policy changed from the use of Americans in the top management positions to the use of country nationals for General Manager wherever possible. As an example, Bruce was replaced with a well-qualified Thai.

There have been many reunions for SEA IBMers since our departure from Vietnam in 1973. The early meetings were in Las Vegas in 1991 and 1994 and although attendance was small (30 or so), enthusiasm for follow-on get togethers continued. The most recent reunion, as of this writing was in 2011 held in Laughlin, Nevada. The camaraderie built from our experiences has been long lasting among this 'family' of men. There was also a periodic newsletter in the 90's with a circulation of approximately 250. Contents of the newsletter came from the IBMer readership and gradually information about where we all went was shared and accumulated. E-mail communications gradually replaced the newsletter and credit for initiating and maintaining communications over the years must go to Mr. Bill Banks. More recently, Bill has established a 'Pac Ops' web site. Thanks Bill!

Whenever I have asked an SEA IBMer whether he would do the same thing again - that is, accept the Vietnam assignment - I have received 100% agreement that "Yes, they would go back tomorrow", and most have said that they are proud of what we accomplished. When I asked one ex-IBMer whether he thought we suffered from discrimination after returning to the U.S., he said, "No, he didn't think so and that he left the company after Vietnam because he felt that many in IBM management had taken their eye off the business in favor of their own social advancement," and he went on to say that, "I wouldn't trade those three years in Vietnam for an IBM vice-presidency." Another said that the work he was given by his management just wasn't very interesting or important compared to what he had accomplished in SEA. Others felt differently about IBM discrimination.

Regrets? Yes, other than wishing that the whole thing had never happened in the first place, I do have a few regrets. I wish that I could have had more time to see more of Vietnam, as some of our men did. Under the circumstances it would have been difficult at best, but I would have liked to visit the highland city of Dalat with its delightful climate, waterfalls, gardens and parks and even visited the old imperial capital of Hue and the Citadel there. I would have liked to spend more time up-country at our remote IBM locations. I would have liked to get more into the minds of the Vietnamese with whom I worked, so as to better understand their attitudes about communism, freedom, the American presence and their innermost thoughts, fears and ambitions. I am sorry I did not travel to Vientiane in Laos or that I did not take the train ride from Bangkok to Chiang Mai or down the Kra Peninsula to Malaysia (like a few of our CEs actually did). I would have liked to know all the facts surrounding the U.S. Embassy's failure to evacuate our IBM Vietnamese employees as promised. Certainly, an early and partial evacuation of many of the IBM Vietnam employees could have been accomplished with better planning rather than the fiasco described above of those final days. And, I am sorry that I have not been able to afford the time and money to return to Vietnam these last years during the writing of this book; the contrast to years past would have been inspiring. Lastly, I still want to visit the Vietnam Wall in Washington D.C. and touch some of the engraved names of the 58,272 names of the men and women who died there.

If you can possibly believe that one of the justifications for entering and escalating the war because of what was called the domino theory - the continuous Communist conquest toward other nations to the south - then it can be argued that the political stalemate and eventual American withdrawal in Vietnam was in part a small success. Communism overran South Vietnam, Laos and Cambodia, but at least it stopped short of Thailand, Malaysia and Singapore.

I found that one of the main saving graces to help retain one's sanity in Vietnam was a good sense of humor. The ability to laugh or save one's frustrations for the SEAWA gong changed many a bad attitude and helped restore one's sense of harmony. Laughter in any tense situation is good medicine.

Our nation has gradually purged itself of the guilt of what we did to a foreign country through mental self-flagellation, too many protests and the passage of time. More and more things have been written about the war (eg. MacNamara's book and *Time Magazine's* twenty-year special report). In light of these writings and many other articles in newspapers, magazines, books and more recently on the internet, I have had the opportunity to review things that I wrote over fifteen years ago for inclusion in this book in order to determine whether there are any contradictions or disagreements with my original observations. My conclusion is no, my writing, and the writings of the others who have contributed, remain intact and true to fact.

Some good things came out of the Vietnam War and these positives are often overlooked because most of what has been written is either negative or soul searching or descriptions of terror, heartache and sorrow. I remember that at each Christmas, our Marines would promote their 'Toys For Tots' program that has been so successful here in the U.S. Military and civilians alike generously donated needed items that the Marines would then distribute to the all too many Saigon orphanages. There was also a great deal of year around volunteer work being done by both the military and civilians in these same orphanages. Help was given where help was needed. I also often think that the skills learned and practiced in Vietnam by the fixed wing and helicopter pilots contributed mightily to our present day private and commercial air services.

All the data processing centers that were left intact after 'The Fall' were requisitioned by the new government. The People's Army took over the S/360 Model 50 at Army Logistics as well as the S/360 Model 40 at Army Personnel and the S/360 Model 30 at PA&E. The S/360 Model 20 at the navy shipyard became the property of the People's Navy. The remainder of the systems were generally left in place and were taken over by whichever communist entity was first to 'liberate' the business or ministry where they were installed. They continued to operate and be maintained by the local IBM Vietnam CEs.

Regarding the S/360 Model 50 system at Army Logistics: A South Vietnamese Army Colonel and an American officer called on IBM

Vietnam on April 28th, 1975 and asked them to de-install and prepare their 360/50 for removal to a safer location. They wanted the job done in two days, which was unrealistic under the circumstances, and they were told no, it was too late! Later, during the first week of May, an inspection and inventory tour was made by a few local CEs, and the new IBM communist management. They found that the 360/50 had been wired with explosives and that the wires were connected to a nearby command post that would have triggered the detonation. However, someone had severed these wires and the 360/50 was spared.

Nghia, the faithful Field Engineering Manager who had been left holding the bag during the last fateful days of Saigon's fall, continued to struggle through the office intrigues of the new regime until he resigned in1980. After working as a mechanic for three more years, he was able to leave Vietnam in 1983. He was then employed, by IBM World Trade Corporation in Europe and hoped to someday return to his beloved Vietnam. I lost contact but hope he made it.

The manager who was put in place to run IBM Vietnam by the communists in 1975 was eventually convicted for stealing state properties; apparently his training as a tanner did not serve him well in business ethics. His wife is thought to have escaped to Europe via an adventure with the boat people of Vietnam. A most fitting end!

# Acknowledgements

This book could not have been written without the help of a number of IBM adventurers and the encouragement of a few close friends. I am indebted to George League, Robert McGrath, Ed Baker, Stuart Schmidt, Curtis Maxwell and Rob Moore, who each contributed a full chapter describing their unique experiences while on assignment in Vietnam. I also give a special thanks to Bill Shugg who intended for many years to write his own book on Vietnam, but elected instead to give me his very sensitive writings which I have generously shared throughout these pages. Thanks too to Gloria Hartre Elle who contributed personal experiences as seen from a woman's point of view. Bruce Tomson played a key roll in the history that follows, and I thank him not only for what he contributed to the last two chapters but also for his encouragement and friendship during the all too few years we worked together. I thank Bill Banks for his dedication in putting together all the PacOps reunions and for his earlier *No Name Newsletter* prior to the present wide usage of e-mail, both of which have helped me remain in contact with those mentioned here. John Leussler has been especially helpful with anecdotes and specific details about Southeast Asia as well as grammatical corrections as sometimes needed. A special and humble thanks goes to Quan Trung Nghia who assisted in updating some IBM Vietnam history and who suffered through the Fall of Saigon and the communist oppression that followed.

Other IBMers who graciously responded to my requests for help include Jim Strandine, Graham Siebert, Bill Ogden, Bob Curtis, George Winter, Fred Hodder, Tom Camargo and Bob Dillon. Each one of these friends played an important role during IBM's presence in Vietnam, and they share some of their experiences throughout the pages of this book. I must mention Rob Moore again; not only did he write most of Chapter

12, but he volunteered to be the someone I seriously needed when it came to making constructive changes, correcting phraseology and punctuation and generally acting as proof-reader and initial editorial manager. Lastly, a special thanks to my wife Erika who patiently encouraged me and made helpful and subtle suggestions during the time that a collection of memories grew to chapters and finally into this publication

# Bibliography

1.  <u>The American Experience in Vietnam</u>, edited by Grace Sevy. University of Oklahoma Press, 1989.
2.  <u>Customs and Culture of Vietnam</u>, by Ann Caddell Crawford, Published by Charles E. Tuttle Co, Tokyo, 1966.
3.  <u>Dictionary of the Vietnam War</u>, edited by James S. Olson, Published by Greenwood Press, Westport, Conn., 1988.
4.  <u>The Elephant and the Tiger</u>, by W.H. Morrison, Published by Hippocrene Books, New York, 1990.
5.  <u>The Fall of Saigon</u>, by David Butler, Published by Simon & Shuster, New York, 1985.
6.  <u>Home Before Morning, the Story of an Army Nurse in Vietnam</u>, by Lynda Van Devanter, Beaufort Books, Inc., New York, 1983.
7.  <u>Tools of War</u>, by Edgar C. Doleman, Published by Boston Publishing Co., 1985.

Dan Feltham is now retired from previous careers and living in Southern California with his wife. *When Big Blue Went To War* is totally non-fiction and has been a long time coming. It is hoped that the stories told here will appeal to historians, computer buffs, IBM employees, students of the Vietnam War and anyone interested in reading about bachelor adventures in foreign lands. Dan has enjoyed extensive international travel and racing sailboats for most of his life. Dan is also the author of two published novels, *Tradewinds Calling* and *The Catalina Connection*, presently available on E-pub devices such as the Kindle or Nook. He can be reached by e-mailing "danfeltham77@gmail.com".